The End of Karma

SOMINI SENGUPTA

The End of Karma

HOPE AND FURY
AMONG INDIA'S YOUNG

W. W. Norton & Company / *New York* / *London*

Independent Publishers Since 1923

For information about special discounts for bulk purchases, please
contact W. W. Norton Special Sales at specialsales@wwnorton.com
or 800-233-4830

Manufacturing by Quad Graphics Fairfield
Book design by Brooke Koven
Production manager: Louise Mattarelliano

ISBN 978-0-393-07100-9

W. W. Norton & Company, Inc.
500 Fifth Avenue, New York, N.Y. 10110
www.wwnorton.com

W. W. Norton & Company Ltd.
Castle House, 75/76 Wells Street, London W1T 3QT

1 2 3 4 5 6 7 8 9 0

For my daughter, with love and thanks

CONTENTS

Nervy, glowering, your daughter
wipes the teaspoons, grows another way.

—ADRIENNE RICH,
"Snapshots of a Daughter-in-Law"

The center was not holding. . . . Adolescents
drifted from city to torn city, sloughing off
both the past and future as snakes shed their
skins, children who were never taught and
would never now learn the games that had
held the society together.

—JOAN DIDION,
"Slouching Towards Bethlehem"

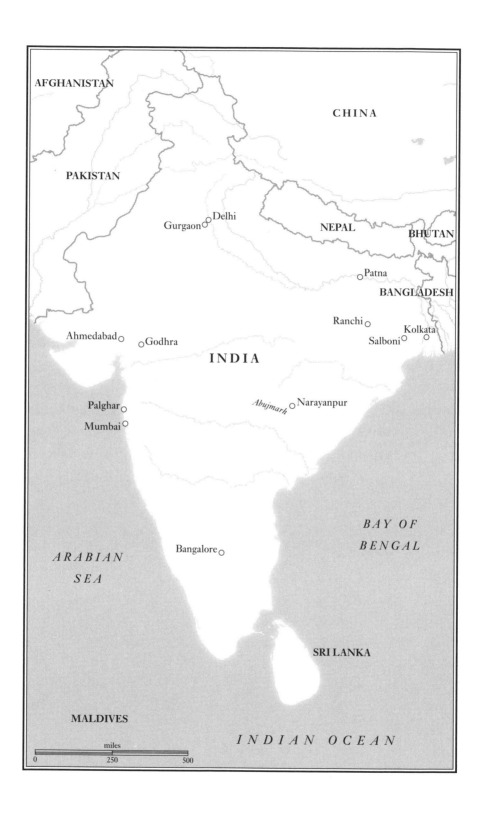

The End of Karma

Author as a child in India.

Aspiration, Like Water

B y the time I turn eight, with a cake from Flurys pâtisserie on Park Street, my parents have hawked some wedding gold, hustled for passports, and procured three plane tickets out of Calcutta.

It is September 1975, steamy monsoon, when rain clouds break late in the day and democracy comes to a grinding halt. By now, our prime minister, Indira Gandhi, has declared a state of emergency for the first time in the history of independent India, which means that newspapers arrive some mornings with an empty front page, dissidents go to jail, and the men of the slums are enlisted in an aggressive government-sponsored birth control program. In exchange for vasectomies, they are sometimes offered a patch of urban slum. Sterilization becomes the most potent symbol of Mrs. Gandhi's emergency rule—and the closest our country comes to totalitarianism.[1]

The emergency forms the backdrop for our move. My parents' decision to leave is material, not political. By this time, inflation has hit 30 percent. Refugees from the war over East Pakistan crowd into our city, erecting vast shanties of tin and tarp across from my grandmother's house. Every day come new corruption scandals about politicians and civil servants. Strikes shut down Calcutta.

My parents are not among the country's deprived. Baba is a midlevel civil servant. Ma teaches math. They make enough to rent a two-room flat of our own, but not enough to splurge at Mocambo as often as they would like. They can pay for my piano lessons, but they're not posh enough to become members of the Calcutta Club.

Their frustrations are the frustrations of what is, in 1975, a tiny urban middle class. Baba gets tired of hustling for a tank of cooking gas. He scours the city for Horlicks, the malted milk powder that is supposed to fortify a skinny, sickly child like me, but which becomes more and more scarce as inflation rises and traders start hoarding. He can rarely afford a pack of Rothmans, his preferred smoke. One night, walking home along Deshapriya Park, he steps over the corpse of a rickshaw puller whom local thugs call a police informant. Calcutta, that steamy metropolis of Victoria and jazz, is fast becoming what a future prime minister would call a "dying city."

I imagine Baba and Ma whispering to each other in the dark, while I sleep: *Is this what you call home?*

My parents want more. They want out.

And so, late one night, long past my bedtime, the three of us board a whirring, air-conditioned British Airways jet, waving and waving to an army of relatives who remain behind. My parents are allowed to bring with them the princely sum of eight U.S. dollars each, thanks to Indian banking regulations at the time.[2]

My parents don't know how they will make it so far from home. They know only that they will not make the more conventional journey to Britain. Baba is convinced that Indians clean other people's toilets in Britain, which is his way of saying that they do dirty, dehumanizing work—that they are, in effect, untouchables. We will not clean toilets, Baba insists. We will go to the New World. I have no idea why he believes Indians don't clean other people's toilets in the New World. But he does, which is why we opt to freeze to death instead.

We land first in a town called Selkirk in the flat cold middle of Canada, where my uncle, my father's older brother, has come before us. We squeeze into his family's apartment, which is across the road from a mental asylum. Only a field of snow separates the hubris on our side from the madness on theirs.

Every year, Ma, Baba, and I pack up and move. We settle into a different apartment, a different school, a different city, until, eventually, we pack up our autumn gold '76 Ford LTD and drive southward across the continent. We stop in Minneapolis, Salt Lake City, the Petrified Forest, Las Vegas. Motel after motel after motel. What are we chasing? I don't have the courage to ask. I am told only that there are palm trees in California and friends from Calcutta.

In my memory, my parents are unmoored and happy. They have a new baby, my sister, daughter of the New World.

East of Los Angeles, on the banks of rushing Interstate 10, we buy a house in a suburb of strivers. Our street is lined with identical L-shaped houses with jutting-out double garages, sloped roofs, oak trees out front. We have avocado green "wall-to-wall" carpeting and a calla lily that someone before us has planted by the door. Our neighbors are secretaries and schoolteachers—whites mostly, some Chicanos, a handful of Japanese-Americans who never speak publicly of the internment during the Second World War. We are the only Indians for miles. And so the questions thrown at me are banal—nothing terrible, just foolish.

"Do you eat monkey brain?"

"Hey, Gandhi!"

"What's that red dot mean?"

Et cetera.

Daughter of the Old World, I tell myself to keep my eyes on the road ahead. Draw a thick velvet curtain over memory. Dillydally, look back, and you're likely to stumble and fall.

This is good guidance, except that nearly every other summer, during school holidays, I am ferried back to Calcutta to commune with the past. I no longer know how to respond when a barefoot child on Park Street tugs at my American clothes, wanting coins. I cringe when Ma bargains with the hollow, barefoot rickshaw pullers. When the electricity goes out, which it does every day, because there's a shortage of power, the ceiling fans stop rasping and the air gets choking hot. What I would have known how to handle, had I grown up there, I no longer know how to handle. As I get older, the Indian oddities are joined by prohibitions: Don't go to the park by yourself. Don't wear shorts. Don't open the fridge when menstruating. Don't touch the untouchable. There are so many rules, more because I'm a girl. They are stultifying. They make me want to run back home.

Except that coming home to California is also awkward. How do I explain a summer in the City of Dreadful Night to friends who have spent their holiday listening to Olivia Newton-John?[3]

This toing and froing, this explaining to one side and then the other, demands considerable dexterity—and occasionally fibs. When Mrs. Gandhi lifts the state of emergency in 1977, only to be ousted in the elections that follow, her political rival and successor, Morarji Desai, appears on *60 Minutes* to extol the virtues of drinking his own urine. It is ancient Vedic practice, he says on prime-time American television. The next morning, I feign a bellyache and skip school. "Indians drink their own pee?" This is not a question I want to deal with during recess.

Perhaps this is when my parents' question starts to become mine: *Is this what you call home?*

For my parents, the question doesn't recede. They just roll up their sleeves and re-create the home they left behind, and, unlike me, they seem to know exactly what that requires. By the time I am in high school, they and their Calcutta friends bring over their most vital piece of home: Ma Durga, the mother goddess herself, who arrives at Los Angeles International Airport, all ten arms intact. Made of plaster of paris on the edge of Calcutta's most storied red-light district, Durga is stashed away in a friend's garage in another Southern California suburb, only to be brought out every fall and worshipped with ululations and prayers. A friend of my parents, a Brahmin by blood right, performs the service. Baba prepares the offering: an enormous vat of slow-cooked, chili-bathed mutton.

I worship other goddesses. I spend hours in front of the mirror trying to feather my hair like Farrah Fawcett. My hair is too wiry to feather like Farrah Fawcett's. I try to brush it like Donna Summer's glossy, wavy tresses. But it is too unruly. My hair is a mess, a daily burden. The part of me I hate the most.

Ma's advice is to tame it with oil, which is sensible, except that greasy hair will earn me about as many social points in high school as talk of drinking pee.

Throughout the 1980s, news of home comes on flimsy, blue, thrice-folded, international aerograms. There's no kerosene in the market, relatives write; the government has banned Coca-Cola; so-and-so's son is also going to America. India's economy crawls at an average of just over 3 percent a year through the decade: Hindu rate of growth, people call it. Occasionally, and only for the most urgent of matters, comes a crackling, rushed phone call. We all speak very loudly, as though our voices have to carry across the ocean. "What? We can't hear you. What did you say?" is how the conversations often go. I learn of my grandfather's death this way. Baba lights the ritual fire in our laundry room; it's the only part of the house where there's no wall-to-wall avocado green carpet.

Nostalgia and desire swim in opposite currents in my parents' lives. They cling to a country they left during the rains in 1975, while India churns.

I'm a high school senior in 1984, the year Prince releases *Purple Rain*. That fall, Mrs. Gandhi is shot dead by her Sikh bodyguards, which prompts deadly attacks against Sikhs across India in one of the worst incidents of communal violence in independent India.

The Berlin Wall collapses the year after I graduate from college. Nelson Mandela, whose freedom struggle shapes the way I look at the world, is let out of jail. Our neighbors tie yellow ribbons around their trees, as America goes to war in the Persian Gulf. Global oil prices soar as a result, sending India to the edge of a foreign exchange crisis. Officials in New Delhi crack open the state-led economy. They ease government restrictions on the private sector. They do it out of necessity. They do it quietly, making no announcements, because they fear unrest. This paves the way for changes that can barely be imagined at the time. Eventually, this also paves the way for a psychic shift among Indians who come of age in the years that follow: they come to believe that they can write their own destinies, that they are not defined by the past, that they live in an age that I begin to understand as the end of karma.

I try to find my place in the world. I work in a blues bar. I host a radio show. I try my hand at community organizing. Nothing quite satisfies, until I land in a newsroom. This is where I discover I can make a living toing and froing, poking my head into one world, then another, having to belong to none. Cognitive dissonance becomes my travel mate. I become a journalist.

I am a fish in water. Home.

Also, I chop off my hair.

The Bhagavad Gita, a dialogic sermon within the *Mahabharata*, the two-thousand-year-old Hindu epic, offers three paths to liberation. One path is through devotion. Another is through knowledge. The last is through karma, which, according to scholars of Sanskrit, roughly translates as the merits (or demerits) that derive from the deeds of one's previous lives. The physical body disintegrates after death, but the bundle of accumulated karma follows each being into her next life, where she might be reborn as a human being again, or a bird—or maybe move on to the realm of the gods.

By this theory, each creature is born with a distinct karma, based on the actions of earlier lives. The earthworm's karma is to break down the soil. The tiger's karma is to scour the jungle for prey. And in the peculiar and degrading logic of the Indian caste system, the Brahmin's karma is to study scripture, the warrior's is to fight, the sweeper's is to collect waste.

But one's role on Earth is not entirely predestined, according to this philosophy. Free will matters. You can choose to be an honest, hardworking warrior or a deceitful, slothful warrior. How you carry out your predestined role has a bearing on where you end up in your next life. Many lifetimes of karma can shape how you ended up where you are.

Hinduism allows you to wipe out bad karma too. Yoga goes a long way in exfoliating the demerits of a previous life, for instance. So does offering food and drink to a Brahmin, as does deep, unbreakable faith.

For all these caveats that temper strength, though, karma remains a potent force in the ancient texts. Wendy Doniger, a scholar of Hinduism, offers one explanation: "karma ex machina explains what cannot otherwise be justified."[4]

In the title of this book, I am using "karma" in its colloquial sense—as destiny. But I also invoke its richer meaning. I mean that the demands of India's young are pushing India to break free of its past. They are no longer willing to put up with their lot. They are also, profoundly, changing the destiny of their country.

In 2005, exactly thirty years after I left as a child, I came back to set up home in India. I was the first reporter of Indian descent to be appointed New Delhi bureau chief for *The New York Times.*

I would be dishonest if I told you this was an easy position to be in. I felt enormous pressure, probably most of it self-imposed. I told myself I had to work harder than those who came before me, never say no to the demands of editors, cover everything. I worked all the time. I worried all the time that I wasn't doing enough.

When I arrived, India was in the midst of a historic turnaround. It was poised to be the youngest country in the world—ever.

With a population of one billion, destined to overtake China in a few years, India had become a noisy, crowded nursery in a graying world: the vast majority of its people were under the age of thirty-five. But unlike the time I left, when they were seen as the wretched of the Earth, by the mid-2000s, India's young were seen as its crowning asset. Also, to India's advantage, the very shape of the Indian population was changing. The fertility rate was plummeting, with the average Indian woman bearing 2.6 children in 2010, down from nearly 6 children in 1960. Over time, India would have far fewer children to care for than ever before—and many more working-age adults—yielding what scholars were calling "a demographic dividend."[5]

Moreover, the economic reforms that began in 1991 had uncorked entrepreneurial energies at home and opened the market for all kinds of goods from abroad. Economic growth rates accelerated, peaking at close to 10 percent by 2007.[6] It was predicted that by 2020, India's economy would grow faster than China's. This begat tremendous exuberance among the Indian elite, exemplified by a piece that caught my eye in 2009, in the *Hindustan Times*, one of the capital's most popular English-language daily papers. The article reported that the Indian economy was projected to swell that year, with an illustration of a bare, flexed arm, the kind one might see in a logo for a men's gym. "Higher Pace, More Muscle," read the headline.

These twin developments—a demographic shift amid economic reforms—became the defining elements of what everyone around me referred to as the New India.

It came against the backdrop of another crucial shift: India was realigning its place among nations.

In 1955, as a young man, my father had stood in a thick crowd to see Nikita Khrushchev appear in central Calcutta alongside India's founding prime minister, Jawaharlal Nehru. It was the height of the Cold War. The Soviet premier pledged support for newly independent India and used the stage to excoriate the West. *The New York Times* editorialized ominously: "Mr. Nehru's toleration of Soviet anti-Western attacks on Indian soil have aligned him so closely with Soviet policies as to put a large question mark behind his professed neutrality."

The speeches of neither Khrushchev nor Nehru could sustain my father. Asthmatic and frail, he passed out in the crowd. His father had to carry him home.

Fifty years later, in Delhi, I sat with notebook in hand at the sixteenth-century sandstone fort called Purana Qila to cover the India visit of President George W. Bush. The fort was brilliantly illuminated. Members of the country's political and business elite listened proudly as Bush pledged American support for this fast-growing nation, going as far as to recognize India as a nuclear power, and as such, a legitimate member of the world's most powerful private club.[7]

His successor, Barack Obama, came in 2010 and endorsed India's desire for a permanent seat at the global table of high power, the United Nations Security Council. "In Asia and around the world, India is not simply emerging," Obama said in a speech to Parliament. "India has emerged." Indian parliamentarians howled with delight. It seemed as though they all wanted to kiss him.[8]

Obama came again in 2015. He spoke to an audience made up largely of young people. "So young Indians like you," he said, "aren't just going to define the future of this nation, you're going to shape the world."

From the moment I arrived in India in 2005, I would hear—from both Indian and American officials—how vital the relationship between these two unlikely democracies was. The United States, once suspicious of India's leftist leanings, had come to regard it as a rising strategic bulwark against a powerful China. The United States wished to be a handmaiden to India's ascent. It helped that India represented a large, lucrative market for American goods. And throughout the 2000s, American companies flocked to India to peddle everything from warplanes to Walmart outlets. Millions of young Indians were hungry for things that were previously out of reach: cell phones, high-rise apartments, cars. McKinsey & Company, the global consultancy firm, predicted in a report breathlessly called "The 'Bird of Gold'" that by 2025, the Indian middle class would grow to 583 million people, making up the world's fifth-largest consumer market.[9]

For a hot second, there were (facile) prognostications that India was becoming almost American.[10]

The opening of the Indian economy went hand in hand with something far less tangible, and something that stemmed from the democratic experiment that began in my father's time, when India gained independence from Britain at midnight, on August 15, 1947. Salman Rushdie memorialized that generation in his mind-blowing novel *Midnight's Children*.[11]

Since then, something had shifted in the Indian ethos. The freedom that was promised in 1947, when India won its independence from British rule, had quietly settled in the Indian imagination. Almost seventy years later, ordinary citizens up and down the social ladder believed they did not have to be bound by their past, that they could escape what had been predestined.

Nandan Nilekani, one of India's most well-known technology magnates and the author of *Imagining India: Ideas for the New Century*, a book about the vast changes in his country, post-reforms, summed it up this way: "For the first time, there is a sense of hope across the country," he wrote.[12]

He published the book in 2008, the year my daughter was born. This was a time of new reckoning. The generation of Indians growing up in the years since economic reforms began in 1991 were hopeful, but also impatient. Their demands were beginning to unsettle the soul of New India. They were pushing their country to deliver on the freedoms promised at midnight.

I call them noonday's children.

India's youth bulge came at a time when much of the rest of the world was growing old. By 2000, fertility rates in Europe had so plummeted that the continent was no longer replacing its population. America, despite its infusion of young immigrants, was aging. Even China, whose own youth bulge in the 1980s propelled its phenomenal economic ascent, was projected to soon have a larger share of old people to care for, and, thanks to its one-child policy, only one child to care for both parents.

India's big youth bulge turned out to be astonishingly big. The median age was 26 in 2012, the latest year for which comparable figures are published. (In China, the comparable figure was 35; in the United States, 37.)[13]

More than 300 million Indians are estimated to be under the age of 15, making India home to more children than any country at any time in human history. More important, every month, between 2011 and 2030, nearly 1 million Indians are expected to turn 18 and join the global labor force. By 2030, India is projected to reach its demographic sweet spot. That's when the majority of its population will be working age, with a relatively small share of children and elderly to care for.

All of them will have their noses pressed against the hopes of a better life. The trouble is, a great many of them will be altogether unequipped to get a job. And, anyway, the manufacturing jobs that blossomed during East Asia's demographic dividend are vanishing. What lies ahead is an increasingly automated workplace and what the demographer David Bloom calls an "unforgiving" global economy.

India faces a formidable challenge: Every year, India must create at least 10 million jobs for them.

Whenever a big bulge of young people comes of age, wherever that is in the world, disruption inevitably follows. American baby boomers sat at lunch counters in the segregated South and protested the Vietnam War: they changed the United States forever. Both the Arab Spring, beginning in 2011, and the rise of the Islamic State a few years later, were spurred by the disaffection of the young; when Tahrir Square burst into protest, the median age in Egypt was 24.8.

India is too big, too diverse for its baby boomers to spawn one coherent revolution. India's youth are not seeking to overturn the societal conventions of their parents' age entirely. Nor are they politically more liberal. But they are fueling implosions big and small, in different directions. You can feel it. It's unmistakable.

India's demographic challenge is complicated by one peculiarity: according to the 2011 census, for every 1000 boys that are born, there are only 919 girls. This represents the sharpest gender imbalance in India's own history—one measure of the degradation of daughters that starts in the womb. This degradation is also the source of turmoil, as young women begin to push, in great numbers, against the rules and ways that hold them back. The more they push, the more violently they are pushed back, often by men as young and hungry as they are.

India's story line would turn. The euphoria that greeted me in 2005—a mood that many of my Indian friends had warned me to be skeptical of—would give way to disenchantment, anger, even bitterness.

By 2011, the economy slowed. Foreign investors began pulling out. The price of food soared. Corruption scandals burst open. A coalition government, led by the Indian National Congress party, was paralyzed. The country was experiencing its worst economic crisis since before liberalization. On the eve of the 2014 parliamentary elections, there were loud calls for change.

Many reasons were offered: the global financial crisis, a fragile coalition government, reckless spending, and insufficient progress in carrying out economic reforms. All of these may have been true to varying degrees. But to my mind, the shift in India's trajectory pointed to more fundamental gaps—and these were precisely the fault lines that its young had begun to reveal. The post-1991 generation had been led to imagine it could rewrite its destiny, that it could shake off the karma of past lives. The country was utterly unprepared for this.

After nearly seventy years of democratic rule, and a decade of galloping economic growth, there is still nothing close to a level playing field—neither functioning schools that would let poor children take advantage of new opportunities, nor parity for daughters to allow women to realize their true potential, nor even tolerance for different points of view. Life for millions of young people remains utterly fragile. About 30 percent of children under the age of five remain clinically malnourished; most women suffer from anemia; one-third of all Indian children are not immunized against preventable childhood diseases; and, despite roaring economic growth and a stream of state-sponsored programs, nearly one in four Indians lives in dire poverty, or on less than $1.25 a day.[14]

India is being propelled from within by what I regard as its most transformative generation—those who have grown up since economic reforms began in 1991. Their demands are reshaping the country. Their ambitions are exposing important fault lines. They are poking at the fable of freedom at midnight.

I have a personal stake in this. My daughter was born in this India.

In the coming years, India can thrive because of its young. Or it can implode. Or both. There's little time left.

"When the world sleeps," Nehru had said in 1947, on the eve of independence, "India will awake to life and freedom."

That was India at midnight.

Were he to come to my daughter's India, he might say otherwise. While the world sleeps, Indians come of age—and holler.

This is India at noonday.

To understand noonday, let's rewind to midnight, to when the story of independent India begins—in a burst of bloodshed.

As British India was partitioned into India and Pakistan in August 1947, the vast province of Bengal, which is where my family is from, was carved into two. The western part of Bengal fell in Hindu-majority India. The east fell in Muslim-majority East Pakistan, which would later become a sovereign nation, called Bangladesh. Millions fled during the time of Partition. Hindus headed west to seek refuge in Hindu-majority India. Muslims moved the other way, to Muslim-majority East Pakistan.

Hemendra Nath Sen, my great-grandfather, my father's mother's father, did not flee. He had no intention of fleeing. He was a lawyer in a small provincial city called Rangpur, in what would fall in East Pakistan. He was a Hindu, well-known, well-off, the father of seven children—five girls, two boys. In Sen-*para*, which is how the neighborhood of the Sens was known, he had built a sprawling bungalow of red bricks and green wooden shutters, with high ceilings to let out the heat and a *jamun* tree that littered the yard with purple berries all summer. This is what he called home.

By 1947, the year of Partition, all seven of Hemen Sen's children had left Rangpur. Most of them had settled in Calcutta, in what became Hindu-majority India. Hemen Sen and his wife stayed on, perhaps for as long as five years after independence—the dates are impossible to verify more than half a century later—until his children insisted that he leave. And so, sometime in the early 1950s, he sold his house to a Muslim family who came from Jalpaiguri, a city just across the border in what had become Hindu-majority India. With his wife, Hemen Sen boarded a Calcutta-bound train. It broke his heart to leave, his youngest daughter, my great-aunt, recalled.

There are stories like this in family after family across north India. Partition seared the consciousness of my parents' generation and left a mark on generations to come, though the facts of what actually happened during that time remain shrouded in mystery and myth. Hindus and Muslims attacked one another without mercy. Between 250,000 and 2 million people are estimated to have died. Up to 10 million people are said to have been uprooted from home forever. Women were raped, though no one bothered to count how many. There was never any accountability for what happened, nor even a truth and reconciliation effort to get to the bottom of the awful things that people did to one another.[15]

By independence, Hemen Sen's eldest daughter, Sushoma, was the mother of five children in Calcutta. The fourth among them was my father. No one is quite sure about his date of birth. It was probably 1941, possibly July, maybe August, definitely during the rains.

Baba was a schoolboy at the time of the Partition. His family lived in a three-room ground-floor flat in a Hindu-majority neighborhood near bustling Gariahat Market. The milkmen of his area were amateur wrestlers who had migrated from the countryside in the neighboring state of Bihar. They were seen as the local toughs you turned to when you needed to keep troublemakers out, and so during the Partition years, it fell on them to lead the neighborhood vigilante group. One day, amid the rumors and fights that were routine at that time, the milkmen-wrestlers stopped to accost an older gentleman, a stranger, as he walked through the neighborhood. Who are you, they demanded to know, why are you here? They stripped off his pants, standard practice to assess whether a man was circumcised, and therefore a Muslim. The stranger was a Muslim, and for that reason, they beat him so thoroughly that he died right then and there. Baba remembers it vividly. He says he watched from the sidelines. Who among his friends and neighbors took part, I will never know for sure.

Baba heard that in retaliation Muslim mobs set upon Hindus in the old man's neighborhood. Like this, violence spiraled across Calcutta. There were several rounds of bloodletting, in 1946 and 1947. Newspapers described corpses floating in the canals. Refugees poured in on trains from East Pakistan. Baba's father—tall, self-possessed, passionate about politics—marched through the neighborhood trying to find shelter for the newcomers. Baba was with him when he persuaded the residents of Jasoda Bhavan, an elegant four-story apartment building across from Gariahat Market, to open up their homes. He turned the courtyard into a communal kitchen. He goaded every household to send a pot of *dal*.

Circumcision and pots of lentils: these are Baba's most vivid memories of Partition. He describes it as a time of trouble. He uses the Bengali word *gondogol*, which is one of those elastic, imprecise words. One might refer to a rumble in the stomach as a *gondogol*.

Baba's sister, who is ten years older, has another memory. She was at a family wedding in a neighborhood near the Hindu temple to the black goddess, Ma Kali. The wedding must have been sometime in the months before independence. And what a strange wedding it was. You couldn't turn the lights on for fear of drawing attention. You couldn't blow the conch. You sat in the dark, as quiet as could be. The priest quickly whispered the bare minimum prayers, and the shutters remained closed. My aunt occasionally peered through the slats. She saw men lunging at one another with knives in a field across the street. The image stamped itself on her memory. "They were cutting each other's heads off," she said.

Close to midnight on August 15, 1947, when freedom officially arrived, Jawaharlal Nehru addressed the nation. His speech was broadcast live on state-run All India Radio. These were among his most famous lines. "A moment comes, which comes but rarely in history," he said, "when we step out from the old to the new, when an age ends, and when the soul of a nation, long suppressed, finds utterance."

Nehru and his fellow members of India's Constituent Assembly deliberated for three years over the language of the constitution of independent India. What they came up with was a document of extraordinarily audacious pledges. India was to be a nation like none the world had seen: secular, democratic, held together by no shared language, faith, or race. The majority of its people were hungry and illiterate. Its social order treated women and outcastes as lesser beings. Never mind all that. The Constitution, which came into effect on January 26, 1950, enshrined the right to equality for all its citizens.

No country had ever pulled this off—except America, and that too, only sort of.

The Constitution of India guarantees every citizen a set of "fundamental rights," which includes the right to freedom of expression and the right to practice one's religion and culture. It compels the state to try to establish a social order in which "justice, social, economic and political, shall inform all the institutions of the national life." It underscores the hope that the state would soon offer free, compulsory education to all children up to the age of fourteen.

Implicit here is a promise that one's path in life would no longer be determined by the past, that all men and women could forge it themselves— that they could escape karma.

Its preamble reads:

WE, THE PEOPLE OF INDIA, having solemnly resolved to constitute India into a SOVEREIGN SOCIALIST SECULAR DEMOCRATIC REPUBLIC and to secure to all its citizens: JUSTICE, social, economic and political; LIBERTY, of thought, expression, belief, faith and worship; EQUALITY of status and of opportunity.

The framers of the Constitution capitalized those words, as if to underscore their own audacity.

For centuries, an Indian's destiny has been scripted in the womb. There, it was determined whether you could go to school or look a policeman in the eye, what work you did, who you married and if you could wear diamond studs in your ears. Bhimrao Ambedkar, chairman of the committee that drafted the Constitution, was keenly aware of this. "Democracy in India," he said, "is only a top-dressing on an Indian soil, which is essentially undemocratic."

Top dressing. Not part of the undersoil.

Ambedkar was not alone in recognizing that a society as stratified as India's could scuttle the experiment with democracy. Many of the men who shaped modern India—and they were by and large men—set out "social revolution" as their most important goal, the historian Granville Austin observed, rivaled only by the need for national stability.[16] These two imperatives—fundamental reforms and a strong state—would set the stage for several crucial battles in the years to come.

Since independence, India has unquestionably proved its democratic credentials. Unlike many of its Asian neighbors, which boasted swift economic growth under totalitarian rule, India has stuck to its democratic path.[17]

Since 1951, it has held free and fair elections for local and national office. Only once, during the emergency rule of Indira Gandhi, did India bow to authoritarianism. The judiciary is independent (though often accused of corruption). Civil society is robust. The press is free and aggressive. The country's many castes and languages are better represented in politics than ever before. India has withstood three crippling wars with its neighbors, battled insurgencies of many stripes, and survived some of the worst terrorist attacks in the world. These are enormous achievements for any country, especially one that was born so poor.

Through it all, the lives of ordinary people have improved on the whole.

In 1951, the average Indian could expect to live until the age of thirty-two; today, life expectancy is sixty-six.

Infant mortality, one of the most telling measures of a country's well-being, has plummeted. In 1951, about 180 out of 1000 infants were likely to die before their first birthday; in 2011, that figure was 44.[18]

Fewer women died in childbirth too, compared with seventy years ago. Many more Indians can read and write than ever before.

But beware. It is impossible to tell one story about how India has fared since independence: its northern, eastern, and central states are the poorest, with human development indicators that mirror those of sub-Saharan Africa, while its southern and western states resemble Southeast Asia in terms of health, education, and well-being.

Taken as a whole, India has one of the world's fastest-growing large economies, second only to China's. Its gross domestic product is the third largest in the world, after the United States' and China's.

Freedom has delivered these things. But has prosperity brought greater freedoms to those who had so little? That is a point of contention, and that will be underscored by the life stories of the people you will meet in the pages of this book.

At the same time—and this is of course impossible to quantify—the idea of freedom has unquestionably taken root, even in the undersoil. In my father's India, so many Indians would dare not question their station in life. In my daughter's India, they expect to shape their destiny. Escape is a given. Democracy has anchored itself in the minds of India's young. It speaks to the triumph of an audacious idea.

One word embodied the bullishness of this generation: "aspiration." Young Indians were repeatedly praised for being aspirational. A wedding *lehenga* embroidered with Swarovski crystals was called aspirational. Cell phones were called aspirational; by 2011, more Indians had a cell phone than a toilet. So too was the budding Indian love affair with the road. In 2008, the year my girl was born, Indians bought a record 1.5 million cars, making it one of the world's most attractive car markets. That year, the Indian conglomerate Tata unveiled the world's cheapest car—a tiny, no-frills automobile, known as the Nano, that was marketed as the very symbol of Indian aspiration. (By 2013, sales of the Nano were far lower than expected. Indians apparently wanted a bigger, more proper car, not this low-priced vehicle marketed to the lowest rung of the ambition ladder.)

Aspiration was a meme that infected India's idea of itself. Consider this advertisement for a vocational school in India, where you could learn to work at an office or a fancy hotel. The ad told you nothing about the courses offered, only about ambition.

"Without ambition," the ad declared, "you're like a wardrobe without jeans, a sky without a single star, a song without words, a lemon with all the juice squeezed out."

And then this devastating punch line: "Without ambition you'll go nowhere."

In the years since economic reforms began in 1991, the gap between rich and poor not only widened, the rich flaunted it. In a classic symptom of oligarchy, new millionaires sprang from industries like mining and real estate, where business success depended on political connections. The upper middle classes checked out of public India altogether; they neither went to public hospitals nor public schools, nor rode the bus. Economic reforms offered them better alternatives. They retreated into new gated enclaves, seeking reprieve from power cuts, water shortages, noise, open sewers, heat, and the psychic brutality of having to live amid the poor. This too was desire for a certain freedom.

There was a lot of talk of the growing middle class. But the vast majority of Indians were nothing like what the rest of the world would consider middle class. Nearly two-thirds of Indians sustained themselves on less than $2 a day.[19]

Since liberalization, poverty also declined, though the number of Indians in extreme poverty remained pretty stubborn. By 2012, more than 300 million Indians lived below the national poverty line, which Biraj Patnaik, an activist, rightly called the starvation line.

Ambedkar was remarkably prescient. India still struggles to be democratic in everyday life. Not long ago, I came across a full-page advertisement in one of the English-language daily papers. The ad was for a new private school. It featured a picture of a little girl, probably five years old, with a broom in her hand and a grinning housemaid at her side. The caption played on the apprehensions of a privileged parent. "While your child is learning the maid's language," it warned, "someone else's child is learning a foreign language." The ad went on to boast of an Olympic-size swimming pool and classes in French and German.

What this ad neglected to show was the aspiration of the maid. Across India, where for centuries a life's possibilities were circumscribed by the caste into which you were born, housemaids, sharecroppers, and bricklayers are sending their children to school like never before. In primary school, there is almost universal enrollment, and for the first time in the country's history, girls are as likely to be enrolled in primary school as boys. On every reporting trip across India, I am struck by this remarkable shift, and when I ask their mothers why they bother, I hear answers as vague as this: I will educate my daughter because I want her life to be different from mine.

The stakes are higher now than ever before. A million young men and women turn eighteen every month. They go out in search of work and dignity. They push their leaders to deliver.

And yet.

India is the land of And Yet.

Ramachandra Guha, the leading historian of modern India, calls India a "fifty-fifty democracy."[20] I take this to mean that it works about as well as it doesn't.

I think of it as a democracy that makes promises it has no intention of keeping.

And this is the tension that prevails in India—and why the noonday generation is so important in rewriting India's freedom story. It is a tipping-point generation in the arc of independent India's history. It makes new demands on India's democracy in at least three important ways: genuine equality of opportunity, dignity for girls, and civil liberties. It pushes India to keep its promise.

Aspiration is like water. It needs a place to go, or else it drowns everything in its path.

By 2014, Indians had elected a man who embodied aspiration itself—a man who also inspired as much fear as admiration. Self-made, iron-fisted, known to harbor zero patience for the country's English-speaking privileged elite, Narendra Modi had risen up the ranks of a Hindu militant group called the Rashtriya Swayamsevak Sangh, or RSS, and helped his party sweep the 2014 parliamentary election. He promised voters a government that worked, no matter what it took. "Good times ahead," his campaign slogan boasted. By now, 40 percent of the electorate was under the age of thirty-five.

There are two kinds of people in my family: those who, having been uprooted early and often, choose to stay rooted and those who keep uprooting. I belong to the second category. I am most at ease when there's a suitcase packed at the door, with sensible shoes and a silk sleeping-bag liner in case I find myself in a skanky guesthouse somewhere out in the world. I avoid nailing bookshelves to the wall because it signals a settle-down that makes me uncomfortable. My favorite apartment of all time is one that abuts the Nizamuddin railway station in Delhi, where the sta-tionmaster's voice announces the comings and goings of trains all night long, and I dream of trips not yet taken.

My toing and froing continues. Before my daughter turns four in the spring of 2012, we move back to the United States. This is the twenty-third time I have moved. My girl is now an immigrant to the United States, just as I was once. Except that America is a different country.

As I return, the United States is struggling out of its worst eco-nomic crisis since the Great Depression. Roads are potholed, one in five American children is hungry, and many, many American mothers are no longer certain that their children's lives will be better than their own. Most striking, the American dream seems further from reach for so many Americans.

The idea of upward mobility—the evidence casts doubt on whether it was ever more than an idea—now seems remote for millions for hard-working families. Inequality, a word that was never really spoken of while I was growing up in California, is greater than it has been in generations, and Americans are talking about it openly. Rising inequality shapes the New York mayoral race in 2013. And as I write this, in 2015, nearly every presidential candidate is having to pay at least lip-service to the growing gap between rich and poor.

My girl settles in quickly. It takes about three weeks for her Indian accent to vanish. She learns to camp in the California redwoods. She learns to love ketchup, which is far sweeter than what Indians call tomato sauce. I sign her up for Sunday morning Kathak class, the sixteenth-century classical dance tradition that has blossomed in cities across America, to cater to the children of Indian immigrants. "That's so N.R.I., dude," my friend in Bangalore tells me. N.R.I. is shorthand for Non-Resident Indian. It is not always a term of endearment.

I am a second-time immigrant to the United States. Toing and froing. Escaping, only to come right back.

"We are like turtles, me and Mama," my daughter says, parroting what she has heard me say. "We carry our homes on our back."

When I set out to write this book, I imagined it would be an American's journey through the old country. Becoming a parent changed everything. For one thing, it took so much longer to write. It also changed course. My stake in India deepened. I wanted to understand the time and place that made my child—and to chronicle it for her. I found myself thinking about what kind of a country it could become as she grows up, and how far it would go to deliver on its audacious, original promise of freedom.

So this book became a highly personal chronicle of today's India, told through the stories of ordinary Indian men and women who represent the yearnings of India's most transformative generation. They are from country and city, and for the most part, they are born and raised, like my girl, in the years since economic reforms began in 1991. Their journeys tell the story of aspiration—its triumph and its undoing—in one of the most important democracies in the world. Taken together, they are meant to be a portrait of the noonday generation.

I have tried to tell their stories with affection and humility. I know they don't represent the whole of India. They are only seven in a billion.

They include Rakhi, a country girl who turns into a ruthless killer, and the ghost of Monica, shot in the head for falling in love. They follow Mani, a young woman who escapes the wasteland, only to face a terrible reckoning in glossy gated India. There's Rinu, who wants to be the next Miley Cyrus, but becomes famous instead for speaking her mind on Facebook, and Varsha, who wants to be a cop, so she can help girls like her feel safe. There's Shashi, the political strategist of my generation, who sells Modi to the young. There's Anupam, the son of an auto-rickshaw driver. Each one of us makes our own destiny, he told me once, as we were sitting on his college steps one afternoon, batting away mosquitoes, and he said it so matter-of-factly, as though it were so obvious, that he looked perplexed when he saw me taking notes.

The story of India at noonday is the story of ambition, and it is a story of ambition thwarted. That story will inevitably shape the world in the years to come: By 2015, India's population had peaked past 1.3 billion, and shortly after 2022, India is expected to surpass China and become the world's most populous nation.

I am reminded of the freedom stories of American women in the late 1950s and '60s. They too were impossibly ambitious. Educated, creative, tough women, they too found their ambitions blocked. In turn, they gave rise to one of the most transformative social movements in modern history. Ambition is ambition. When it's thwarted, it can unleash demands for change, perhaps even a new freedom struggle.

My parents were among midnight's children. Their India faced a test that no other modern nation had before: how to build a democratic republic from a hungry, fractured, feudal society. India at noonday faces a tougher test: how to make democracy something other than topsoil.

"HI-FI"
How to Outrun Fate

Anupam Kumar grows up in a three-room house made of naked bricks and tin, along an unpaved alley popular with stray pigs, in an ancient city that has come to be known as India's most disorderly, called Patna.

His papa is Srikrishna Jaiswal, a small man of few words who, for as long as Anupam can recall, has plied an auto-rickshaw through the streets of Patna twelve hours a day, seven days a week, inhaling exhaust fumes, dodging careening buses, sometimes getting a whack from the pistol butt of a local cop.

Also for as long as he can remember, Anupam has wished not to be his auto-rickshaw-driving father's auto-rickshaw-driving son. Since childhood, his single-minded goal has been to outrun that destiny. Mummy has been his chief co-conspirator.

At age seventeen, his escape plan involves getting into what is possibly the most competitive university in the world and studying the possibilities of life on other planets—Earth having become too dirty, in his view, and too crowded. Look around, he says in the spring of 2005, when he is preparing for the college entrance exam at home. His narrow unpaved lane is bordered by a shiny, black ribbon of raw sewage. The air reeks of piling rot. By monsoon all will melt to muck. The brick-and-tin houses are pressed so hard against one another you can practically hear the drunks burping nearby.

What makes his escape plan all the more audacious is that Anupam is a Class 4 dropout. He is nine years old when he comes home and tells Mummy that his teacher cannot read a textbook properly. So he teaches himself, hunching over books morning, noon, and night, usually by the light of a kerosene lamp, since the electricity supply in Patna is even shoddier than its schools. His mother pounds the pavement for private tutors. She hushes the younger children so Anupam can study. She never, ever rolls her eyes when he tells her about his dreams, like wanting to explore life in outer space. She never clucks her tongue when he says he would like to conduct research, even though she's never heard of the word "research." Naturally, because he is a boy, she never orders him to sweep the floors or roll chapatis. When he tells her he'd rather study than attend a family function, she makes excuses for him. He'll go mad, her relatives say, he'll go blind.

She knows Anupam is her golden child. And a golden child is different. Also, a golden child needs someone to watch his back. And so, during the hottest mosquito-ridden afternoons, she sits behind him on their hard wooden bed while he studies, keeping him cool with a handheld bamboo fan.

She doesn't have to tell him how she feels. He can see it in her eyes. Mummy looks to him to outrun his destiny—and take them all with him.

"I feel a lot of pressure," Anupam says the summer of the college entrance exam. "It's from inside."

Coiled, anxious Anupam.

At seventeen, his hair has flecks of gray.

During British rule, on the vast, fertile Gangetic plains of Bihar, the north Indian state whose capital is Patna, grew fields upon fields of poppy. In the nineteenth century, an opium factory was erected along the banks of the Ganges, not far from where Anupam grew up. Steam ships traveled downriver to the port in Calcutta, from where their precious cargo was ferried to Shanghai as part of a lucrative opium trade.[1]

Indigo came from Bihar too, engorging cotton in vivid blues for the cloth mills of northern England.

Bihar's plantation economy was marked by exceptionally large landholdings. The powerful *zamindars* who owned them lorded over a hierarchy of traders, teachers, cattle herders, cobblers, tailors, candle makers, farmworkers, and so on. One measure of Bihar's misery could be seen in the large numbers of Biharis who left home for a life of indenture on the other side of the world. By the mid-1800s, as the transatlantic slave trade began to be abolished in the European colonies of the Caribbean, laborers from Bihar left by the boatloads for the sugar plantations of the New World. If you crossed the black ocean, it was said that you lost the caste you were born into. Thousands and thousands of people were willing to do just that—even if they were born to the highest caste of all, Brahmins.[2]

By independence, in 1947, Bihar was one of the most feudal parts of India, with a prosperous *zamindari* class plus many, many landless peasants. Its sharecropping system meant that tenant farmers and their children were often bonded for life to landlords or moneylenders. Peasant uprisings were ruthlessly put down. One landlord was known to have thrown rebellious peasants into the maws of his pet tigers: For this, he was called the Maneater of Manatu.

By the late 1970s, when Anupam's mummy was still a child, Bihar's stubborn feudal system came face-to-face with modern, democratic wants. Then began nearly three decades of violent caste wars, pitting landless peasants against those who had lorded over them for so long. The landowning upper castes, known as the Rajputs, had their own militias. So did the Yadavs and Kurmis, communities that were several rungs below on the caste ladder. Each militia was armed with country rifles and fanciful names: Bhoomi Sena, Sunlight Sena, Ranvir Sena. They clashed, often over land, leaving a trail of terror in the countryside. Dalits, as those at the very bottom of the caste ladder called themselves, were often the most brutally assaulted.[3]

In a typical case, in a village called Parasbigha in February 1980, a dispute over who had the rights to a plot of land led an upper-caste militia, Brahmeshwar Sena, to torch the mud huts of Dalit peasants in the dead of night. At least eleven people were killed, among them four children. Some burned to death; others were shot. This was the Bihar of Anupam's parents.

Srikrishna Jaiswal was born shortly after independence, in 1955, in a town encircled by lychee orchards called Muzaffarpur. The family sat on the lower reaches of the caste ladder, part of a community known as Kalwars. His father, who had made his living as a small shopkeeper, died when Srikrishna was young. The family shop was sold, and the proceeds were divided among four sons. Srikrishna, the youngest, quickly spent his small share, taking his mother to visit Hindu temples here and there and, just as quickly, becoming the butt of family jokes. He would amount to nothing, his brothers said. He would have to go around with a begging bowl to earn his keep. Anupam was raised on the story of his father's humiliation. He held it close to his chest, as though it were an amulet.

Srikrishna was in his thirties by the time his marriage was fixed to a girl named Sudha. She must have been around fifteen at the time. Small and lean, she had bright, fast-moving eyes, and though she had attended school only up to Class 6, she had a good deal of practical good sense. We may not amount to much, she told him, but our children can rise. With this, she persuaded him to leave Muzaffarpur for Patna, the state capital, where Srikrishna hired an auto-rickshaw, black and yellow, noisy and noxious, with two wheels in back and one in front. What he earned, he turned over to his wife. He had learned his lesson with money.

The Patna they came to in the 1980s was in the midst of political turmoil. Some of Mrs. Gandhi's loudest, most prominent opponents came from Patna. Their protests had prefaced Mrs. Gandhi's emergency, and their victory in the elections that followed, in 1977, transformed the political landscape. Among the new leaders to emerge was a charismatic student activist from Patna University named Lalu Prasad Yadav. He soon became the most outspoken leader Bihar had seen from the lower rungs of the caste ladder.

He came from the Yadav community; their traditional occupation had been to herd cattle, but by now they had accumulated land, guns, and a large constituency of voters across the state. On the caste order, they were somewhere near the bottom, though not considered "untouchable." In the finely graded categories that delineated the caste order (Americans might recall our own absurd racial categories, like "octoroon"), they were officially classified as one of the so-called Other Backward Classes, meaning that they were socially and economically disadvantaged compared with those who were considered "forward."

Also on the list of "backward" castes was Srikrishna Jaiswal's Kalwar community.

Yadav leveraged the caste stereotypes brilliantly. Portraying himself as a champion of the downtrodden, he dressed in the countryman's white cotton wraparound dhotis rather than the city man's pleated trousers. He gave speeches in colloquial Bhojpuri and Hindi. And he stitched together a winning patchwork of voters who felt dispossessed by the big political parties that were, by and large, led by upper-caste men.

Yadav was elected chief minister of Bihar in 1990. His ascent marked a crucial shift in the postemergency political order. Never before had a man from the "backward" castes taken power like this. Bihar was one of India's most populous and therefore most politically influential states, and so his new Bihar-based political party became a force to contend with in national politics. Never again—at least not during Anupam's coming-of-age—would small parties like his allow either of the two major national parties, Indian National Congress and its rival Bharatiya Janata Party, to enjoy a monopoly on power. Indeed, for the next thirty years, both national parties would have to rely on these third parties, based on region and caste, in order to rule India. Power had to be shared.

Upper-caste Biharis called Yadav uncouth. His own people saw it differently. A man who was then a student at Patna University recalled of that time that, finally, he and others known to have come from "backward" communities no longer had shoes thrown at them in class. They were now in charge.

In December 1987, when Yadav was beginning to make his mark in politics and the cold mist rose so late in the morning that mothers swaddled their babies in blankets and mufflers until close to lunchtime, Sudha bore her first child: a boy, thanks to God's grace, whom she called Anupam. She can't say exactly how old she was. She thinks she was around seventeen. It had become customary at the time to not burden your child with a caste name. So she didn't bother to write Jaiswal on his birth certificate. Sudha wrote his name simply as Anupam Kumar, introducing him to the world as simply Anupam-the-young.

In quick succession came another boy and a girl. Enough. Sudha had her tubes tied and set her mind to building a home. She saved, prayed, borrowed, until finally, there was enough to buy a plot of land, in a working-class *mohalla* near Gaighat, where the British had once built their opium factory. Sudha bought a few bricks at a time, then sheets of corrugated tin for a roof. From a sister, she picked up hand-me-down window frames. She installed iron bars to keep out thieves.

The house slowly came into being.

If she could have put an electric fence around it, she would have, so fiercely did she want to make it a sanctuary from the disorder outside. She barred her children from playing cricket, tossing marbles in the lane, going to the movies, loping through the bazaar—or in any other way loitering on the street. When she went to the market, she padlocked the front door from outside, keeping the kids inside. She was terrified of the street. She was terrified that it would suck the marrow out of her children's bones, that it would fill them with chaos and vice.

She had reason to be nervous. During Anupam's childhood, Bihar was a dangerous place. The state accounted for one in five murders committed with an unlicensed gun in all of India. Anyone who was seen as wealthy risked having a child kidnapped. Educated professionals left in droves. Sudha had no such escape route. She knew only she had to keep an owl's eye on her young.

In Gaighat, gang fights broke out often. Thugs who enjoyed Yadav's patronage were rarely prosecuted, which explained the success of a gangster who lived nearby and ran a lucrative hooch business from the back of his house. His portly wife, back-fat spilling out of her blouse, often sat on the front porch as though on neighborhood watch. Sudha taught her children to bow each time they crossed her path.

Sudha's tin-roofed house trapped the heat of summer. The power supply was unreliable, so it didn't make much difference that they had no ceiling fans when Anupam was a child. The water pipes were dry more often than not. Across the lane, an enterprising family produced bags of noodles from a noisy makeshift ground-floor factory. Pigs foraged in an empty lot next door, which served as a neighborhood trash dump.

Anupam's destiny was most certainly scripted in Sudha's womb. She willed Anupam into being. She believed in him. She guarded him. She prayed each morning that he would outfox fate.

"It was a mutual collaboration between me and my mom that brought the magic" is how Anupam once put it.

Anupam studied all the time. It rubbed off on his younger brother and sister, Anuj and Chandni. Mummy made it clear that they were to emulate his ideal.

That Sudha had a Class 6 education was no doubt crucial to Anupam's success. She could read, which meant she could hustle for school forms, caste certificates, tutors—whatever her children needed. She could manage the family's finances on her auto-rickshaw-driving husband's perennially erratic income.

Sudha was typical in this respect. The children of educated moms, regardless of their economic circumstances, are less likely to be malnourished, more likely to be immunized against childhood diseases, and they are more likely to succeed in school.[4]

* * *

Anupam's childhood coincided with Yadav's reign. Yadav became chief minister of Bihar in 1990 and with the exception of a brief period when criminal charges forced his resignation in 1997, he remained in power until 2005.

Bihar's fortunes tumbled during his tenure. Throughout the 1990s, its economic growth rate slipped to an average of 2.87 percent a year, less than half of the national average of over 6 percent.

At the same time, its youth population soared. Bihar, one of the most populous states in India, became the youngest state in the union, with a larger share of its population under the age of twenty-five than any other. As such, it became an emblem of the mismatch of labor supply and demand: lots of young people, coming of age in a sluggish economy.

During Anupam's childhood, this scenario came to define most of India's northern and eastern states. The country's south and west were a stark contrast: there, fertility rates fell steadily, thanks to advances in women's education and health. In the southern state of Tamil Nadu, for instance, its fertility rate dropped so much that the population growth pretty much stabilized, while its economic growth rate was among the highest in the land.

Yadav, shrewdly for his time, focused his priorities on social empowerment, promising dignity rather than the nitty-gritty of economic development. He built no new schools in Anupam's crowded neighborhood. Teacher vacancies were left unfilled. Highways disintegrated from lack of state investment. Vast swaths of the state were not connected to the electrical grid at all, and other places, like Anupam's Gaighat, lived through hours of power outage every day. It's what Anupam grew up with—he didn't know anyone who lived differently.

Yadav wore his populism on his sleeve. He invited commoners to visit the lawns of the chief minister's villa in Patna's onetime British enclave. He installed stables for his buffalos.

One day, Yadav sat in his office, surrounded by cabinet members from a variety of upper castes. He slipped his foot out of a sandal and regaled those present with a story about how he lost a toenail. "Look at my foot. See, I am missing a toenail. . . . This is *democracy*." After a dramatic pause to let this bewildering statement sink in, he continued:

> I lost this toenail when I was a poor boy living in my village. We barely had enough to eat and I used to herd buffalos all day, sometimes so late that I would fall asleep on the back of a buffalo on my way home. One day, a buffalo that I was herding stepped on my foot and I lost the toenail. . . . Now look at what a tall chair I am sitting in [the chief minister's chair]! I have proven that ballot boxes are more powerful than machine guns. Votes can decide whether a man will be in the dust or riding in an airplane.[5]

As far as Sudha was concerned, there was no question of putting her children in public school.

In Gaighat, the government schools were falling apart. Indeed, at the school where Anupam was nominally enrolled, bricks tumbled off the façade. Anupam remembers that it was painted red, "like a police station." Teachers rarely showed up, or when they did, they didn't do much more than take attendance. Kids played hooky or marbles—or they made themselves useful, snatching gold earrings or serving tea to the rickshaw drivers under the Mahatma Gandhi Bridge.

Sudha pounded the pavement for a private school she could afford—which wasn't much with what her husband brought home from his rickshaw route. Anupam went to school dutifully, until one day in Class 4 when he came home, put down his book bag, and told Mummy: My teacher can't read properly. What good is a teacher like that?

She did not doubt his word. She did not tell him to keep quiet and go back to school. She let him drop out. Then she pounded the pavement some more.

In the next *mohalla*, she found a "coaching center," which was another name for a private, unregulated non-school school. Some coaching centers are afterschool tutoring centers. Others, like the one Sudha found, offer full-day programs. This one established itself in a ground-floor flat, shielded from the street by a high wall of bougainvillea. Rows of children sat on the floor, rocking gently back and forth while memorizing math.

Every morning, at quarter to eight, Sudha packed Anupam a *roti-sabji* lunch and whispered prayers over his head. The boy left home, bowed to the hooch dealer's wife, walked past the shuttered snack shops and under the Mahatma Gandhi Bridge, where the auto-rickshaw drivers assembled. He studied at the coaching center from eight in the morning until eight at night, six days a week. The subjects offered were math, logical reasoning, and general knowledge, enough to crack the state-run matriculation exam in Class 8.

That exam was the only reason Anupam enrolled in the nearest government-run school, which was across the street from the coaching center. He showed up once a month, so his name could remain on the attendance rolls.

On Sundays, he did homework.

It was a typical Indian work-around. By 2011, one-fourth of all Indian parents shelled out money for tutors outside school, according to the Annual Status of Education Report, an independent survey of education trends carried out by a national nonprofit called Pratham. It was one telling measure of how little kids learned in school.

This survey, conducted every year across rural India since 2005, also pulled the veil off of one of India's best-kept secrets. It found that while the vast majority of children were enrolled in school—India was boasting of near universal school enrollment—they were getting very little out of it. The latest survey results, from 2014, showed that most Indian children in Class 5 are functionally illiterate. More than half cannot subtract.

That is to say, even though education is now democratic, its quality is abysmal. Vast numbers of children are going to school, and coming home with little to show for it. It is a perfect snapshot of what aspiration has wrought, and how aspiration is defeated, one child at a time.

I will never forget what a social worker who worked for Pratham told me after we spent the day in a typical Bihar village, where his colleagues were conducting the survey. We had watched dozens of children stream into school early in the morning. We had watched them trying to read by themselves. We had listened to the headmaster complain bitterly about having to handle so many kids, and with so few teachers, that it was impossible for him to do anything. The social worker looked utterly dejected by the end of that morning.

"When they get older, they'll curse their teachers," he said of the children. "They'll say, 'We came every day and we learned nothing.'"[6]

Anupam displayed an unusual acumen for numbers. Word spread in his *mohalla*. Another tutor stepped in during high school. He armed Anupam with more hat tricks to ace math tests.

Srikrishna once suggested that Anupam become an Indian Administrative Service officer, a bureaucrat with a government-issued Ambassador car with flashing red lights on top. That would be sweet revenge against all those cops who had pushed him around all those years on the streets of Patna. Anupam confessed to having no interest in becoming a bureaucrat.

Anupam told Mummy that he wished to study at one of the Indian Institutes of Technology, the IITs, an intensely competitive chain of colleges established by India's first prime minister, Jawaharlal Nehru, to train engineers for a new nation. By Anupam's time the IITs had exported armies of engineers to build the global technology industry in California's Silicon Valley.

Sudha broached the idea with her husband. Neither of them knew anyone who had attended the IITs. They hadn't even heard of the IITs. It didn't matter. It was enough to know there was a world beyond their world—and that Anupam would take them there.

In one respect, the education of Anupam is a portrait of Indian neglect. It is equally a portrait of how to hack a way around it—how to adjust.

As Anupam was coming of age, caste was fast losing its original currency. That is to say, it defined less and less what you did for a living. More and more, caste did not dictate which water tap you could use or whom you ate with; those distinctions didn't vanish, they just mattered less in many parts of India, especially cities. Caste remained central in marriage ("Take water, not daughter," it was said). And it became entrenched in politics. ("You don't cast your vote," it was also said; "you vote your caste.")

In the years after the lifting of the emergency, caste carried more and more weight in who you backed at the polls, and for good reason. If your man (or woman) got elected, it could mean jobs for your people, or a road through your part of the village, or a government contract for a cement dealer in your community. People voted along caste lines not out of an antiquated sense of tribal loyalties, but often for the prospect of real material gains.

The Constitution guaranteed set-asides for those on the very bottom of the social order. Those who were considered untouchables, or Dalits, and those who were regarded as outcastes, because they were India's indigenous people, or *adivasis*, were entitled to a fixed share of elected seats in parliament. They were also entitled to a fixed share of government jobs and seats in college.

By the 1980s, as the "backward" classes rose in political power, they too sought quotas in jobs and university admissions—but gauging who was "backward" and how many they were became enormously tricky. To determine backwardness, the government sometimes relied on the peculiar observations of nineteenth-century British ethnographers.

One H. H. Risley, a Briton writing in the late 1800s, described Anupam's community of Kalwars as a "liquor-selling, distilling, and trading caste of Behar." He averred, "The social rank of Kalwars is low. Brahmans and members of the higher castes will on no account take water from their hands."

And in 1896, a treatise placed Kalwars under the heading "Manufacturing or Artisan Castes that are Regarded as Unclean Sudras."

John C. Nesfield, a British census officer serving in the North-West Provinces and Oudh in 1881, observed that Kalwars were higher in status than oil pressers, because liquor distilling required "more skill and less dirt."[7]

In 1990, when Anupam was a baby, a government panel, relying in part on these writings, concluded that indeed, his community was deserving of "backward" status. They too would be eligible for quotas in university admissions and government jobs.

That immediately unleashed protests across the country by "forward" caste students. More set-asides meant fewer seats for upper-caste students. Competition was fierce for government jobs too, which were about the only jobs that were available around that time, before economic liberalization. In the anti-affirmative-action protests, some upper-caste youths went as far as to set themselves on fire. The first among them died in 1990. It was a turning point in the story of how much caste would continue to matter for Anupam's generation.

Anupam eschews caste distinctions. He believes it shouldn't matter, either in how you treat people or in who does what for a living. He is wary of affirmative action, which is understandable, given how "backward" kids like him are ridiculed by "forward" kids for getting into university on reservations. In his view, admissions should be based solely on test scores, he says, especially at elite institutions like the IITs.

This is not always so straightforward, as a pair of American scholars discovered when they set out to measure how children's self-awareness of caste differences affected their educational performance.

Karla Hoff and Priyanka Pandey, both economists, conducted an experiment with Indian schoolchildren modeled after experiments on racial self-awareness in the United States. They tested two sets of boys in middle school on a set of mazes. One set of boys took the test without knowing who belonged to which caste. Another set of boys took the test after being told who was high-caste and who was low. When caste was not revealed, there were no differences in the performance of the two sets of boys, the researchers found. But when caste was publicly announced, the lower-caste subjects performed measurably worse. Their ability to solve the mazes dropped by 23 percent. That is to say, the lower-caste students performed measurably worse when they knew that others knew that they were lower-caste.[8]

I asked Anupam what he thought about this experiment. He was unusually introspective, but he didn't refer to himself at first. He wrote in the third person about "people" who belong to this caste or that:

> As people know their castes since they are born, they start interpreting their status based on that. A person belonging to a higher caste feels privileged which instigates a wave of self-confidence in her. On the other hand, a person belonging to a lower caste feels deprived which fills her with inferiority complex. As a result of this, higher-caste people do well in their lives and lower-caste people become laggard, but, a person from a lower caste can also excel and even outperform higher-caste people if she does not let the feeling of inferiority complex overpower herself.

I asked how he dealt with those feelings himself. He sent back his usual upbeat message of drive and motivation. "Yes, I also felt inferiority complex at various points of time," he wrote. "But, I was able to overpower it because I maintained an inner drive to break my family out of the vicious cycle of poverty. I was motivated by the hardships which my parents went through and the immense hope which they had in their eyes about my bright future."

He was not always so upbeat. I remembered the seventeen-year-old Anupam I had first met in the spring of 2005, when he was applying to the IITs. That was the serious, coiled Anupam. Flecks of gray in his hair. "I feel a lot of pressure" is what he said then.

Nehru regarded the IITs as a symbol of "India's future in the making." They represented his own faith in science and technology to guide the development of this improbable new nation.

By the time the IITs entered Anupam's dreams, every major Silicon Valley firm had an IIT alum: from Vinod Khosla at Sun Microsystems and Padmasree Warrior at Cisco to Sundar Pichai at Google. Anupam knew all their names.

But how to get into the IITs? Nearly two hundred thousand students took the entrance exam for fewer than five thousand seats. A boy in his *mohalla*, a lot like him, had tried two years earlier. He didn't succeed. Then he hanged himself from his ceiling fan.

On his first try, Anupam didn't score high enough either. But he didn't surrender. Nor did his mother. She found a tutor who specialized in getting kids into the IITs.

Anand Kumar was his name. Hundreds were flocking to his test-prep center, paying good money. But Anand gave away his tricks for free every year to thirty very poor, very smart kids. Super 30, he called them. He did it because he was once like them. He was so poor that he had had to help his mother sell homemade *papads* on the streets of Patna so the family could eat. He was forced to abandon his dreams of studying math at Cambridge University.

Anand's prep center sat on a cracked, dry field on the outskirts of Patna with two armed guards at the gates. The gates led into a large makeshift lecture hall, open on all four sides, shielded by a sloped tin roof. There were rows of benches on bare ground.

"Find the domain of the following function," Anand hectored on the morning of my visit, as he scribbled digits on a blackboard. His microphone was scratchy It was hard to make out what he was saying. He repeated it several times, like an invocation. "Find the domain of the following function." His hair flew in many directions, in urgent need of a trim. His beard was unkempt. He paced in front of the blackboard, wiping the sweat from his head with the back of his chalky hand. The tin roof inhaled the midsummer's scorching sun. Hundreds of students sat on wooden benches, pressed tightly against one another, hunched over notebooks. Their faces glistened with sweat. They scribbled, looked up, wiped their foreheads, scribbled some more.

There were very few girls among them.

Anand established an enviable track record. Every year, several local kids whom he coached made it into the IITs. He drew press attention from far and wide and eventually the wrath of rivals in the coaching business. Once, a homemade bomb was hurled at his open-air compound, after which the guards were hired.

Anupam studied like he had never studied before. For seven months, as part of the Super 30 program, he lived in Anand's house. He slept on a mattress on the floor. He ate what Anand's mother served. He attended Anand's lectures every morning, studied all afternoon and evening. There was no television, no football, no marbles, not even talking to Mummy every day.

He was an exceedingly withdrawn child. He spoke enough English to be ashamed of his lack. He did not look strangers in the eye. He looked at his feet when he spoke. His shoulders were hunched, as though they were pulled down by the weight of that amulet that held Papa's humiliation.

The morning of the IIT entrance exam, Sudha prayed at her altar. Srikrishna went to work on his auto-rickshaw, looking for passengers. Anupam sat through six hours of mathematics, chemistry, and physics.

He aced it.

Instantly, he became an icon of young India's aspiration. I wrote about him in *The New York Times*.[9] Letters of congratulations poured in from all over the world. His picture appeared in the Patna papers: hair greased to one side, eyes shielded by square, unfashionable glasses, the face of a boy utterly baffled by having to walk along this new road he had chosen.

A few weeks later, with Mummy at his side, Anupam rode the train to the original IIT campus built by Nehru's government, in a town called Kharagpur, just west of Calcutta. Anupam had his eyes on studying astronomy.

As it happened, the same year Anupam went to college, Indian democracy sprang a new surprise. In the Bihar state election, voters booted Yadav from the chief minister's office. Shrewd as he was, he had misread the mood of the electorate. It was no longer enough to deliver dignity. Voters now wanted more. They wanted some of what they had seen in the rest of India: electricity, roads, public safety, schools that function.

*   *   *

Super 30 had prepared Anupam to get into IIT. It hadn't quite prepared him to survive there.

His first few months in college, Anupam stumbled. The challenges were more social than academic. It was his first time away from home. It was his first time being around kids who were not from homes made of naked bricks and tin. The lectures were all in English, which he had a hard time following. He had never really been outgoing. He felt deeply lonely.

And like so many of us do when we are crippled by loneliness, Anupam tried standing closer to God. This disoriented him even more.

It happened like this. One day, some older students, no doubt sensing his alienation, invited him to a lecture. They were from the Hare Krishna movement. He cannot explain exactly why he agreed to go, except that he had a hard time saying no to anyone. The Hare Krishnas told him to forget his parents. They told him to think of only their lord: Hindu mythology's first auto-rickshaw driver, a charioteer from the *Mahabharata*, named Krishna.

The Hare Krishnas chanted Krishna's name. They held their arms aloft and danced. Anupam found it bewildering.

"I couldn't believe educated people, engineering students would dance like that," Anupam said.

More baffling, he joined the dance himself. "I suppose I wanted to feel close to God," he said.

He began following his Hare Krishna mentors to temple every morning and evening. It helped that they served sweet, buttery *halwa* at the temple, and he could eat all he wanted. All the dancing and chanting and *halwa*-eating made him too tired to study. He lost focus. He lost his way. He bombed his tests.

His initiation into the movement required that he not tell his family what he was doing. "I wanted to feel something," he said of his search for the divine. "But I didn't."

Despite his best efforts at deception, his mother knew something was wrong. He was behaving strangely. He wasn't in his dorm room when she called early mornings. He was asleep earlier than usual. On the phone once, he mentioned something about a temple, which raised her suspicions even more: The boy had never been much of a temple-goer.

One day, without warning him, she got on a train to Kharagpur and showed up at his dorm room. One look at his face, and she knew he was in trouble. A few minutes of grilling, and the truth spilled out of him.

God.

Halwa.

Loneliness.

Sudha was furious. She wondered: Had the Hare Krishnas drugged her son? Would his hazy spiritual quest flush away all her hard work all these years? No. She would not let that happen. She would get him out of here.

Anupam wanted to stay. He would repeat his freshman-year courses, he said. He would shape up. His grades weren't good enough to study astronomy, but still. This was the IIT. This was everything he had worked for.

Sudha wasn't having it. She wanted him to leave this college, and Anupam knew he could not defy her. He knew he had let her down. This is what felt worst of all.

The following year, Anupam transferred to a new college, the Indian School of Mines, in a gritty coal-mining town called Dhanbad, a coveted university though one tiny notch below the prestige of the IIT. Instead of exploring the prospects of life on other planets, he would now plumb the depths of the Earth.

At the IIT, out of Mummy's grasp, he had discovered something about himself. Now, at the Indian School of Mines, he would begin his discovery of India.

His first summer internship took him to a coal-mining district in West Bengal state. Around those mines, Anupam saw an India that he didn't know existed. Children walked around with bloated bellies that screamed hunger. Drinking water was contaminated. When the coal trucks rumbled past, you had to cover your nose from the swirls of coal dust that flew through the air. No one had toilets at home. Few sent their kids to school. It was eye-opening. Mining had done nothing for these Indians, he concluded, except pollute their water and soil. And if anyone uttered that thought aloud, he learned they were labeled a Maoist.

Anupam was no stranger to want. He grew up in a ghetto in Patna. But the more he saw of his country, the more he was appalled. It was difficult to shut it out.

In college, there was a lot of talk about the Maoist rebellion in India's mining belt. He found himself sympathetic to their grievances. But he abhorred their violence. He couldn't understand why they destroyed everything around them. The young women and men who joined the rebellion, he said, must have been "brainwashed."

Poverty wasn't his only discovery.

One year, while applying for a passport to travel to Bangladesh, where he had procured an internship with the Grameen Bank, he discovered another of his country's ills. The passport application required a police clearance and the police clearance required an unofficial fee at the local station house: two hundred rupees, or about five dollars by the exchange rates of the time. He didn't want to—but he paid. "It is a tradition" is how he described it. "You don't pay. You don't get your passport on time."

A few months later, he was again asked to pay a bribe, this time just to be able to file a police report for a stolen mobile phone. Anupam had wised up by now. He stared the cop in the eye and told a bald-faced lie. He claimed to know a senior Patna police officer. The cop backed down.

This was one of the most important dividends of his education: Anupam, son of a rickshaw driver who had been pistol-whipped by the cops, could look a policeman in the eye.

His most vital discovery came on a pilgrimage. One year, during summer holidays, Anupam took himself to Bodh Gaya, an ancient town in Bihar where the Buddha achieved enlightenment. There, he studied silent meditation, which meant that for the first time in his life, he didn't talk to his mother for ten days straight. It was a pivotal moment. By the time he emerged from the retreat, he realized he had lost his faith in the gods. No divinity controls my destiny, he concluded. I make my own.

From Patna, it's a short drive along a national highway to an unre- markable town of narrow lanes and open drains called Fatwa. There sits a hothouse of dreams: a government girls' school, with classes filled to the rafters.

In every classroom, every bench is full of girls. Bony hips press against bony hips. Classes spill out onto the covered patio. Girls sit cross-legged on the floor.

The headmistress is also a Class 4 teacher. Never in her twenty-two years of teaching has she seen so many children pouring into class, she says. Some of them know their letters. Some of them don't. She is hav- ing a hard time teaching anything at all. In any case, there aren't nearly enough teachers to go around. Right now, she says, there are four teacher vacancies, including the post of headmistress. On this morning, teach- ers sit at their tables, mostly hunched over papers. Students variously chat, read, stare out the windows. In the back courtyard, one girl picks through a pile of dead leaves. Another plays hopscotch with a pebble balanced on her foot. Several mill around—and it's not recess. "Safety pins," I write in my notebook. Safety pins hold up oversize dresses on the backs of skin-and-bones girls. Safety pins are ubiquitous in places like these.

I've come here in the summer of 2009 to see what is arguably the most important school reform project in the history of independent India. It is carried out by the nonprofit group Pratham, and it is shaped by the data that it collects year after year on what kids learn when they come to school.

Pratham has carried out an ambitious set of experiments to improve basic math and reading skills of primary-school children. It has recruited tutors, coached teachers, organized remedial sessions during the school day and after the school day. It has sought to measure what works and what doesn't, and then buttonholed bureaucrats with data so they might be persuaded to do things differently.

The effort is marked by a faith in evidence rather than good intentions. This makes it all the more depressing.

For nearly ten years, the numbers have changed very little, except a little for the worse since 2011. By 2014, the most recent year for which figures are available, among children enrolled in Class 5, 52 percent could not read sentences from a Class 2 textbook; about half could not handle a simple subtraction problem.[10]

Attendance was hovering around 71 percent. Children enrolled, but they weren't coming to school regularly. In 2011, a separate government-commissioned report found that about 40 percent of children were dropping out between Class 5 and Class 9. Among those who made it to Class 10, another 40 percent left school within a year.[11]

Compared to other countries, India does not spend much of its national budget on schools. But Rukmini Banerji, Pratham's chief executive, doubts that the abysmal state of Indian public education is not for lack of money. As India has prospered, the government has levied new taxes for the purpose of building new schools and hiring teachers. The physical infrastructure has improved. One survey found that between 2004 and 2010, the share of schools with electricity grew from 20 percent to 45 percent, while the share of schools with free lunch programs grew from 21 percent to nearly 80 percent. Even teacher-student ratios improved. In 2004, there was 1 teacher for every 47 students; in 2010, there was 1 teacher for just under 40 students.[12]

Unfortunately, these teachers weren't always teaching. Perhaps they were ordered to help with other tasks—like drives or registering voters. Or perhaps they just hadn't bothered to come to work. Pratham found that about 15 percent of teachers were absent on the day their survey takers made their unannounced visit. Other assessments of teacher attendance have found that around 25 percent of teachers are no-shows on any given day.[13]

That so many children are streaming into school reflects a profound hunger. Half of all primary-school children in government schools,

Banerji has found, are born to mothers who cannot read—moms who have no idea what their kids should be learning in school. Their children are tromping off to school, after all. They must be learning something. That's what they told Banerji when she asked.

We were sitting in her basement office in Delhi one evening. She pushed back her chair, rose to go to the cabinet behind, and riffled through a stack of slim, brightly illustrated books Pratham has published.

She chose a book for my daughter. Small, glossy, about a boy named Moru who loves numbers but who is discouraged at school by a mean killjoy of a teacher. Banerji had written the story herself.

She wondered how she would feel if she had gone to school and hadn't learned to read. "I'm going to have a huge chip on my shoulder if I'm a failure, if I amount to nothing," she said. "And all because the adults—my parents and my teachers—have failed me."

This might surprise those of you who look at India as a bottomless well of clever, hardworking math nerds who are about to steal good jobs from Americans. Actually, fewer than 15 percent of college-age Indians even go to college. The vast majority of kids coming of age are in no shape to compete in the global economy. India's education system is a failed promise of enormous proportions.

How did Indian schools become what they are today? At independence, India's founding fathers took great pains to establish top-rate universities, including famously, the IITs that Anupam had worked so hard to get into. It was hoped that these universities would groom a modern technocratic national elite who in turn would pull the new nation into the modern age—an Indian equivalent of W. E. B. Du Bois's notion of the Talented Tenth.

Nehru and his peers did not throw that same weight behind primary education. It's not that they were blind to the need. They knew tradition conspired to keep education beyond the reach of many—including women and outcastes. At the time, more than four out of five Indians could not read. "The national leadership had realized that what the educational situation needed was a revolutionary approach," recalled J. P. Naik, the education adviser to Prime Minister Nehru.[14]

A revolutionary approach they certainly did not take. As Naik rued, Nehru's administrations—he won elections to three consecutive terms—devoted neither the money nor the imagination to strengthen primary education. Schools remained beyond the reach of most Indian children, constitutional promise be damned.

There are at least two theories for why this was the case.

One is a charitable explanation. At independence, the state was too poor and too overstretched to take on the luxury of educating so many millions of children. Drought and famine loomed over the land. World War II had ravaged two continents, and India's founding fathers were as anxious about fascism in Europe as they were about communism next door in China. At such a time, who could think of schools?

There is also a less charitable explanation: that the failure to invest in basic education reflected the most pernicious effect of caste.

Myron Weiner, an American sociologist, made this argument in an influential book called *The Child and the State in India*. He pointed out that several modern nations took on education as a moral and legal duty when they were as poor as India. South Korea, for instance, in the 1960s, enforced compulsory education laws and invested heavily in primary schools. The investment paid off. Industry took off. The country was transformed.[15]

Today, South Korea's adult literacy rate is 100 percent. The Indian literacy rate is 74 percent among those over the age of seven: that figure is based on the number of people who say they and their family members can read when a census field-worker asks them, and education experts say it is likely to be an overestimation. Even so, that puts India's literacy rate slightly above Europe's in the 1850s, before the end of the Industrial Revolution, and far below those of other countries with which it is often compared, like Brazil or China.[16]

Weiner, rather provocatively for a foreigner, ascribed India's neglect of primary education to the culture of caste. Indian elites across the ideological spectrum, he argued, feared that too much education would disrupt the social order. "The Indian position rests on deeply held beliefs that there is a division between people who work with their minds and rule and people who work with their hands and are ruled, and that education should reinforce rather than break down this division," he wrote. "These beliefs are closely tied to religious notions and to the premises that underlie India's hierarchical caste system."[17]

Education remained the monopoly of high-born Indians with names like Sengupta and Banerji, who sit at the very top of the heap. We have long been entitled to learn. It is expected of us. Amartya Sen, the Nobel Prize–winning economist, once described it as one of the most insidious legacies of caste.

Weiner, if he were coming to India today, would no doubt notice a churning in the undersoil. Those who work with their hands are as keen to educate their children as those who work with their heads.

School enrollment trends bear this out. In 1950, when my father was studying in a government-run neighborhood school in Calcutta, 40 percent of primary-school-age children were enrolled in school. In 2013, when my daughter entered kindergarten, enrollment had swelled to over 96 percent.

In my daughter's India, it is widely understood that everyone is entitled to learn—and that educating your children is key to improving their lot in life. The data bears this out, again and again. Even a bit of early childhood education improves an individual's earning power as an adult; girls with six years of schooling are significantly more likely to seek prenatal care and immunize their children, in turn improving their children's life chances.[18]

Karthik Muralidharan, an economist at the University of California at San Diego, wanted to know who was learning what between the time they entered kindergarten and when they finished Class 5. He began to follow a cohort of ten thousand children in one hundred different schools in the southern state of Andhra Pradesh as they made their way through primary school.

Muralidharan's findings echoed what Banerji's annual survey had concluded nationally. By the end of Class 5, only 60 percent of the students could perform Class 1–level work. That meant that over a period of five years, 40 percent of students had not learned what they had been expected to in the first year of school; in effect, they got nothing out of five full years of schooling.

Muralidharan's study revealed something else extraordinary. He found that only the top 10 percent of students could keep up with the syllabus from year to year, so that by Class 5, they were able to do Class 5 work. The bottom 10 percent seemed to stop learning after Class 2. The remaining 80 percent "muddled along," as Muralidharan put it, making some progress but reaching nowhere near what the curriculum expected.[19]

Drilling down further, he noticed that learning levels were really flattening out starting in Class 3. It was bewildering at first, but it soon made sense. Class 3 is when kids are expected to be functionally literate, when they are expected to read on their own from class texts. So, those who weren't yet able to read couldn't keep up at all. They would likely also fall behind in every subject—science, Hindi, history, you name it. Muralidharan's data suggested that the school curriculum was serving only a narrow slice of students: those who could read.

"It's an education system that is catering to the top 10 percent of kids. The bottom 10 percent are learning nothing, absolutely nothing, even though they're spending five years in school," he concluded.

A new gulf had emerged.

"You may have reduced inequality in school enrollment," Muralidharan said, "but that inequality has moved to massive inequality in learning outcomes."

The Indian School of Mines campus is a peaceful oasis in grimy Dhanbad, on the train line between Delhi and Calcutta. Built in 1926, it remains an architectural throwback to the British colonial era, with its thickets of old shade trees and red-brick buildings whose wide arcades offer respite from the heat.

The first time his parents came to visit, Anupam took them to Dhanbad's newest, snazziest attraction: a department store, called Big Bazaar. It was part of a national chain that modeled itself after Walmart. It pitched a vast collection of refrigerators, school bags, toys, cooking oil— you name it—to India's aspiring middle class, and was itself a symbol of the middle class's new wants. The loudspeaker blasted discounts. The fluorescent lights were lit bright as a wedding tent.

Mummy was thrilled to be here. She pointed to a plywood dresser that she would one day love to have in their home. And a sofa that guests could sit on, instead of the big platform bed under which they kept their winter blankets in heavy steel trunks.

Papa looked at the price tags and grumbled. He thought it was all a waste of money.

They rode the escalator up to the top floor, to the food court. It was nothing like the narrow lanes of Gaighat, where an ancient *jeelebi* maker jostled next to a food cart selling Nepali *momos*. No. The Big Bazaar food court had hot trays of Chinese noodles and crispy fried *bhel puri*, even veg burgers topped with tomato sauce. The servers wore plastic hats to keep hair from falling on the food. You got your tray and sat down at a table and chairs, instead of standing around the lane and swatting away flies.

It was all deep-fried, starch-packed deliciousness. Who wouldn't want it?

Anupam took me to Big Bazaar food court too when I came to visit. He ordered the Chinese chow mein noodles, veg of course because he remained, as Mummy had raised him, a strict vegetarian. He slurped it noisily.

I asked him about the boys who sat behind us in the food court, wearing slouchy shorts and disheveled hair, hunched over the plates, laughing. These are rich kids, Anupam said. The kind of kids who would go down to Café Coffee Day once or twice a week and drop forty-five rupees on an Americano. He would never waste his scholarship money on fancy coffee. Whatever he had left over after books and train money, he gave to his mother. She used some of it to fix the house in Gaighat. She bought a ceiling fan. Eventually, she replaced the tin roof with cement and began building rooms upstairs. This was his last year in college. He said he was doing well. He said he had made friends.

His brother and sister were doing well too, although the IITs were not in their range. Anuj had gotten into a private engineering college in Kerala, along with a student loan to pay for it.

His sister, Chandni, went to an expensive coaching center to prep for engineering-college entrance exams. Anupam pitched in some of his scholarship money to pay for it.

In so many ways, Anupam was a changed man. English came easily to him now. He could look a stranger in the eye. He no longer looked down at his feet when he spoke. He laughed with delight, throwing his head back. He walked with a straight back. His shoulders no longer slouched.

In Dhanbad, he felt it was time to give something of himself back to kids who were like him. Right next to the calm colonial-era campus was a higgledy-piggledy *mohalla* that reminded him of his own. Among its naked brick and tin houses, amid the children with matted, brassy gold hair and the piles of trash, was something that called itself a "private school," not unlike the one that his parents could afford for him back in the day. The children were led to believe they were taught English. But they couldn't string words together. Anupam and a few friends from college established an afterschool center. They came up with lesson plans. They tacked them on the wall. This week, it was to take a noun, and then use it in a sentence as a descriptive word, first as an adjective, then an adverb. Today's noun was "honesty."

Without English, the children of slums like this would get "demotivated," he said.

"Without English, they'll never get out of the slum."

He had come up with a catchy name for his center: English Speaking Course and Personality Enhancement. ESCAPE for short.

English of course has nothing to do with caste, except that those who don't speak English are increasingly seen as outcastes—so much so that a Dalit activist from Delhi once suggested erecting a temple to the goddess of English, whom he said every outcaste should worship.

The hunger to learn English is hard to miss. English conversational classes sprout in slums across India. Private schools for the poor promise English-medium instruction. The satellite dish company that brings me a bouquet of television channels offers a spoken English program aimed at parents who are "embarrassed when your children's friends' parents speak English."

There was one thing that I could never get Anupam to really explain: the intensity of how much he missed being home in Gaighat. It's not like he had friends there. It's not like there was a cinema that he missed or a pool hall or a café or anything like that. No. All he could tell me was that he missed the taste of his mother's food. He missed her voice. He missed the closeness of her companionship in the tiny house she had worked hard to build.

He was the only one among his siblings who felt this way. His brother refused to come back home after college. His sister couldn't wait to get out.

"I can't even step out of the house in my jeans," Chandni scowled once, barely looking up from the television in the dark middle room of the house. There were hoodlums out there, *faltu* useless fellows, with nothing to do but ogle and yelp at a girl wearing jeans. Anupam didn't contradict her assessment. He didn't have any friends who could defend her, and he certainly wasn't going to take them on. Chandni was anxious to get as far away from here as she could.

Anupam told me later he was disappointed in her. He didn't think she was applying herself as hard as she could be. She preferred to go shopping with Mummy rather than study, he said when she was out of earshot.

As it happened, Anupam had misjudged his sister. She blossomed as soon as she left home. She aced her first year in engineering college, scoring near the top of her class. He admitted to having been wrong. Out of forty-five students, she had scored second highest. "I am feeling elated by her remarkable feat," he wrote in an email.

Anupam never once considered striking out on his own, without his family.

At no point did he ever bring up whether this would complicate the life he might have with a wife one day, or in some way arrest his path to adulthood.

Truth is, Anupam wasn't much of a player in the ladies department. As a teenager, he was too shy to ever talk to a girl. And by the time he began to shed his fear, there were hardly any women around him. In his college, women made up barely 9 percent of his class.

Toward the end of his stay in Dhanbad, Anupam faced a painful reckoning. He was going to a college designed to prepare mining engineers, but this was not a career he was the least bit interested in. What he really wanted to do was to get a postgraduate degree in business management, India's equivalent of an MBA, and that too in the country's most prestigious business school: the Indian Institutes of Management. That would mean another two years of school for him—and another two years of rickshaw driving for his papa.

This worried Sudha. At fifty-five, her husband was becoming frail. She could see that. But how could she thwart Anupam? She never had. She admitted to feeling stressed. There is a bit of "tension," she said.

The decision plagued Anupam. On the eve of his interviews for business school, he said: "My father has been working for almost thirty years without any rest or holidays. He says that he can manage for another couple of years, but I think that it's high time for me to take the burden off his shoulders and come at the front."

Anupam erred on the side of his dream. He enrolled in the graduate program at the Indian Institutes of Management campus on the edge of Calcutta, which was now officially called Kolkata. He graduated in 2013, at one of the worst moments of reckoning for the Indian economy. Growth rates had plummeted to below 6 percent that year. The roaring optimism that was in the air when he entered college had faded.

Now there was anger. Politicians were exposed for having stolen millions of rupees from government contracts. The death of a young woman who had been gang-raped in Delhi unleashed angry protests in cities across the country.

Even Yadav, the once invincible chief minister of Bihar, went to jail that year, in connection with his role in the misappropriation of public funds from the state animal husbandry department. It was poetically known as the "fodder scam."

"So, I am getting myself prepared to strive for the best, but to face the worst," Anupam said.

In the final few months of business school, he dutifully attended all the job placement talks, appeared for interviews, and looked high and low for jobs in finance, which is where he wanted to be. His business school peers scooped up plum assignments before him. He was no less smart than them. He knew that. For the first time he was beginning to confront the constraints of his past.

If recruiters were looking at his final exam scores from Class 12, he was at a clear disadvantage. His scores were lousy. He hadn't really focused on those exams. He had single-mindedly focused on the other exam, the one to get into the IITs.

Perhaps his extraordinary ambitions weren't enough. His country had starved them.

Finally, in the last round of interviews, Anupam did get a job, with an iron ore mining company based in Kolkata. It was not what he wanted. He said he felt "disheartened."

Nonetheless, he could not afford to turn down the job offer. He needed to work now. And anyway, his starting pay would be roughly fifteen times what his father earned after a lifetime of driving an auto-rickshaw. Papa could finally retire.

Later that year, he read Nassim Nicholas Taleb's *Fooled by Randomness: The Hidden Role of Chance in Life and in the Markets*, which I had bought him. I thought it was a smart book on economics, and Anupam had been interested in economics.

The book struck a chord with him. At the time, he was nursing his wounds for not getting the sought-after jobs that his friends from business school had snatched up before him. But reading Taleb prompted him to reassess where he was. Relative to so many others of his generation, he said, he had profited from a great education. He had an MBA after all, from his country's most famous business school!

He sent me an upbeat email. "It was a nice read," he said, "and forced me to think about life in a different perspective altogether."

Reward came soon.

By the end of the year, Anupam was hired by the state regulatory agency that controls the securities market in India. It meant he could leave mining and get into the financial sector, which excited him much more. His parents were thrilled too, but for another reason. It was a government job, which meant that it was a job for life. His parents padlocked the house in Gaighat and moved across the country to join him. He rented an apartment in Navi Mumbai, a grove of high-rises across the water from the island city of Mumbai. "Now we'll be able to live together, after a long gap of nine years," he said.

Mumbai was so different from Patna. "Wide roads, innumerable flyovers, twenty-four-hour electricity and water, and of course, huge population," he reported.

And it rained. Oh, how it rained. For days, sheets of rain blew off the Arabian Sea. He had never seen anything like it.

Anupam bought a sofa for the living room and an iPad, on which his mother played Candy Crush for hours each day. By then, Sudha was batting away marriage offers for Anupam. One family approached her with a dowry of 50 *lakh*, or 5 million, rupees, which is a lot of money in Gaighat. Anupam told his mother to turn it down. He said he didn't believe in dowries. And anyway, Chandni would first be set up for a match.

Anupam is no Horatio Alger. His country is not a country of Horatio Algers. No. Anupam is a prodigy, blessed with rare talent and pluck—and equally, a mother of rare faith and pluck.

Anupam's is a story of audacious ambition. Equally, it is a portrait of how his country conspires to fail young people like him every step of the way—and his own gradual awakening to that knowledge.

Likewise, he is an emblem of a profound psychic shift. There are millions just like him, who shake off the past to say, "And why not me?"

Democracy has allowed that shift to take place. Yet India's successive democratically elected governments have not put the fundamentals into place. Schools don't work. Every day, 1600 children die of diarrhea and pneumonia alone. Three out of ten children are clinically malnourished.[20]

Anupam is determined to be a member of his country's elite— "ee-light," as he pronounces it—and to cross over into their world not just by getting rich but by acquiring so much knowledge that no one will be able to put him down. No one will be able to say that he is any less capable.

This is one of his most remarkable traits. He is supremely self-confident. He is as certain about how far he has come as he is about what he is capable of. He doesn't ever seem to second-guess himself. And perhaps because he is not a daughter, he has never been circumscribed at home.

"I won't have difficulty proving myself," is how he put it. "I know as much as a hi-fi person would know."

GATES
Keeping Out the Lives of Others

The wedding begins after dark, once lightning flashes across the sky and a spitfire of a storm lashes the trees. When the rain stops—"the clouds ran out of batteries," is how my daughter explains these hard monsoon bursts—the air suddenly cools. It is a good omen, people say. Perhaps the rains will be good this year, enough to slosh the fields. Perhaps there will be rice, enough to fill half the belly.

Close to midnight, two hours behind schedule, a shiny black Mahindra jeep turns off the highway and comes trundling down the muddy red dirt lane, bringing the bridegroom and his crew.

The bride's party advances up the lane to welcome him. The old men, *lungis* draped around their waists, pound on drums held in their armpits. The young men are dressed in low-slung jeans and Kangol caps of 1980s hip-hop. They tap a mean, fast rhythm on snares. The tempo picks up speed, grows agitated. The men dance, young and old, heads down, hips thrusting. They cast enormous shadows on the trees, as though some gyrating forest giants have come out to play.

Mani stands out in this crowd. She does not dance. She does not even stir her hips. She wears the quietest sari of all, orange chiffon with a narrow band of green sequins along the border. Her hair is held back in a braid, as always. Her back is straighter than all the others. Her face gives away nothing.

Only when I needle her does she admit to wanting to get married one day—but, she stipulates, in a smaller, more modest ceremony. This is the most lavish wedding the family has ever organized. It is in honor of the last daughter in the clan—the last not counting Mani, who is the family spinster, its reliable worker bee, its migrant, whose wages uplift them all.

After the rain, the sky bursts with stars. This is what Mani misses. The infinite sky. The clean air. Home.

This is why she comes back, once a year, every year, to her mother's house, in a village pressed hard against the jungle in Jharkhand, the state next to Anupam's Bihar. Usually, she comes this time of year, in May, when the hot season breaks for rain. The rest of the year, Mani works as a maid in Gurgaon, in a forest of steel and glass on the edge of the nation's capital, Delhi. There are armies of women like her, mainly *adi-vasis*, India's indigenous people, working as maids in Gurgaon.

Mani is a child of noonday, born in the late 1980s—she's not exactly sure of the year—and raised in the years since the economy creaked open in 1991. The fourth of nine children, she too seeks to shape her own destiny. So she leaves home when she is around eighteen. A family friend, an older woman who works as a maid, brings her to Gurgaon. Soon, Mani too is working as a maid, moving in with one family, then another. Some of her employers slap her when they are dissatisfied with her work. Some of them give her enough to eat. It is never so bad, Mani says, that she feels compelled to go back home. And anyway, at home they need the money.

By the time I meet her, in 2011, she is a live-in maid for a stay-at-home mom named Supriya, in a seventh-floor apartment in a gated condominium complex called Central Park. Mani watches Supriya's two young children, rolls the dinner chapatis, washes dishes, hangs the laundry. She has her own room, which opens out onto the service balcony, and food and water around the clock. She gets along with Supriya, who, like Mani, is something of an introvert. Mani finds her to be a fair employer. She is courteous. Most Sundays, she lets Mani take the day off to go to church.

Mani saves practically all the money she makes. With her earnings, her family is able to rebuild their mud-and-tin house, buy goats, and pay off debts. Three sisters are married off. The youngest graduates from a private high school; Mani pays the fees.

Until calamity strikes.

One day, in the summer of 2011, during the season of the *loo*, when the hot wind blows in from the western desert and stings the skin, Mani comes to Supriya in a state of panic. Mani says her fourteen-year-old niece has been abducted from home, in a village deep in the jungles of Jharkhand, and forced to work as a maid somewhere in or around Delhi. Mani tells Supriya she has no idea exactly where, though she has somehow tracked down a phone number and spoken to her niece, only to learn that the girl is being held against her will in a neighborhood she knows only as something-or-other Puram. It could be anywhere in this concrete jungle of 20 million people. The girl has never been out of Jharkhand.

Mani's story chills Supriya's blood. Supriya has never been to a village in the jungles of Jharkhand, never really thought about them, to be honest. And now suddenly she is thinking about them all the time. She wonders what the girl's village looks like. She wonders how a mother who has to work in the fields, fetch water, and gather firewood can possibly keep her children safe at home. She shudders at the thought of how precarious life must be in Mani's village. "Not a day goes by," Supriya says, "when I don't think, Oh! What if my child went missing? What if someone just took one of my children away?"

Supriya resolves to help Mani rescue her niece. And in so doing, she opens a door that, like most of us, she is accustomed to keeping closed. She steps across a line, ever so briefly, into the lives of other mothers, in the other India. It burdens her with more knowledge than she bargains for.

In stepping across that line, Supriya temporarily upsets a delicate psychic balance that confronts women of her comfortable social class. It is a balance that becomes all the more tricky to maintain in the India of noonday, where the gap between rich India and poor India is wider than ever before. A friend of mine, in Bombay, says this growing gap also correlates with a noticeable diminution of compassion. The rich seem to increasingly regard the poor as an embarrassment, she tells me, and as "a burden on the aspirations of their betters."

Had I not left India as a child, Supriya is the woman I might have become. She is of my generation. She grew up in Calcutta. She went to Welham, a girls' boarding school a few notches above my own Modern High School for Girls, but likewise designed to prepare modern girls to become modern wives. She is open-minded and friendly but also a bit of a recluse. She reads a lot and despises idle gossip. She is conscientious about composting, and she enjoys hiking in the hills.

She met Arvind, her husband, at a Delhi advertising firm where they both worked. She wasn't into her job nearly as much as he was, so when they got married, it was she who got off the career track.

Their daughter was born in 2002, then a son in 2007. Soon, they moved to Central Park, a neat new set of multistory buildings overlooking a golf course, encircled by gates. Supriya immediately felt a sense of relief. Inside its gates, she no longer worried constantly about where her daughter was. "I could let her be in the park and not keep a hawk's eye on her," she said.

By the time I first met her, in 2011, Supriya was a devoted, full-time mother, although she let it slip every now and then that a small part of her also fantasized about what else to do with her life, once the kids were a bit older.

Supriya and Mani were in each other's company perhaps more often each day than they were in anyone else's. They were not likely to confide in each other. Nor was theirs a relationship of equals—Supriya was Mani's employer, after all. But in the rhythms of their daily lives, the two women relied on one another. Supriya needed Mani to run the household. Mani needed Supriya in times of trouble. They were not irreplaceable to each other, but vital.

Supriya drove her kids to Kumon math sessions and dance classes. If they had to go to a birthday party outside the gates of Central Park, she accompanied them herself, rather than follow the common practice among moms of her class: sending them with nanny and driver. She planned healthy meals. She supervised homework. She combed the Internet for books to help her daughter practice her handwriting. She was strict about limiting the children's screen time.

Central Park—its tagline is "Expect the world"—catered to college-educated, English-speaking professionals like Supriya and Arvind. It sponsored Diwali parties for residents and brought in a consultant to help kids apply to colleges in Texas and Singapore. It did not rely on the paltry services that the city of Gurgaon offered. Central Park's generators came on the instant the municipal power went down, which it sometimes did for nearly a third of the day. It provided ample water, plenty of parking, a lush green playground, guards at the gate to keep out the *thela-wallahs* peddling everything from onions to buckets. It required maids to carry identification tags. It kept plumbers on call 24/7 in case the pipes got clogged. Some of India's best private hospitals and schools were within a short drive. There was a Mercedes showroom across the street, and a microbrewery.

Central Park, and the dozens of gated communities like it across the country, reflected, simply, an aspiration to live not only with basic material comforts—round-the-clock water and power—but also in safety, protected from the distress of the rest of India, which might be just across the road or miles away in the hinterland, where there was no clean water to drink, where children were stunted from hunger.

Supriya called Central Park a "manicured paradise," an oasis of safety amid vast disorder and want. For this she was grateful: Her day was not wasted waiting to turn on the water pump when the city water supply began to flow, nor stocking fuel for a generator, nor reminding a servant to sweep the remnants of a dust storm off the driveway. These were the headaches she referred to when she said, "We don't have to worry about *motor chalao. Diesel khattam ho gaya. Driveway saaf karo.* It's not worth it."

She was all too aware of the psychic costs, which made her ambivalent about the life she had chosen. This also made her unusual among her peers. She told me about the time her daughter was at her parents' house in Delhi, when the power went out in the afternoon—and stayed out for hours. The child, then eight years old, was shocked. What do you mean there's no electricity, she demanded of Supriya's mother. "Our lives are a bubble," Supriya said. "Our children, they should know how others live."

There were also times when the gates of Central Park offered only a gossamer curtain between this India and that, when it occured to her that the security she had procured for her own children was beyond the reach of others.

Supriya and I were talking one afternoon while her kids raced through the playground in Central Park. Her quiet, gentle son played by himself. Her daughter, the extrovert, laughed as she ran through an open sprinkler with her friends. Supriya led me to the back fence, dividing the verdant lawn on this side from the dry brush on the other. There, one night a year ago, Supriya said, a young woman was raped and left naked one night. A security guard at Central Park, hearing her cries for help, ran over, gave her his coat to wrap around her shoulders, and called the police. Supriya knew nothing more about the girl or her rapist, except that such a thing happened here, just beyond the fence from the tidy, well-watered playground where her children play every day at sundown.

In Supriya's childhood and mine, India's privileged were far more likely to live face-to-face with its poor. Across the street from her comfortable Calcutta house was a slum, where an old woman sat on her haunches and sold lumps of coal. The woman arranged her coal into neat, symmetrical piles, each one roughly the same size, for sale at the same price. With the coal dust she drew swirly designs around each pile. Supriya watched her for hours.

As a mother, in Gurgaon, Supriya could wall herself off. Only occasionally, like a hot squall, did the lives of others blow in and disturb the order of things. Private India was only so good at keeping the disorder away. Then you had to quietly shut the gate again. You had to learn to see distress, and also to not see distress.

That psychic equilibrium settled on me slowly, imperceptibly. I became aware of it only after I had become a parent. It became impossible to ignore each time I got in a taxi with my daughter, and we stopped in traffic, and a gaggle of children came banging on the window, peddling dirty roses, or pirated copies of American books ("The world is flat, madam," they shouted, waving Thomas L. Friedman's best seller), or nothing at all except their bare hands.

Occasionally, I would bring a five-rupee packet of Parle-G biscuits to offer, but more often than not I'd forget. Shriveled by heat and traffic, I would find myself closing the car windows just before thin, grubby fingers crawled inside. I would look the other way. I couldn't believe I was doing this: I would aimlessly look at my phone in order not to have to look at them.

I noticed that my girl, when she was two years old, would wave and smile. At age three, she was old enough to turn to me and ask: "Mama, what are they talkin' about?" By three and a half, she was talking back at them, with a voice that would make me wince, a voice that signaled that she was *us*, not them. "No, we don't need anything today! No. I said we don't need anything today!" A voice she learned from me.

I would say nothing when the driver barked at the beggars. They would make a face, flip him off, and skitter like lizards.

Gurgaon is the city that aspiration built: a Xanadu of a New Indian imagination.

It rose next to Delhi, on a rocky stretch of dry earth and acacia trees, in the shadow of the Aravali Hills, where peasants once coaxed grain out of hard soil. In the season of the *loo*, great hot wheels of dust swirled in the air. Women shielded their faces with wide muslin *dupattas*. The men's white cotton turbans doubled as pillows for afternoon siesta.

Land and life here required a certain toughness. Honor mattered. Caste mattered. Guns were plentiful. And a preference for male heirs gave the state of Haryana, in which Gurgaon sits, a peculiarly stilted gender ratio. According to the 2011 census, there were 834 girls for every 1000 boys, the worst sex ratio in the country. The sex imbalance reflected the region's prosperity too: families could afford ultrasound tests to check the sex of the fetus, and abort unwanted females.

Gurgaon's destiny changed forever when a developer named Kushal Pal Singh started visiting from Delhi, starting in the 1970s. He made acquaintance with the local farmers. He drank tea with the menfolk. He attended family weddings and visited ailing relatives. He took his time to earn their trust. Then he started buying their land.

On these parched fields, Singh conjured a new metropolis. He persuaded Indira Gandhi's government (it helped that he was a family friend) to tweak the route of a new national highway so that motorists could zip from Gurgaon to the airport, on the southern edge of Delhi. He persuaded the American executive Jack Welch to open an outpost of General Electric's business-process outsourcing unit in Gurgaon, turning it into the hub of a booming Indian industry. He bought. He built.

Up rose a building that looked like a ship's helm: the headquarters of Singh's company, DLF Limited. Then came a grove of high-rise apartment blocks, encircled by high walls. By the mid-2000s, Gurgaon was pocked with construction canyons. Singh's example had inspired a host of developers to erect office buildings, shopping malls, hotels, golf courses, and cluster after cluster of gated apartments with dreamy names: Cyber Greens, New Town Heights, Nirvana Country.

Soon, DLF would build a private monorail that looped around its properties; Central Park was among the six stops. The company also announced plans to build the country's largest mall in Gurgaon, even though, as the Indian papers lamented, it was already surpassed in size by China's largest mall. (That competition with China is a fixture of the Indian elite's imagination, one that India repeatedly loses.)

Singh became one of India's richest men, while his dream city became a metonym for New India's ambition. Gurgaon drew scores of ambitious, educated men and women to write computer code and harangue American debtors from round-the-clock call centers. It drew scores of equally ambitious but uneducated men and women to serve them, as cooks, press-*wallahs*, electricians, tea sellers, auto-rickshaw drivers, layers of roof tiles, security guards, and *ayahs* to take care of the children.

Like Mani, many of the workers were *adivasis*, who came from the poorest swaths of the country. Their rivers had run dry. Their jungles had thinned out. So they left their homes, traveling for days in cramped trains to sweep and swab the floors in Xanadu.

I had watched Gurgaon come into being. There were construction sites everywhere. Day and night, women ferried bowls of sand and mud on their heads. Men stacked bricks. Children rolled in the dust. Steel beams poked higher and higher into the sky. Some days, in a certain hazy late afternoon light, they looked like so many skinny fingers pointing up, up, and up. I wrote about it for the *Times*.[1] I was drawn to it again and again.

Gurgaon became an emblem of a country in the dizzy, post-economic-reforms era. Its population doubled in ten years, to an estimated 1.5 million in 2011, and is projected to exceed 4 million by 2020.

There was only one problem. Gurgaon was dangerously short of water. The central government's water authority warned that its water reserves would run out by 2017. The water table was falling by 1.5 meters each year. By 2012, the Gurgaon government could provide only about half of the water that its residents consumed. The rest came from wells that were bored deep into the ground and that drained the aquifer.

Water wasn't the only service that Gurgaon's gated community residents obtained privately. In 2012, about one-fourth of the electricity they used came from diesel-fired generators; the government electricity board couldn't meet their full demand. As for the waste they produced, only 30 percent of the population of Gurgaon was connected to the public sewage network. The rest was rescued by a thriving private sewage industry. Condominium associations hired tanker trucks to extract the waste of its residents, ferry it across town, and dump it into streams and ditches.

In short, Supriya and her fellow Gurgaon residents procured privately what the state did not provide. They were among a new class of upwardly mobile professionals who had risen up the ranks of India's booming services sector. Their success reflected not only the government's failure to provide basic services but also the widening inequality that came to define India at noonday. This too aspiration had wrought.

India is home to one in three poor people worldwide. This means that any effort to reduce global poverty has to start with India. And it has. Indian poverty rates have declined measurably since independence in 1947, though the question of whether it has gone down fast enough since economic reforms began in 1991, especially for the poorest of the poor, remains a matter of fierce dispute.[2]

The decline in poverty is in part because of the sheer expansion of the economy; steady growth has driven down poverty in India, as it has in many countries, including in China a generation ago.[3] But this is only part of the story. For one thing, living standards have improved far more slowly in the countryside than in the cities, which explains why women and men like Mani pack up and leave home. In addition, despite the promising reductions on paper, poverty continues to deprive millions of Indians of the very basic provisions, including enough to eat. Less apparent, even as millions of Indians have climbed above the official poverty line, the vast majority is nowhere near a middle-class existence. In 2011, even after twenty years of steady macroeconomic growth, 59 percent of Indians lived on under $2 a day.[4]

Then there's the gap between the rich and poor. In the last twenty-odd years since the economy opened up, inequality has risen sharply. Economists who have plotted the gap between what the richest and poorest segments of the population consume—from the money they spend on food and school fees to motorcycles and mobile phones—have found a clear trend line: Inequality in India went down slowly and steadily between 1951 and 1991, only to spike upward after 1992, both in urban and rural India.[5]

Living standards between the bottom 40 percent of the population and the rest of their compatriots have also widened. And even though consumption levels have grown overall, they have not grown as fast for those at the bottom as they have for the rest.

As for the poorest of Indian citizens, the bottom 10 percent saw barely any improvement in the first ten years of economic reforms, according to an analysis by the World Bank. (They have fared better in the later years.)[6]

Strictly by the numbers, inequality in India doesn't look as bad as the imbalance between the rich and poor in the United States—or even China; in both countries, the Gini coefficient, the conventional measure of economic inequality, is higher than in India.[7] But numbers don't tell the whole story. Inequality in India presents an acute challenge to the idea that democracy can offer even a semblance of equal opportunity. An Indian child born to a poor mother is far less likely to be immunized against childhood diseases, for instance. Also, a poor child is twice as likely to be clinically stunted.

In a democracy of the poor, rising inequality is a recurring challenge for politicians. It explains why at election time over the years, they propose a variety of government initiatives for the poor: cheap rice in some states, free blenders in others, free school uniforms elsewhere. In 2005, the Congress-led coalition government put into motion one of the world's most ambitious programs to employ millions of those who teetered on the starvation line: a massive public works program that promised a hundred days of employment to men and women in the countryside.

Some of these government programs leaked like old faucets. Barely half of the subsidized food grains that were supposed to feed the poor actually reached their intended beneficiaries, according to one official audit. This was not insignificant; nearly half of all Indians buy grains from these ration shops, often paying bribes to get a ration card. Nor was graft limited to ration shops. About 60 percent of the food meant for an early-childhood feeding program was found to have been siphoned off, according to another audit.[8] Widows' pensions sometimes vanished into the pockets of local bureaucrats—including, for many years, the payment that Mani's mother was entitled to. Dead people collected scholarships.

The mounting evidence of corruption finally prompted the government to try, in 2012, an ambitious biometric identification project designed to funnel benefits to the right people. By 2015, India went a step further. It rolled out the world's largest cash-transfer program for the poor.

If Gurgaon represents India's glossy new riches, Mani's village, Birhu-Patratoli, in the state of Jharkhand, represents its vast distress. I have asked her many times, in many ways if she was coerced to leave home. No, she says each time. She chose to leave. She chose to be someone.

Mani's Jharkhand spreads out next to Anupam's Bihar. Parts of the state are jungle; other parts are rocky and arid. Jharkhand is among the most destitute states in the entire country, but it is rich in minerals, especially coal. Day and night, trucks clatter along the highway that abuts Mani's village, ferrying black gold from the coal mines to power plants across the land.

Despite its abundance of coal, there is no electricity in Birhu-Patratoli, nor in many *adivasi* villages like it. Evenings are illuminated by flashlights and kerosene lamps—and in the last few years, by the blue glow of cell phones. Nearly every home has a cell phone, but to charge the battery, you must walk over to a shop that sits on the highway and is connected to the power grid. Once the phones are charged, they bring Bollywood songs, cricket scores, and the election-time promises of politicians by SMS. When they are dead, there is only the stirring of trees and the trucks clattering down the highway.

The village where Mani's niece, Phoolo, grew up is not as blessed as Mani's. It is deep in the woods, up in the dry, red, hardscrabble hills. There is no highway nearby, nor a paved road for miles. No place to charge a cell phone easily.

It was there that Phoolo was walking home from school one afternoon, in early 2011, when a local ne'er-do-well by the name of Harko followed her. Harko had been stalking her for a while. He belonged to what Phoolo called the *mama-log*, literally the uncles, but which here meant that he was affiliated with Maoist insurgents who roamed freely in those parts. According to Phoolo, Harko came that afternoon with two friends, a pistol, and a less than charming pick-up line: Marry me or I'll kill you. It was the second time he had proposed to her. The first time, her mother heard about it and chewed him out. But on this day Phoolo's mother was not home. She was attending a wedding in a neighboring village. Phoolo's brother was out drinking with the *mama-log*. Phoolo's home was empty.

According to Phoolo, Harko and his friend told her to come with them. Was she forced? It's hard to say. No doubt she was afraid. These were men with guns. She did as she was told. She boarded a car that waited on a dirt road outside the village. Two other girls got in the car at another village farther down, and they were taken to the train station in Ranchi, a couple of hours away. They were told to get into a train so packed that they all had to sit on the floor. This was the Sampark Kranti Express, the train used by thousands of Jharkhandi migrant workers to travel to Delhi and back. Phoolo put her head on her knees and fell asleep. She was still wearing her school uniform: a white button-down shirt, a blue skirt, and a belt.

The train to Delhi took a full day. There, she says, she was first detained in a two-room flat with dozens of other women and men. They were all *adivasis* from Jharkhand villages close to hers. One by one, they were dispatched across Delhi to work as domestics. Phoolo landed with a clan of six in a neighborhood on the northern frontier of the city. She swept floors, washed dishes, laundered and pressed clothes, and rolled chapatis at whatever hour her employers felt like eating, which was generally late. She was told to sleep on a straw mat on the kitchen floor. She was not allowed to step out of the house.

I could not corroborate Phoolo's version of events. She had no address for her employer. There was no police record. What I do know is that Phoolo told this same story to members of her family. I also know that her predicament is not uncommon.

Advocates say trafficking has been rising steadily in the 2000s, as urban Indians prosper, move out of extended family homes and into their own apartments, fueling the demand for more maids.

Many of them are children. By the government's own estimates, nearly 4.5 million children work for a living in India; the United Nations Children's Fund says the numbers are far higher.[9]

Like Phoolo, an estimated 20 percent of all child laborers between age five and fourteen—both boys and girls—work as domestic servants. Their parents may or may not be fully aware; or they may not want to know. (Children work in brick kilns, carpet factories, and brothels too.)

A United Nations report published in 2013 found that parents were sometimes offered cash up front for their children, plus promises of a better life.[10] The U.N. investigation went on to say that *adivasi* villages were among the most fertile places for employment agents to recruit—and the recruiters, as in Phoolo's case, were *adivasis* themselves. Family members, the report concluded, rarely lodged complaints with the authorities if their children were missing.

Jharkhand is believed to be among the worst affected states—except there are no precise figures, because state officials have not bothered to submit missing children's data for the national crime statistics database since 2009. A state plan was drawn up to combat trafficking, but it wasn't implemented.

To be clear, the law prohibits child labor. The law prohibits trafficking. The law is often disregarded.[11]

I am roundly discouraged from visiting Phoolo's village, which is called Sokoy. People say it will be hard to find. They say it will be a waste of my time. No one there will talk to a stranger. They tell me it is full of *mama-log, jungle ka-mama-log*, and *bhai-log*, as if just uttering the word "Maoist" might invite danger from one side or another.[12]

Of course, all this naysaying makes me all the more determined. Luckily, my driver is game, and so is a Ranchi-based journalist whom I have persuaded to help me on this reporting trip. And so we set off from Ranchi early one morning, picking up a case of bottled water and a guide who speaks the local language from the nearest district headquarters town, and try to find Sokoy. It is nowhere near a highway, nor on a map. The directions from locals go something like this: drive up that red dirt road, veer left at a banyan tree, turn right at a tombstone, drive past a Shiv temple, go deeper into the bush until the road ends at a giant tamarind tree.

Sure enough, the road ends at a giant tamarind tree, which is full of bats—screeching, argumentative bats. In its shade stands a row of crooked gravestones and a toothless woman of imprecise age, sitting on her haunches, dismembering a jackfruit. Scrawny chickens peck at the ground. The bats keep screeching. The village otherwise is a hush.

The warnings are accurate. Sokoy does not reveal its secrets. No one wants to talk to a stranger. Who knows who they think I am. A cop? a do-gooder? a ghost, shaped like a woman, skin like an Indian's, a notebook in hand, asking questions in an odd language.

Eventually, I confirm that Phoolo and another girl were forcibly taken away the year before. I learn also that two boys, suspected of having abducted them, were subsequently stoned to death. Public stonings are apparently not so rare. Police rarely show up here. The villagers don't want to tell me the names of the boys.

Deeper inside the village, I find a work gang prospecting for water, part of the national public works program designed for the very poor. Two years of drought have sucked the wells dry. The village is short of even drinking water. Also, two years of drought have meant no one is able to sow rice in their fields. The villagers have had to borrow money to buy rice that comes from far away. They have sold their animals, if they had any. They have sent out their able-bodied children to find work elsewhere.

Digging the new well this morning are four men, armed with sledge-hammers, their bare chests glistening with sweat. It has taken them four months to dig down to thirty-two feet. They are now close to the reward: a small pool of brown water sloshes around their feet.

Nearly seventy years of freedom, I discover, has not brought Sokoy electricity, irrigation canals, or even a reliable source of drinking water.

It wasn't supposed to be this way. When the leaders of newly sovereign India debated the language of its constitution, one of the sole *adivasi* members of the Constituent Assembly, Jaipal Singh Munda, gave a haunting speech. He introduced himself as the original Indian, the *jungli*, the man of the jungle. Everyone else, he said, correctly, was a newcomer to the land. He said he trusted the newcomers. He cited the prime minister by name.

"I take Pandit Jawaharlal Nehru at his word," Munda said. "I take you all at your word that now we are going to start a new chapter, a new chapter of independent India where there is equality of opportunity, where no one would be neglected."

His faith was misplaced.

If the Constitution promised equality of opportunity—indeed, if it promised to uplift those who had been neglected for generations—free India has failed on this promise very badly.

Today, two generations later, there are an estimated 84 million *adivasis*, around 8 percent of the population of India. They are technically outside the Hindu caste system—literally, outcastes—and their social, economic, and political status is the lowest of any other social group in India, lower than Dalits, who sit at the bottom of the caste ladder.

The *adivasis'* greatest curse is to live on India's richest lands, which are full of coal and iron ore, bauxite and uranium. Those commodities have been coveted since the early days of independence, when Nehru's government sought to industrialize the nation. The demand for those riches has sharply grown as India has prospered. *Adivasis* have paid a high price. Dams have flooded their lands. Mines have gutted their hills, including blatantly illegal ones. Among the millions of Indians displaced for industrial and infrastructure projects, *adivasis* are disproportionately represented.[13]

Rich as their land is, *adivasis* on average are India's most destitute. According to 2012 figures, 44 percent of them live below the official poverty line, compared with 27.5 percent of Indians as a whole. And poverty among *adivasis* has fallen more slowly than for any other social group— including for Dalits.

Child deaths are disproportionately high among *adivasi* children. *Adivasi* mothers are significantly less likely to get prenatal care. *Adivasi* children are less likely to have access to care for basic childhood ailments like diarrhea and respiratory disease. Hunger hits *adivasi* children the hardest too.[14]

Being underweight means more than being scrawny and short. It means being far more vulnerable to everyday childhood illnesses—and to be destined to be intellectually stunted for life.

I should point out here that while the figures are particularly bad in the *adivasi* belt, childhood hunger remains inexplicably high in India, even after two decades of galloping economic growth. According to 2014 government figures, 30 percent of Indian children under the age of five are clinically underweight. Nevertheless, this percentage is a vast improvement from the last figure, released in 2006, which found a child malnutrition rate of nearly 43 percent. On a global index, produced by the Washington-based International Food Policy Research Institute, India's improved numbers place it somewhere near Angola and only slightly better than Bangladesh, which is far poorer.[15]

This is entirely a man-made problem. Hunger in India is not like hunger in barren countries where nothing grows, like Yemen or Niger. India as a whole produces more than enough food to feed its people. But the food doesn't reach the people it should.

That is to say, there are vast parts of my daughter's India where the aspiration story is hard to swallow, where hunger is such an everyday curse that the promise of freedom seems not so much undelivered as grotesque.

Children no longer die of hunger as much as they did in Jaipal Singh Munda's day. They live with it. They grow up short, frail, disease-prone, less capable. Cursed in India's most prosperous era.

*   *   *

It's not that the government doesn't try to address the problem. It's just that many of its programs—even ambitious, well-meaning ones—are poorly designed and destined to do very little.

On the drive back from Sokoy, I stop to speak to Dr. Anjulan Aind, a government doctor who runs a clinic for the sunken-eyed and skinny-boned children of the *adivasi* belt. Her Malnutrition Treatment Centre is housed in the main government hospital that serves this wide swath of *adivasi* hamlets. This district, which contains both Mani's and Phoolo's villages, is among the one hundred worst districts in the country for childhood hunger.

The kids who come into Dr. Aind's care are in some ways the luckiest. They have been identified by a village health worker. (India has a vast network of village health workers, but their job descriptions are so pyrrhic that to really fulfill their responsibilities properly, you would have to have a master's in public health and work twenty-eight hours a day.) Their mothers have been persuaded to bring them to the clinic. They have escaped death, for now.

The clinic itself is no more than a room with five metal beds. There, Dr. Aind weighs the children, measures them from head to toe, and records the circumference of their arms. She squeezes peanut butter into their mouths if their guts are strong enough to digest it; rice porridge, if they are not. She tests them for anemia and tuberculosis. She has never seen a child who is not anemic.

Much depends, as always, on a mother's fate. A 2011 study of the hundred worst districts, conducted by an Indian advocacy group called the Naandi Foundation, found that malnutrition was significantly higher among mothers who cannot read, which is the case for nearly every woman who comes to Dr. Aind's ward.[16]

Mothers are paid a hundred rupees a day to bring their children here. It's meant to be an incentive, as much for them as their families, who otherwise may not let them come to the treatment center at all.

Dr. Aind is one of Jaipal Singh Munda's people, born and raised here in Jharkhand. She speaks a smattering of Mundari, an *adivasi* language, and when she can speak to patients in their native tongue, their eyes light up, and they take in what she says a bit less reluctantly.

The Malnutrition Treatment Centre is a well-intentioned program. But it is also a stark portrait of how a democratically elected government cheats its poorest, most vulnerable citizens. The mothers' time with Dr. Aind is brief and restful—and very often, pointless. They and their malnourished children are in her care for fifteen days. Usually, that's long enough for her to rescue the children from the brink of death. Then she sends them out into the wasteland again. She has no way to know who among the children lives or dies, nor a way to help their families take care of them better.

The first time I visit her clinic, I meet a boy named Jeevan Munda, who is in the bed closest to the window. He contracted pneumonia when he was around three months old. He started vomiting. He couldn't keep down food. His mother says she gave him whatever she had on hand—saltine crackers, rice—but Jeevan, whose name means "life," didn't have the strength to chew. His mother didn't have the strength to produce much breast milk, and she watched him shrivel steadily for a year.

By the time he landed in the hospital, his big eyes had sunk into his head. His arms were like twigs. He was so weak he could barely sip the water that his mother gave him from a steel bowl. It chilled me to look at him. At eighteen months, Jeevan weighed 3.8 kilograms, barely 8 pounds. He was 61 centimeters (24 inches) long, no bigger than a scrawny cat.

Why didn't you bring him here earlier? I ask. There was no food at home, his mother whispers, so she and her husband went to work in a factory in a neighboring state. The child was already weak, and there were no doctors there, at least none that she could afford. And so, even as they left home to stave off hunger, their child shriveled from hunger. By the time a village health worker sent her to Dr. Aind's clinic, Jeevan could no longer take in any food.

This is what happens to a child who lives with hunger for so long. The body prepares to shut down.

The Naandi Foundation study found that the overwhelming majority of mothers surveyed hadn't heard of the term "malnutrition," in whatever language they spoke. This is the most striking thing about child hunger in the Indian wasteland. If every child around you is scrawny and sick, how would you even know that yours is malnourished?

I return to Dr. Aind's clinic a couple of years later. I ask whether she knows how Jeevan Munda is doing. She does not. Her malnutrition treatment program does not track the progress of its patients. She knows only that she treated him for fifteen days, pumped him with milk and peanut butter, and cajoled his mother to take small steps to keep him well. Give him rehydration salts if he gets diarrhea. Don't wait until he is screaming for food; take a bowl of rice with you when you take him to work with you; feed him several times a day; try to buy an egg for him now and then. Anything more, the doctor knows, is out of the question. The family can rarely afford meat. There is no question of fresh fruits and vegetables on a regular basis. Nor milk. It is too expensive.

Malnutrition's stubborn hold is the most hideous measure of how little India's phenomenal economic growth has meant to those at the bottom of the country's traditional pecking order—and it also attests to the persistence of that traditional pecking order. Aspiration has not dissolved the hierarchies, nor the state's ambitious efforts to break them.

How does India's record of improving the lives of its poor rank? Terribly—and especially terribly for a democracy of the poor.

Consider, for instance, a 2009 study carried out by Martin Ravallion, a Georgetown University economics professor who sought to measure what impact economic growth had on poverty and inequality in India, compared with Brazil and China.[17]

The results offered stark contrasts. In China, he found, the poverty rate diminished most dramatically during its period of high macroeconomic growth, from 84 percent in 1981 to 16 percent in 2005. But even as poverty went down in those years, economic inequality soared.

India reported a similar trend. As the economy grew, the share of

Indians living below the poverty line fell from 60 percent in 1981 to 42 percent in 2005. During that same period, economic inequality widened, though neither the fall in poverty nor the rise in inequality was as sharp as in China.

In Brazil, he found a very different picture. Its economy grew too, but not quite as fast as China's. Brazil's poverty rate fell by more than half between 1981 and 2005. But unlike India or China, Brazil's notoriously high inequality rates narrowed. Ravallion found that was due, in part, to an ambitious government redistribution program that handed out cash to poor mothers so long as they could prove that they took care of their children—immunizing them, for example, against childhood diseases. Brazil's conditional cash transfer program—something that India has sought to replicate in recent years, linked to a biometric identification program to stem corruption and cheating—was credited with helping poor families improve their health, education, and social well-being.[18]

In other words, a high rate of economic growth was not itself enough to help the poor. A rising tide could lift some boats. But whether they stayed afloat depended on how the government used its new riches—and indeed on what sort of a society it sought to create.

S upriya can't pinpoint exactly how she became conscious of the dehumanizing inequity that pervades daily life in her country. She knows only that she became conscious of it after she became a parent, and that it makes her something of an oddity among her peers.

She notices how the ancient logic of caste pollution plays out at the birthday parties of her children's friends in modern, glossy Gurgaon. Usually, the children and their parents (if they come) are invited to a buffet table piled high with food—strawberries, samosas, chicken salad sandwiches cut into triangles, pizza, bagels, cake. They are invited to help themselves to as many servings as they want.

The buffet table is not for the nannies and drivers. They are not to use the same plates or cups. They are to eat separate boxed meals—

individually apportioned, to be touched by them only, and then thrown in the trash.

This peculiar form of segregation rests on the notion that what the untouchable touches risks polluting everyone else—and also on the assumption that servants are likely to be low-born, perhaps Dalits, and employers likely not. It is an unspoken rule, passed down from one generation to the next.

These taboos are not limited to servants. They might apply to a concert musician as well. My friend Ashutosh Sharma, a music promoter who also lives in Gurgaon, recalled that in the summer of 2013, he had invited Lakha Khan, an award-winning elderly musician, to his hotel room in Udaipur, a popular tourist destination in Rajasthan, about an eight-hour drive west of Delhi. The hotel waiter refused to serve tea to Khan. Never mind that the Indian government had lavished him with awards: Khan, as the waiter well knew, belonged to a community called the Manganiyars, who for centuries have served as court musicians for the royal families of Rajasthan, and are considered untouchable.

Infuriated, Ashu summoned the manager. To his shock, the manager stuck by his waiter. Ashu was told this was hotel policy: Khan, a Manganiyar musician, would not be served tea. Ashu says he was close to wringing the manager's neck. He gathered himself and said coolly that he would tell his friends to never patronize this hotel; Ashu owns a travel agency. The hotel manager shrugged. Suit yourself, he said. No untouchable would be served tea in his hotel.

Supriya grew up with this segregation. Her mother used to run her household by this logic of the separate tumbler system: one set of cups for the masters, another set of cups for the help. This logic applied to furniture also. Servants were not to sit on their masters' chairs. They could squat or stand or, at best, use an old stool reserved for them in the kitchen. Supriya never gave it much thought. It's what everyone did. She did it too.

Slowly, at the children's birthday parties, it begins to needle her. She thinks: Why should ayahs eat from separate plates every day at home, when they cook and clean and watch after our children every day? Why should they be served out of paper boxes? One year, she quietly rewrites the rules. At her daughter's birthday, she lays out one table of food for everyone. No more boxed paper meals for the help. To the ayahs she says: Help yourselves.

She figures some of the other mothers might find it strange, which is fine by her. She isn't forcing it on anyone. She just wants to make the change herself—quietly, which is her style.

Over time, she also notices the inexplicable segregation within the gates of Central Park. There are benches on the perimeter of the playground. But the ayahs, who invariably accompany the kids to the playground in the late afternoons, are prohibited from sitting on those benches. They must sit on the ground, even when it is cold or wet, or the grass is prickly dry. It is an unwritten policy, Supriya learns, and enforced by the guards. As a result, the benches are usually empty, piled with children's water bottles. They are reserved for parents, who rarely come.

Supriya finds this bizarre. She takes it up with the residents association. Why should the ayahs have to sit on the grass when the benches are empty? The members of the association offer a variety of justifications. To Supriya, each is as strange as the next.

One of them wonders: What's wrong with sitting on the grass? We also sit on the grass sometimes.

But *we* are free to choose, Supriya replies. *They* are not.

This is how it has always been, another member says.

Supriya quickly understands she isn't going to persuade anyone. Central Park may have made it easy to retreat from the inconveniences of the past, but not its customs.

She is telling me this story while we are out shopping for chocolate cake mix at Modern Bazaar, one box for each of the twenty girls who are invited to her daughter's birthday party the next weekend. It will be in their goody bag—the "return gift," as her kids call it.

I ask if she expects these sentiments to change by the time her children host birthday parties for their own kids. Supriya clucks her tongue. "These things are so deep-rooted I don't think it will change," she says.

The practice of "untouchability" is outlawed. Still, in a survey carried out in 2010, one out of four Indians said they followed this custom, keeping the cups and plates in their homes out of the reach of those whom they regarded as untouchable.[19]

Shortly after I moved to India in 2005, Helene Cooper, a colleague from the *Times*, came to visit Delhi and joined me at home for dinner.

Like me, Helene had moved to the United States as a child—in her case, from Liberia. And like me, she remained deeply connected to her country of birth. She wrote a brilliant memoir about Liberia, before and after its civil war.[20]

"Do you feel like you've come home?" Helene asked.

I scrunched my face. "No," I said. "This does not feel like home."

I had arrived in Delhi only a few months earlier. I found the city too loud, too in-your-face, too feudal. The sprawling bungalow that I inherited as the *Times* bureau chief came with an army of domestic staff. There was a cook who did not clean, a cleaner who did not cook, not one but two gardeners (the yard was big and beautiful), a driver, a washer/presser of clothes, and a "bearer," whose job was ostensibly to bear things on trays. I winced every time one of them called me "mem-sahib," which is how you would refer to a foreign woman—the madam, or wife, of a sahib.

I was unfamiliar with Delhi's social rules. Occasionally I would wait for an interview at a government office, only to be asked when the *Times* bureau chief would arrive. They seemed not to have expected to be inter-viewed by a small Indian-American woman. At a dinner party, shortly after I arrived in Delhi, I was asked, "What does your father do?" My father is a *chowkidar*, I was about to say, which was not a lie, for one of my father's many jobs in the New World was to work part-time as a security guard—until I saw my husband flashing me a look. Don't be snarky, the look said. I swallowed my words. "He is an engineer," I replied instead, which was equally true and which sufficed to shut up my interlocutor. He had found me a place on his pecking order: I was a N.R.I., as my ilk was known, whose father was an engineer in America.

A well-heeled editor in Delhi once snorted that N.R.I. should really stand for Not Required Indians. The country had done just fine without us. She was right.

I was a stranger in Delhi. I had not lived through its ups and downs. I did not know its rules.

So, I remember being emphatic that night when Helene came for dinner and asked. No, I said. I don't feel at home.

Until I do.

I move out of that sprawling villa with its army of staff. When my posting as the *Times* bureau chief comes to an end, I rent a third-floor walk-up in a neighborhood named after Nizamuddin Auliya, a thirteenth-century Sufi saint.

I stop being a full-time reporter. For nearly two years, I am a full-time mom, aided by a highly capable housekeeper, Kiran, who has spent her entire life working as a domestic so that her daughter—her only child—doesn't have to.

Nizamuddin is a special neighborhood. It draws parakeets to its trees and pilgrims to the Sufi saint's shrine. Train whistles blow day and night.

This becomes my daughter's domain. Driving in from the main road, she sees the sandstone dome of the Khan-e-Khana monument at the gates of Nizamuddin and she sighs in relief: "We're home!"

She waves every morning to the couple that irons clothes under a tree. She mimics the *kabbadi-wallah* who cycles by collecting old newspapers. The fruit seller offers her a banana every time she passes by his cart.

One day I watch her waddle into our corner store and haul herself up on a tiny ladder to sit next to the storekeeper, long enough for him to open his drawer and pull out a forbidden piece of candy. Her eyes light up. Her head bobs from side to side, and I know she will be offered another until I intervene to say, "No more sweets before dinner!"

My girl is at home here. And while I suspect she will feel at home wherever we go, I wonder if she will one day ask what I still sometimes ask: Who might I have been had I stayed?

Khejoorperwala Park, named after the date palms that line its edges, is where she goes to play every day, between the time she wakes up from her afternoon nap and a muezzin's call for the evening prayer. Summer. Winter. Even in the rains. This is where she chases mynahs. This is where she goes hunting for ladybugs. This is where she and her Nizamuddin pals wrestle and race.

She is three years old when the two of us lather up with mosquito repellent one summer afternoon and head to the park. I watch her waving to the women sitting in a circle on the grass.

"Whose mama is that?" I ask her. My girl shakes her head.

"Those are *didis*, not mamas," she says.

Didis—literally, "older sisters"—is how polite children refer to nannies and maids. They are Indian, just like the mamas. They too wear *salwar* suits, occasionally jeans with a tunic.

"How do you know they are *didis*?" I ask.

She shrugs, leaps out of her stroller, and runs across the grass to play.

She just knows. Three years old and she can distinguish between *didis* and mamas, servants and masters, them and us. Good thing we will not live here forever, I tell myself. I am unprepared for what awaits us back home in America.

Growing up in America, I didn't know anyone whose family hired domestic staff. I associated it with India. In our Southern California suburb, we kids washed dishes, loaded the laundry, mowed lawns, and babysat for our neighbors for extra cash. No one I knew back then had a nanny.

Of course America has always had servants—it was founded on chattel slavery, after all. But servants were not really a part of the middle-class suburban economy I grew up in. If you had enough money, you hired someone to mow your lawn—and he was inevitably a Mexican migrant worker. If you were lucky enough to have a pool, you hired someone to clean the pool—also, invariably, a Latino man.

But by the time I am a parent, I have inched up the American social ladder. I belong to a far more privileged class. Members of my class have grown accustomed to domestic help of all kinds. Perhaps this is one of the most glaring elisions of the American feminist movement. Instead of making men shoulder the day-to-day drudgery of domestic work, or even forcing our government to offer child-care benefits to working parents, privileged American women like me have dumped that work onto other women, poorer women, whose families are sometimes elsewhere.[21]

I notice this sharply when I move to New York City at the end of 2013. Nannies take babies to the playground, and quite routinely, mothers report to other mothers on what they see a nanny doing to a child on the neighborhood parents' Listserv. Housekeepers come to vacuum and dust. The neighborhood laundromat sends men to pick up dirty laundry. Other men deliver takeout Chinese, Thai, Mexican, and Indian. Even in the worst New York blizzards, they ride their bikes through snow and slush, ring the bell, and wordlessly hand you a receipt, faces frozen. You don't even have to know their names. You don't ever have to wonder what happens in their villages, whether there is a drought this year or if a niece has been kidnapped. You tip them, you thank them, you shut the door. Technology fuels this impersonalized boom. As one mobile app specializing in food delivery orders boasts, it is "seamless."

Inequality—a term once considered unseemly, even unpatriotic—haunts the zeitgeist. New York City, the ultimate beacon of reinvention, becomes the most unequal city in America, so much so that the 2013 mayoral race becomes a referendum over its yawning wealth gap. A clever New York City subway ad reads, "Address inequality. Teach Math."

In fact, social mobility was never actually as great as the myth of Horatio Alger had made it out to be. Ancestry always mattered. Neither modernity nor capitalism had truly dissolved its powerful effects. Your lineage determined not just how much money you could make, but even how long you would live.[22]

Perhaps because I knew something about India, I could detect America's caste system. America was—and is—a highly unequal society. But the psychic costs of living in privilege in America and India are different. We Americans have mastered the art of walling ourselves off completely from the lives of others. In India, that's much harder. It requires an entirely different calibration of compassion and its lack.

When Mani tells her about the abduction of her niece, Supriya feels a chill down her spine. What if someone came and took her child? What if she couldn't even figure out where her child was, or whether she would ever see her again?

She throws herself into the job of rescuing Phoolo. She consults her building manager, who regularly deals with the Gurgaon police. She asks her husband to work his contact in the Delhi police; his advertising firm once developed a branding campaign for the department. She is glad to have the guidance of her father-in-law, a retired Indian Air Force officer who is visiting for a few days, and who can deal with cops much better than she can.

The surprising good news comes on a hot afternoon in late April, when the curtains are drawn to keep out the sun out, the air conditioner set to a cool 17 degrees Celsius, and Supriya is on the sofa, caressing her son, who is curled up against her, groggy with fever. Supriya's cell phone trills. She listens more than she talks. She stands up from the sofa, paces across the living room, thanks the caller, and dials her husband. "Can you talk?" she prefaces. "We have a situation."

The situation is that the Gurgaon police, armed with the phone number Mani procured, has tracked down the address of the house where they suspect Mani's niece is being held. If she is in fact being held against her will, the cops are willing to get her out. But they need two things: a set of wheels to travel there and back (it's unclear why they do not have a police vehicle available) and some cash to make it worth their while.

Supriya has never faced a situation like this. She has no idea how to bribe a police officer, nor how much to give. She paces across her living room, visibly nervous. She changes out of track pants into a loose cotton *salwar kameez*, so she can accompany the police. Dad-in-law takes one look at her face and offers to go instead. To this, Supriya easily agrees. Mani will have to go too. She is the only one who can identify her niece.

It is almost evening by then. In rush-hour traffic, it will take hours to reach the north Delhi enclave where the police suspect the girl is held. Supriya packs cold water bottles and biscuits for the trip. There is a brief discussion with her dad-in-law over how much to pay the two officers assigned to the job. On his way out the door, he assures Supriya that a bribe is justified "on humanitarian grounds."

Miraculously, they find Phoolo. According to Mani's version of events, the police tell her employers that a police complaint will not be filed so long as they identify the employment agent who has brought the girl to their home. The cops find the agent. They persuade her to pay the girl what she is owed: 9000 rupees in all, which amounts to no more than thirty dollars for each of the six months that she has worked. Phoolo hadn't been paid a single *paisa* until then.

No police case is filed. No one is prosecuted.

After Arvind gets home later that evening, he makes arrangements for the policemen to be given what is referred to as a gift. Supriya doesn't want to know how much cash they get. She doesn't want to deal. She is just relieved that another mother, far away from here, will have her daughter back.

Supriya is a cautious, protective mother. The safety and well-being of her children are her greatest aspirations. Supriya learns from Mani's ordeal how precarious, how fragile that proposition is for another mother. The membrane is so thin between the comfort on this side of the gate and the distress on the other.

A few weeks after the rescue, at the end of May, Mani returns with Phoolo to Birhu-Patratoli. This year, the fields are cracked and dry. The rains haven't come for two years. In the heat, the jungle swells with fruit: *jamun* and jackfruit, *kusum*, for hair oil, and *karanja*, to keep the mosquitoes away. Rice can be planted once the rains come, if the rains come. And then, women and men will stand ankle deep in flooded fields, bending toward the earth like a row of question marks, and sow. For now, there is nothing to do but climb a tree and steal a neighbor's mango. It is also wedding season. Mani's baby sister, Kalawati, the one lucky enough to have studied in a private school, is getting married.

On the night of the wedding, Mani's home is brightly lit. The family has procured what folks in Gurgaon rely on every night: a diesel-guzzling generator. It powers a row of bright tube lights in the courtyard. Christmas lights are strung around the house. Every room inside the house is brightly lit, as though there was never any darkness at all.

Mani has swept and leveled the courtyard. She has arranged the altar at which Kalawati and her man will exchange vows. She has prepared the wedding trousseau: a bell metal water pitcher, a steel cabinet in which Kalawati can keep her belongings, plus a respectably large goat as a gift for the in-laws.

I am standing in the courtyard with Mani when the chef lopes over to offer a precise count of the wedding feast. He has prepared 50 kilos of mutton, 20 kilos of chicken, and 105 kilos of rice, along with *dal, parwal*, and a chutney of apples and dates. Weddings are when you get your fill of protein in places like this. The entire village turns up to eat.

Kalawati's wedding fills Mani with a new yearning. She thinks: Why not me? Shouldn't I be married too? No one in her family has bothered to arrange a marriage for her. So she chooses a man for herself. His name is Azad—"freedom," in Hindi—and he calls her on her cell phone for months and woos her. On something of a whim, she says, she agrees to marry him, in a small ceremony, at his house in a village in Bihar, way up by the Nepal border. Mani tells no one but her mother. There is no official recording of the union.

Marriage turns out to be Mani's undoing.

Shortly after they are man and wife, Mani says she feels like she is being treated like his bank machine. He asks her for a loan, and then another and another. Mani drains her savings, borrows from others, and a few months into the marriage, realizes he will never pay her back.

Six months into married life, Mani says she feels like a fool. "How was I to know that he wanted to marry me just for money?" she tells me. She seems as angry with herself as with him.

He moves to Gurgaon by then to share an apartment with a half-dozen other Bihari migrants. Mani stays on at Supriya's home. They can't afford an apartment of their own. They argue a lot.

The following year brings an even greater calamity. Azad leaves without telling her. Mani hears that he has gone back to Bihar to marry someone else—and she is infuriated. She tells Supriya that she is determined to track him down, just as she once tracked down her niece.

Mani quits her job at Supriya's, because she doesn't know how long this mission will take. She packs a bag, rides the train all the way to Azad's village, and soon persuades him that it's in his interest to return to her. Be my husband for real, she offers, or else I will press charges with the police. Mani says Azad falls on his knees and begs her for forgiveness. It is a victory, of sorts.

This is all Mani's version of how she got him back. I tried to reach Azad. But Mani was reluctant to introduce me to him. It is possible he has another version of what happened. My takeaway from all this is Mani's determination to not be made a fool.

She knows she will not get her money back from him. But at least another woman won't get it. And no matter how much they fight, she prefers being Azad's wife rather than the wife he left.

For a while, Azad tries to stop her from returning to work in Gurgaon, but she refuses. Her financial independence is too important—and anyway, she can no longer imagine being a housewife, taking care of his elderly parents, in his dark village, without lights, way up near the Nepal border.

Supriya helps Mani find another job as a live-in maid for an elderly woman, in another gated community in Gurgaon.

In the weeks after the rescue, Supriya learns more about Phoolo's abduction. She discovers that there are other girls like Phoolo, taken from their villages and made to work in the city against their will. For a while, this haunts Supriya. She has managed to get one girl out. Even if she gets a second one out, maybe a third, then what? She begins to look at the maids in Central Park a little differently. She wonders whether to ask her neighbors if they know the backstories of how their maids had ended up in Gurgaon. She decides not to ask.

The more Supriya learns about what had happened to this girl, the more burdened she feels. For a while, the feeling balloons inside her. "I feel heavy," she says.

The feeling doesn't last long. She shuts the door.

Otherwise the heaviness would burst.

GUERRILLA
Paying for Broken Promises

On a stifling night at the end of May 2010, when the red earth is parched for rain and the cashew grove heavy with fruit, Rakhi's head is pounding. Tonight, she will have to kill a man. Rakhi is the commander of a guerrilla squad at war against the largest democracy in the world. She is roughly twenty-one years old, and a Class 8 dropout. She has planned executions and given orders to kill. But she has not yet carried out one herself. It is now her turn. She knows it. Her squad knows it. It feels like their eyes are boring through her skull.

The evening begins fortuitously. An informant calls to say that Rakhi's prey, a man who belongs to the local ruling political party, works for the village government council, and is therefore a designated class enemy, has been seen boarding an auto-rickshaw a few miles away. This is good news. This fellow has eluded her for months. He must know that his name is on the kill list. But now, here he is, coming up the road. It is her job to figure out how to eliminate him while sparing his fellow passengers. Only designated class enemies are to be killed. No one else. Those are her orders.

In quick succession, as expected, more calls come in. A series of informants report on the movement of the vehicle. Rakhi's squad is prepared by the time it approaches. They leap out onto the road, stop the driver, and order everyone to march into the darkening woods. There they tie them up.

Rakhi keeps them bound and gagged until nightfall. When it is pitch-dark, she frees all but the man she is supposed to kill. Him she orders to march up the empty country road. She keeps her eyes on the back of his head. She feels her comrades' eyes on the back of hers. When she gives the signal, one of her subordinates thwacks the man on the head. He falls—facedown, thank god. Another comrade hands her a machete, borrowed earlier in the evening from a villager. Rakhi holds the machete handle tight with both hands, swings it up, and brings it down, as steady as she can. She does not see where the blade lands. She hears a dull thump. She feels a spray of warm blood on her arm. She runs. Someone else will finish the job.

The killing of this man ends, as all such killings do, with a story about the killing. Rakhi walks to the nearest market, wakes up a sleeping shopkeeper, pays for paper and red paint, and writes in large block letters, putting to work the fruits of her Class 8 education: "A police informant has been killed. Communist Party of India (Maoist)." Next to it, she draws a red hammer and sickle.

It is the rebel army's rudimentary, pen-and-ink version of a Twitter post—a coda to the actual slaughter, part ritual and part propaganda. The note is left next to the corpse, which is left on the road. It will serve as a message, each piece of the tableau as important as the other: a pool of blood, a smashed head, a handwritten note.[1]

Every killing reverberates like this. By the first light of dawn, word spreads. Maybe the police come to retrieve the body—or, in this lawless patch of the country, maybe not. Villagers say as little as they can to one another. No one wants to admit that they heard something the night before. No one can be sure who will snitch to whom. The rebellion makes people distrustful, quiet, afraid of everyone. It is like living under the Stasi, except that here in rural West Bengal, there is no indoor plumbing.

Rakhi tells me her story a year later, sitting in a cool, curtained room in a heavily guarded police compound, where she has been staying since surrendering to the authorities. She wears a hot pink *salwar-kameez*, made of scratchy nylon, with a spine of sequins running down the middle. India Shining, I write in my notebook. She stares at her fingernails, also painted pink. She sips water from a recycled Sprite bottle. She seems to be narrating this story mostly to herself, as though in the telling, she might better understand who she had become.

Rakhi agrees to speak to me on condition that neither her name nor her village be identified. She fears retaliation by former comrades. She fears especially for her mother back home. And so hers is the only alias in this book, a concession to the fact that she is in an unofficial witness-protection program in a part of the country where the government's writ does not always run. Likewise, I've left out the name of the man she describes killing. Her story is corroborated by interviews with police and her family, as well as by newspaper accounts.

It has taken me months to find her, and then to persuade police to let me speak to her. I searched for her because I wanted to understand why young Indians of her generation have chosen a path of insurgency. I *wanted* to know how much of it is driven by conviction and how much by ennui—and equally how this vibrant, prospering democracy can breed such rage among some of its children.

I am drawn to the story because Rakhi's rebellion was born around the time I was born, in the late 1960s—and returned hotter and deadlier thirty years later, in an era awash in riches and hope. In the story of this rebellion lay a different kind of ambition among Indians of noonday—this one as ruinous as lava.

"I feel terrified when I think about those things now," Rakhi says. "What did I do? Who was I? Did I become like a don?" A don, as in a mafia don, a gang leader, is a familiar figure in Bollywood. There is a 1978 Hindi movie called *Don*, and a remake, also called *Don*.

A sip of water. A short breath. And Rakhi picks up the story. The machete is washed of blood and returned to its owner.

"Why not just keep the machete?" I ask.

Rakhi looks at me like I am an idiot. The Maoists never keep a machete, she says. They're expensive. Villagers need them. There may be a chicken to slaughter the next day, or firewood to be chopped. Fighters are instructed to clean the blood and flesh off of the machetes they borrow and return the tools to their owners.

The slaughter that Rakhi led that evening in a village in West Bengal state, a half day's drive from my birth city, Calcutta, and just across the state line from Mani's Jharkhand, is multiplied across the vast jungle belly of India. The insurgency blossoms during India's golden age, reflecting a perfect storm of inequity, incapacity, and greed.

At its peak, in 2010, Indian intelligence officials estimate that Maoists operated in more than one-third of India's 600-odd districts, from Bihar in the north to southern Andhra Pradesh. That estimate is likely to be exaggerated, designed to draw in extra government funds to those areas that claim to be Maoist-affected. No matter what its real scale, the insurgency is concentrated in India's central and eastern states, including West Bengal and Jharkhand. Those are the very states that hold the country's natural resources—timber, coal, bauxite, uranium—as well as its most deprived *adivasi* hamlets.

In the five-year period from 2006 through 2010, which is also a period of record economic growth, the war between state forces and the Communist Party of India (Maoist), as the rebels are called, kills 4212 people. It is the deadliest of India's sundry rebellions in this period; the more widely known insurgency in disputed Kashmir province results in 3184 deaths during those same years.[2]

The Indian Maoists once called themselves Naxalites, after a peasant uprising that kicked off in 1967, the year I was born, in a village called Naxalbari, nestled in the tea plantations of West Bengal. At the time, Communist guerrilla movements were flourishing across Africa, Asia, and Latin America. In India, Mao's Little Red Book was fashionable among young educated city folks.

My mother's youngest brother was in engineering college when the Naxalbari rebellion erupted, and like so many middle-class youth at the time, he ran away to join them. My *mamu*, as I called him, grew a beard, went underground, and cloaked himself with one alias after another. His mission was to organize sharecroppers to rise up, demand their rights, and, on occasion, kill their overlords, preferably with their bare hands (which was in keeping with Maoist doctrine of the time) or, if necessary, with the aid of everyday sharecropper tools—like machetes. They were not to use guns. They didn't have the money to buy many guns anyway. Once they had vanquished their feudal masters in the countryside, they were to encircle the city and raise their red flag.

The sharecroppers were no fools. Once, when my *mamu* introduced himself as a man from a nearby hamlet, one skeptical villager pointed to his wrist. "*Dada*, what's that mark there?" the man asked, pointing to the band of skin that was a shade lighter from years of wearing a watch. In 1967, no one in these villages wore a watch. They knew my uncle was not one of them.

Every now and then he and his friends would turn up unannounced at my parents' apartment in tidy, middle-class Calcutta. They would come for the luxury of a proper bath, to eat a piece of fish, or to reassure their loved ones that they were alive. They would bring with them the smell of cheap cigarettes and the distress of the countryside. They would bring stories from the bush, and in lieu of nursery rhymes, they would teach me revolutionary doggerel. I had no idea what the verses meant. But I relished them anyway, so I swallowed them whole and I memorized them. Sometimes, this got me in trouble.

A story about my mischief has circulated in my family for forty years. It has been recycled and retold so many times that a few details are no doubt misplaced or made up. It takes place in or around 1970, just before Durga Puja, the most important festival of the year among Bengali Hindus. I was tagging along with my mother, as she went shopping for Puja saris in Gariahat Market. Ma plunked me down on a shop counter as she began her deliberations. Sari after sari was unfurled, each one's provenance and price discussed, whereupon I burst into song, swinging my legs in tempo. Ma no longer remembers the lyrics—only that they were something about liberating the motherland, which was hazardous coming out of a three-year-old's mouth, in a crowded sari shop in Calcutta at a time when cops were hunting for Maoist skulls.

I was scooped off the counter, hurried out of the shop, and plunked into the nearest rickshaw. The saris must have remained unfurled on the counter. Ma's heart must have raced in fear. Her mouth must have been wide open, as it often is when she encounters the unknown.

Mamu's revolution turned out to be short-lived. By 1973, during Indira Gandhi's administration, a tough counterinsurgency effort quashed the Naxalites with little resistance. There were unexplained extrajudicial killings. There were no tribunals to get to the bottom of who did what, no accountability.[3]

My uncle received amnesty from the state. Many of his friends were jailed. A neighbor across the street was killed. The most privileged among them, I was told later, were escorted by parents to the international airport in Calcutta and sent off to universities in America. There were still many idealists, as Mamu recalls, but their movement splintered into numerous ideological shards.

Still, over the next three decades, some of those Maoists quietly regrouped. They acquired guns and satellite phones. They expanded well beyond the few pockets where they had been active during my childhood. This time too, they were led by college-educated men and women, including at least one who had been educated in Britain. Their foot soldiers were young men and women from the hinterland, mostly *adivasis* who had been cheated for generations in free India.

The rebellion blossomed once more at noonday. This time it was deadlier, more damaging. It showed how devastating it can be when young people are promised so much, and given so little.

The volatile cocktail of rich lands and poor people has produced ugly conflicts elsewhere. The civil war in the Democratic Republic of the Congo is a fight over the control of copper and gold. In Nigeria, gun-toting gangsters have fought over control of the oil-rich delta. I have covered both. I have seen the devastation firsthand.

In India's case, the demand for natural resources—especially coal and iron ore—accelerated in the period after the economy opened up in 1991. In turn, it fueled an insurgency across an *adivasi* belt that stretched from the Jharkhand villages that Mani and her people call home through Rakhi's rural Bengal and farther south into Orissa and Chhattisgarh. In my *mamu*'s time, *adivasis* were among the worst off in India. In my daughter's time, they remain so.

Here in West Bengal, it helped the rebels' cause that *adivasi* villages had seen little improvement in seventy years of freedom. Complicating matters, the West Bengal state government had been run for three decades by politicians who also called themselves Communists. Their local apparatchiks behaved like thugs. Jobs went to the politically connected, if there were jobs at all.

The guerrilla insurgency—and the state's response to it—only made things worse for ordinary citizens who struggled to get by. For example, security forces turned schools into garrisons, which prompted the Maoists to raze them altogether.[4] Astonishingly, if schools were rebuilt, they had to abide by Maoist specifications, with sloped tin roofs that security forces could not use as defensive bastions. Otherwise, villagers told me, the Maoists threatened to raze them all over again. That the rebels dictated the design of schoolhouses indicated how little authority local government officials had over government services.

In some states, the government machinery responded to the rebellion by clamping down on law and liberty: Preventive detention laws were enacted. Suspected troublemakers—including journalists, activists, and even a doctor who for years had operated a clinic in an utterly neglected *adivasi* corner of central India—were picked up and thrown in jail, sometimes for years.[5] The insurgency held up billions of dollars in investment in roads, mines, and factories.

Most important, the conflict forever changed daily life in these villages. Fear hovered over everything. Neighbors could no longer trust one another. Corpses appeared on remote country roads. The casualties included cops, teachers, politicians, farmers, as well as suspected insurgents. Passenger trains were derailed. Land mines were planted on strategic roads. Mothers who subsisted on harvesting leaves and berries feared wandering into the forest. In some parts of the country, people scooped up blankets and water pots and fled deeper into the bush. At one point, in 2006 and 2007, as India's economy was galloping, an estimated 50,000 villagers were displaced in Chhattisgarh state, as Maoists battled state-funded anti-Maoist militias.

Dust and brambles blew through the empty villages when I visited Chhattisgarh in the summer of 2006. My goal was to see a Maoist commander inside the Abujmarh forest, which served as the rebel base. Getting that interview involved many months of negotiations by phone and email through a chain of minders and emissaries, followed by an initial, fruitless foray into the bush, followed, finally, by the coveted promise of a face-to-face meeting.

I received my instructions in snatches. Fly to the state capital, Raipur, and wait. Drive to such-and-such tea shop two hours outside the capital and wait. Eat parathas. Wait. Follow those motorcyclists in your own car and wait. Board that jeep. Ask no questions.

There were five of us on this trip: my colleague from the Delhi bureau, Hari Kumar, a photographer on assignment for the *Times* named Namas Bhojani, plus two journalists from the British newspaper *The Guardian*. We squeezed into a dark red jeep. We spent several hours being driven along a paved road, and then several more on unpaved roads, until it became dark and we had no idea where we were. We may as well have been driven around in circles. At some point, late in the evening, we were told to disembark and follow our guides into the jungle. We walked silently until we reached a shallow, gurgling stream. I took off my shoes and socks, rolled up my jeans. The water came up to my knees.

On the other side of the stream, motorcycle chauffeurs waited for us, procured by the Maoists to ferry us over a narrow dirt track through a pitch-dark forest. My chauffeur was a young man who said he had been conscripted for the evening. If he had a strong opinion about the Maoists, he certainly didn't tell me. How could he? He was in their service.

They ruled these jungles. He did muster the courage to ask me quietly as he maneuvered his bike through the inky black trees: "*Didi*, tell me, why do they blow up the roads all the time? It would be good to have some roads around here."

Our chauffeurs deposited us at an abandoned house. Being the only woman in our crew, I got my own room, with my own wooden platform for a bed, covered in cobwebs. I unfurled my purple sleeping bag liner and crawled inside, fully dressed. I turned on my headlamp and wrote in my notebook:

> *frogs*
> *stars*
> *roads with trenches to keep away unwanteds*

I slept.

Our minders woke us up when it was still pitch-dark. Wordlessly, they led us through the forest and deposited us as dawn broke at a small clearing circled by bamboo. The forest stirred. In the first indigo light of day, I could make out figures moving around me. The People's Liberation Guerrilla Army (PLGA) cadres were beginning their day. They brushed teeth. They washed pots. They mostly wore standard-issue forest-green uniforms—pants and button-down shirts—with flip-flops instead of army boots. Their socks dried on tree branches. Someone turned on a transistor radio, crackling with news from the BBC Hindi Service. The company commander, who called himself Gopanna Markam, shaved.

Slowly came light, revealing the guerrilla encampment. Flecks of morning sun warmed the forest floor. Someone blew a whistle, which was a signal for the cadres to gather around the cooking pot. Breakfast today was sweet, milky tea and puffed rice. Markam snapped his finger and a cup of hot water materialized for my Nescafe. Sleeping bag liners and Nescafe were among my vital supplies. No matter how long I lived in India, I could not bear milky tea. Nor could I function at dawn without coffee.

The Maoists had brought us here today to witness a song-and-dance revue that Markam's crew was putting on for the locals. After breakfast, the crew rehearsed. They went over their lines. They practiced their dance steps. They reminded me of cheerleaders. Instead of "Go Team" they chanted "Red Salute." They looked like children—fourteen, fifteen years old maybe—but when I pointed this out, Markam insisted that they were all adults.

Such performances, Markam said, were an effective way to draw local kids. Indeed. Which kid in the world wouldn't skip a day spent drawing well water and collecting firewood to dress up instead and sing?

I was given clear rules of engagement. I was prohibited from talking to cadres. I could ask questions only of Markam. And his story had been carefully curated, skeletal in its details, deliberately everyman. Gopanna Markam was most certainly not his real name.

Markam described himself as a farmer's son from neighboring Andhra Pradesh. His family had the means to send him to college, where he joined something called the Radical Student Organization. "I was a little educated," he said. "I thought the future was dark. I thought I would join to make a change."

This was his version of how the Maoists organized. By 1980, he went underground as a "full-timer," as it is known, for the People's War Group, or PWG. Throughout the 1980s, in Andhra Pradesh, the PWG would make its name by slaying some big landlords and forcing a bit of land reform. The Andhra Pradesh authorities struck back with a powerful counterinsurgency force. Many Maoists, Markam included, slipped into the poorly policed jungles of Chhattisgarh. They shifted focus to winning over *adivasis*.

Those first few months in Chhattisgarh, whenever the locals saw Markam, they fled into the forest. It didn't help that he was armed. It didn't help that he didn't speak the local language, Gondi.

In time, he said, he learned that language. He learned about what the local people wanted. He helped them negotiate higher prices for their principal crop: leaves of the *tendu* tree, which they gathered from the forest floor and sold by the bundles to be rolled into country cigarettes, called *bidis*. Occasionally, the Maoists hauled the *tendu pata* traders into Maoist-run "people's courts," roughing them up if they refused to pay peasants for the crop. The Maoists' principal targets, though, were police and any civilians they labeled as police informants. Markam recruited locals, training them to shoot (but also to conserve bullets) and to use machetes.

On this morning, I noticed some of his subordinates were teaching one another to read. Others were tinkering with an improvised explosive device, as other teenagers elsewhere might tinker with model airplanes. There were plenty of young women in the ranks. Hair oiled and plaited. Belts clinched around the waist. Soldiers.

Markam said the Maoists organized by forming armed village squads, known as *dalams*, and local governance units, known as People's Revolutionary Councils. They took on village priests and headmen, the traditional sources of local power. They kept the cops out. They collected taxes, sometimes a slice of the *tendu* collection. They tried to discourage drinking, but they weren't terribly successful. Maoist leaders like Markam could be a self-righteous, teetotaling lot. A defector once told me that it was the Maoists' joylessness that finally drove him out—as he put it, they didn't know how to enjoy an ice cream cone on a hot day.

Markam told me he had also tried to persuade people not to vote. But this was not terribly successful either. Indians like to vote. Even out here, where choosing your leader brings so little.

While the Maoists stepped up their organizing, the government authorities played right into their hands. In 2005, Chhattisgarh raised a militia to fight the Maoists. The state recruited mostly teenaged boys and young men for its anti-Maoist militia, handed them rifles and a license to be thuggish. The summer of my visit to the Abujmarh forest the widening conflict between the two sides had driven tens of thousands of villagers into refugee camps or deep into the bush. I wrote about it in the *Times*.[6]

I asked Markam about the movement's failures. He said he regretted that they hadn't pilfered as many arms from the security forces as he would have liked, nor launched as many offensive strikes on security forces. Some of the cadres, he admitted, had unnecessarily killed some civilians.

The song-and-dance show began later that morning. Men pounded on goatskin drums. Cadres led chants denouncing imperialism. Under an enormous mango tree they sang a Gondi version of "The Internationale."

Then, the PLGA cadres came down from the hills; I counted nineteen uniformed fighters. Alongside came a second rung of fighters who tended their fields most days but who could be called upon to help the PLGA in battle—like a reserve force, dressed this afternoon in cheerful tie-dyed, wraparound *lungis* (I counted thirty men). In unison, they raised a hodgepodge of weapons—shotguns, antiquated .303 rifles, country-made pistols. They marched. They stood at attention. They circled the field in mismatched flip-flops and oversize sneakers, kicking up red dust.

The audience, all locals instructed to attend the program, sat still in a semicircle. One woman held up her baby, so the child could have a better view. Some broke into giggles as the PLGA charged in a line, their weapons pointed at a chicken scurrying across the field.

Abujmarh—"unknown highlands" in Gondi—spreads out across 3900 square kilometers of rolling hills, thickly covered with bamboo and the sweet berry of *mohua*.

The very top leaders of the Communist Party of India (Maoist)—its sixteen-member leadership council is called the Politburo—hid up in these hills, directing the activities of the rebel organization in the rest of the country. Throughout the mid-2000s, as the Maoists stepped up the insurgency, the rebel group amassed more weapons, blew up trains, and executed politicians. They funded the rebellion in part through a lucrative extortion scheme. Anyone doing business in the Maoist belt had to pay a rebel tax.

In April 2010 came the deadliest attack in this war. In Chhattisgarh, several dozen federal paramilitary troops with the Central Reserve Police Force (CRPF) were ambushed as they returned to their base after an all-night patrol. The Maoists first blew up an armored personnel carrier. Then they sprayed the troops with bullets, killing nearly all of them, seventy-six in all. The Maoists had been watching the federal forces from a strategic ridge just above the road.

An official investigation into the ambush showed how unprepared the security forces were. They had little body armor to protect them. They were sleep-deprived and stressed. They were on unfamiliar terrain. And in an inexplicable tactical misstep, they were returning from their reconnaissance mission along exactly the same route they had taken on their way in. They were easy prey.

A few days after that attack, I traveled back to the same patch of Abujmarh. I got nowhere near the Maoist base. I found instead a rattled CRPF battalion, trapped inside what used to be a residential school for *adivasi* children and was now a garrison for security forces.

The men were boiling with anger, as much at the rebels as at their bosses who put them here. They spoke to me from the other side of a brick wall. They said they dared not venture out. They stayed awake all night in case of a Maoist ambush. They took turns sleeping during the day. This week the rebels had held up even their milk deliveries. So the troops had been reduced to drinking black tea. They said it was like being in jail.

A long line of *adivasi* villagers listened quietly as the troops spat their grievances over the brick wall. The villagers had walked down to the main road that day to collect their government-subsidized food rations for the month. Ration trucks were no longer permitted to go up into the hills. So the hill people had to come down to collect the rations they were entitled to. It took three hours to get down here on foot, and longer to go back, what with the sacks of rice and salt on their heads. But there wasn't much of a choice. If they didn't come, they wouldn't eat, they said. They knew what that was like—not eating.

Rice, flavored with wild greens. That was their daily staple. If they were lucky and someone managed to slay a deer, there was meat. On what they called long days (summer days), they aspired to eat two meals. On short days, one.

Of the thirty-five kilograms of rice they would procure this day at the ration shop, they said the Maoists would take five.

* * *

On this trip I met an orphan who called himself Manher Singh. This is the story he told me.

It was a winter's evening in a hamlet nestled inside Abujmarh. The boy had just returned home from herding his uncle's cattle, when men with guns stood in front of his house. They were from a platoon of Maoist guerillas. Come with us, they said.

They took Manher to a neighboring hamlet, tied him up in a bamboo grove, and presented him before a village assembly. The boy could see their eyes shining in the dark, like so many surprised deer. The Maoists accused him of snitching to the police.

Manher said he was innocent. He said he had nothing to do with the cops, that he had lost his parents long ago and lived with his uncle and occasionally went to school. To make himself useful, he herded his uncle's cattle and gathered firewood for the evening meal.

His captors were unconvinced. "They said if I wanted to leave, they would have to kill me. So I said, 'Okay, I'll stay.'"

And that is how the boy, fourteen at the time, became a beast of burden in a guerrilla war against the Indian state. He trekked through the jungle with a Maoist platoon, past small, remote villages and across rivers, easily avoiding police stations, health clinics, and government offices—because in Abujmarh there are very few of these institutions. For all intents and purposes, the Indian government did not govern here, not before the Maoists came and not after.

The boy carried rucksacks filled with wires, explosives, and tarpaulin for the rainy season. His platoon roamed from village to village. They held meetings, sometimes solved local quarrels, and requisitioned rice from villagers, occasionally a chicken.

He learned how to make a bomb and how to set off an improvised explosive device. He learned how to crawl on his belly in case there was a gun battle. His first lesson on firing a gun ended disastrously. He pulled the trigger and immediately lost hearing in his left ear.

"Did they tell you who the enemy was?" I asked.

"The police," he said.

"Did they tell you what you were fighting for?"

"To get their guns," he said.

"Did they tell you what would happen once your side won the fight?"

Form a "people's government," he was told. First, they would take over Chhattisgarh state, then the whole country. He had never been anywhere outside the forest.

Manher soon got bored. He got tired. Every day he was made to walk so long and carry such heavy loads. One moonlit night, while on sentry duty, he ran away. He took two hand grenades, three rifles, and a muzzle-loading country weapon. The platoon commander slept with his gun, so he couldn't take that. Nor, he told me ruefully, could he get his hands on the pile of money that the commander controlled—500,000 rupees, about $10,000, he guessed wildly. He did somehow procure the commander's notebook, with entries of how much money his platoon took in and spent. He started walking.

He buried two guns in the forest, kept a third, until he passed his village, where, in jubilation, he tossed it into a stream. Naturally, he couldn't go back to his uncle's house. His captors would find him and kill him. So he kept walking, clutching the hand grenades.

"I never went with them out of choice," he said of the rebels. "I didn't like them. They said if I tried to leave, they would kill me."

By morning, Manher reached a police station in the nearest town, Narayanpur. He turned over the hand grenades and the commander's notebook. Then he led the cops back to the jungle where he had stashed the two additional guns. They were all good, actionable pieces of intelligence. The cops patted him on the back and gave him a cot to sleep on in the police barracks. He was still there six months later, in 2010, when I met him. He wore an orange bandanna around his face, which he pulled down only when he was inside the police superintendent's office. He never left the barracks. He couldn't even go to the weekly market in town. Maoists were crawling all over the market. If they spotted him, he was dead.

You would think that the cops would have been grateful for his cooperation. But no good deed went unpunished here, not for a poor, half-deaf orphan. As a reward for leaving the rebels and turning over their weapons, Manher received 20,000 rupees—about $400—or roughly one-sixth of the money to which he was entitled.

The police superintendent, Rahul Bhagat, said his department claimed the rest in fees for his room and board in police barracks.

The one time I met him, Manher said he was utterly bored in those barracks. He begged the cops to let him work. He offered to become an intelligence agent. They said he wasn't old enough.

The state-funded anti-Maoist militia was soon dissolved. Public interest litigation was filed in the Supreme Court of India by three citizens, including the historian Ramachandra Guha, arguing that the state should never have armed its own citizens. The court sided with the litigants, concluding that the Chhattisgarh government had violated the Constitution. The Maoists, meanwhile, pursued extrajudicial measures. In 2013, they assassinated the politician who founded the militia, an *adivasi* member of the state legislature named Mahendra Karma.

Throughout the 2000s, the Maoists drew from a vast pool of young people who were among the least equipped to survive in the new economy, even as they had their noses pressed against it. In their villages, satellite dishes had been perched on top of mud huts, bringing national news and entertainment to the back of beyond. Migrants who went away every year to build shopping malls elsewhere discovered the country beyond theirs—and the riches that lay out of their reach.

A journalist writing for the Indian newsweekly *Outlook* in 2011 looked at around 150 arrest reports to glean something about who the Maoist rebels were. Most of those arrested were under thirty-five; the largest bloc was *adivasi*. What surprised me most was that many more of them had gone to school than those who described themselves as illiterate. A majority, like Rakhi, said they chose to join the insurgency; only a few admitted to being coerced.

Aspiration is not only for the likes of Anupam, who single-mindedly studies, and Mani, who leaves the country to scrub the floors in the city. It also spurs a woman like Rakhi to cut an entirely different path. Unlike their parents and grandparents, young people growing up in the wasteland know what else is out there. They know what they have been denied for generations. They too are taking their destinies into their own hands, except it's fueled more by nihilism than by hope. And they become cannon fodder in a fight led by old-time ideologues singing revolutionary rhymes.

In my *mamu*'s time, when the Maoists briefly flourished, India was a desperately poor country. The Maoists of noonday resurfaced during India's golden age, at a time of unprecedented prosperity. West Bengal, where the Naxalites first emerged in my childhood, became one of the bloodiest theaters of the Maoist conflict, changing Rakhi's life forever.

On a bright Sunday in November 2008, Buddhadeb Bhattacharya, the erudite, elderly chief minister of the state, who often looked like he would rather be writing literary criticism than running one of India's most impoverished states, was seated in the back of a white, state-owned Ambassador car.

Bhattacharya's Communist Party of India (Marxist)—sworn enemy of the guerrilla Maoist organization, which eschewed electoral politics—had ruled West Bengal state since 1977, winning election after election with a tight, often intimidating network of local party bosses. The party dominated everything in every village, deciding who got ration cards or a schoolteacher's job. All the while, the state ranked among the worst in India on hunger, health, and unemployment. Water was scarce in the *adivasi* districts. Thousands migrated every year to work in more prosperous parts of the country, as maids and rickshaw pullers and diggers of ditches. They saw what they didn't have.

On this morning, as part of his quest to resurrect industry in his struggling state, Bhattacharya was on his way to a town called Salboni, to inaugurate a new factory by one of India's biggest companies, known as JSW Bengal Steel. Salboni was a prime location for a steel plant.

The land here was brimming with iron ore. The highway offered easy access to the port of Kolkata, from where it was a short journey by sea to Guangdong, China, where steel was in fabulously high demand.

Bhattacharya came here to lay the ceremonial foundation stone for the steel plant. Standing before television cameras, he spoke of reviving Bengal and promised jobs for sons of the soil. Then he got back inside his Ambassador. Red lights blazing, he headed back to Calcutta.

Police jeeps led the convoy. Sirens screamed.

The convoy traveled barely twenty kilometers when—*bang*—there was an explosion. A homemade land mine had been laid for Bhattacharya: a milk jar, packed with ball bearings. Someone crouching in the paddy fields pulled the switch just as the chief minister's convoy passed. It exploded.

The casualties were minimal: six state police officers were injured, the chief minister unharmed. The impact, though, was spectacular. As the news spread, it set off a chain of events that could have sprung only from a Maoist tactical playbook.

In the days that followed, police scoured neighboring villages for suspects. They hauled off young men and boys for questioning. This infuriated the villagers. For years they had been neglected, and now the cops came barging into their homes, picking up their boys. The drama built up, exactly according to the Maoist script. Years of pent-up rage burst. In one melee, as villagers battled with the authorities, a police officer's rifle butt punctured an old widow in the eye, partially blinding her. The one-eyed widow became a symbol of the confrontation of peasants against the state.

Lalgarh, as the region is known, became a battlefield.

The Maoist leadership deftly manipulated the rage of Lalgarh. One afternoon, hundreds of *adivasis* descended on Dalhousie Square, once the heart of the British East India Trading Company in Calcutta—and now the seat of Bhattacharya's administration. They were armed with bows and arrows. They were tattooed and angry and some of them were barefoot. It was an incongruous picture: the furious wilderness in the old imperial heart of Calcutta.

Lalgarh itself turned into a fortress. Villagers poured out of their houses and blocked the roads leading to the area. They felled trees to keep cops out. One day in June 2009, in a village called Dharampur, they grabbed a local apparatchik of Bhattacharya's political party, lynched him in the village square in broad daylight, and left his body to rot under the summer sun. Neither the cops nor the local government bureaucrats, nor even a hospital ambulance, came to Lalgarh to collect the corpse for days.[7]

The anger of the villagers was aimed at many things. Their wells were dry, there were no irrigation canals, they barely eked out one harvest a year. Their roads were broken. Their children wanted jobs. They were suspicious of the Chinese-style tax-free industrial zones that the government was promoting in the area, including for the JSW steel plant.

Lalgarh offered fertile ground for Maoist organizers. Here were armies of young men and women with a surplus of time and rage. For a while, the rebels controlled the area. They were led by a Politburo member who had spent years organizing for just such a moment. He went by the name Kishenji. He was from southern Andhra Pradesh, just like Gopanna Markam, the Maoist commander I had met earlier in Chhattisgarh. Kishenji had lived in Bengal long enough to speak fluent Bengali. He was something of a show-off. At the height of the Lalgarh insurgency, he liked to appear before television cameras, covering his long, gaunt face with a checkered cotton handkerchief and taunting state officials. One night, on prime-time news, he read aloud his cell phone number, inviting the Indian home minister, who was in charge of fighting the Maoists, to call him for talks. The home minister did not.

Before the rebellion, Rakhi's life is nothing remarkable. She is born to a relatively comfortable family in a village near Salboni, surrounded by a grove of luminescent gray-green *sal* from which the town got its name. Rakhi's family is blessed to have a pond behind their mud-and-thatch house. When the rains come there is water. In the kitchen garden grow cabbage and papaya, radishes and chili peppers. They have chickens and so they have eggs, which is a luxury. "We always had rice to eat," she recalls, which is her way of saying she was never hungry.

The family's good fortunes may have something to do with her father's political acumen. Rakhi recalls that he made sure to pay off both the local Communist Party bosses and their political rivals.

When Rakhi is a teenager, her father suffers a fatal stroke, which, in a country with no safety net, devastates the family. The funeral eats away their savings. An older sister has to be married off—and soon, Rakhi's brother has to organize a celebration to mark the birth of his first son. More feasts. More expenses. The family is forced to pawn off some land. Rakhi can't concentrate at school. She drops out. It is just before her Class 8 exams.

There's some confusion about what happens next. Rakhi's mother, whom I visit one afternoon, tells me she had found a groom for her daughter when Rakhi was about sixteen, a boy from a nearby hamlet. This takes me by surprise. Rakhi hasn't mentioned a husband. When I ask her about it later, she angrily denies it.

I can't say for sure whether Rakhi was married. Her mother seems to have no reason to lie. What I do know is that Rakhi is electrified by the agitation in Lalgarh—so much so that she runs away one night in the early days of the uprising. She hawks Maoist propaganda at first. She isn't an *adivasi* herself, but she has grown up among them, she speaks their language, and she proves herself to be an able organizer. Never before has Rakhi felt so charged, so wanted.

So when the leaders ask if she would like to learn how to fire a gun, she readily signs up. She learns how to shoot, how to burn down a house, how to lay a land mine, and how to beat up a class enemy with her bare hands. She rises quickly up the ranks. She learns to ride a motorcycle. She is given a mobile phone, as well as a gun—with orders to conserve bullets. She is appointed squad leader.

Then begin the killings. Each leaves a vivid memory. The time of day, the season of the year, the name of the victim.

She can chronicle them all.

There is the man named Bhagwat, who is drinking in the courtyard of his house one night when she and her squad ride over and quietly slip over the fence. "Who's there?" shouts Bhagwat's wife in the darkness, only to scream when she sees Rakhi and her squad. Shaken from his drunken lull, Bhagwat dives into a pond. It is winter. So the water is frigid. Rakhi and her comrades circle the pond, firing at their prey, watching the bullets skip on the water like pebbles. It sounds to me like a Keystone Cops episode. She clucks her tongue as she tells me the story. So many bullets wasted, she recalls. Finally, one of the fighters jumps into the pond, pulls the drunkard out, and shoots him dead. The commotion wakes up the neighbors, who then pelt Rakhi and her squad with stones, so they have to fire in the air as they run. More bullets wasted, Rakhi says. She shakes her head, as though she was still keeping count.

There is the man named Ashok, a village thug who would sleep in a different house every night and brag publicly that the Maoists could never kill him. Rakhi's squad carry out a two-month-long reconnaissance. They discover that no matter where he sleeps, he relieves himself at 6:00 A.M. every morning at the same ditch. This turns out to be Ashok's fatal habit. Rakhi orders one of her squad members to wait for him at his morning spot. He is shot dead as soon as he drops his pants.

And then there is Neelmoni Murmu, an old woman who is seen serving water to the police, a heinous crime in the eyes of the Maoists. Rakhi marches into the courtyard of her house and slaps the old woman. This would be unthinkable in normal times—a young woman slapping an elderly woman! But the normal-time rules have broken down.

"Tell us about the policeman who came to your house," Rakhi demands, which makes Neelmoni Murmu throw herself on her husband. The old couple cling to each other so tightly Rakhi has to beat them both with a strip of bamboo to tear them apart. She drags the woman out onto the main road. "We're going to kill you," Rakhi warns. The woman is so terrified, she wets herself.

Rakhi lets one of her comrades slash her throat. Next to her corpse, Rakhi writes in red ink, "Police informant."

The tales come out of her in a long stream of consciousness. I'm still not sure why she opens up like this. Perhaps she isn't sure herself. After that first long conversation, every time I call her, she sounds angry at having told me anything at all.

She is most enraged when she discovers that I have gone to see her mother. You come and go, she spits on the phone. My mother has to live there, with those people.

In the end, it is a man who drives her out of the movement—a hot-headed member of her own squad who, she says, spreads lies about her among her colleagues. He lets it be known that she is squandering the party's money. He defies her orders. "He broke me" is how she puts it.

By then, she is also growing disillusioned. Villagers are killed indiscriminately. She gets tired of being on the run. And then one of her female comrades is sexually assaulted by a commander.

And so, two years after she decided to join the rebellion, Rakhi decides to run away. She knows this is far more dangerous. If she goes home, the Maoists will kill her and her family. If she goes to the authorities, the cops could also kill her—or, she figures, they might let her live. She takes that risk.

One night, on the pretext of fetching water, she leaves her encampment, slips out of the tracksuit that has become her guerrilla uniform, changes into a *salwar kameez*, and hides in a hilltop temple until nightfall. She tosses her mobile phone into a stream, walks all night until she reaches a railway station, and boards a train to a neighboring district, where she is less likely to be recognized by locals. There she walks into the office of the police superintendent and surrenders. "I'm a Maoist," she says.

For the cops, she is extremely valuable. The police commander in charge of the counterinsurgency in this area tells me Rakhi has offered actionable intelligence. Soon after she surrenders, police enter a forest near her village, known as Bhallookbasha—literally, "bear's lair"—and after a four-day gun battle, retrieve a laptop computer. Police say the laptop contains account ledgers that show how much money the Maoists have at their disposal: 12 *crore* Indian rupees, or around $2.5 million.

When I first meet Rakhi, in the summer of 2010, she lives in a two-room apartment in a police compound with another ex-fighter who has surrendered and two cops who guard them around the clock.

Rakhi spends her days mostly watching television. She eats well. She worries about getting fat. Mostly she worries about her future, which is as uncertain as ever. She knows she cannot stay in police custody forever. Nor can she go back to where she comes from.

"We can never eat rice at home" is how Rakhi puts it. This is a literal translation of a Bengali expression that refers to a sense of being cast out, of not being able to share a meal with your people anymore and so, not belonging either.

The police say she is entitled to vocational training, except that nearly three years later, when I check, she hasn't received any. She says there is one lesson she has learned since leaving. "I want to live now," she tells me. "I want to have a decent life, like you have. Before, I didn't care if I lived or died. Before, I was at war, always at war."

To me, this says much more about how little she once had to lose.

State security forces begin to chip away at the guerrillas. One by one, senior leaders are killed or imprisoned. In 2010, the Maoists' national spokesman, who goes by the name Commander Azad (Commander Freedom), is shot dead by police. In 2011, security forces kill Kishenji. His real name is Mallojula Koteshwara Rao; he is a Brahmin and a law school dropout.

By this time, the senior leaders who are still at large are believed to be staying deep inside in the Abujmarh hills, where the orphan named Manher lost his hearing. Many rank-and-file cadres are killed on the battlefield. Some surrender. Big, dramatic Maoist attacks become less and less frequent.

The Maoist message may have lost its urgency for now—or maybe forever. But something else could tap into the well of anger just as easily. More important is whether the Indian state will heed the demands of young people in the parched hamlets where the Maoists have flourished all these years. No longer is the idea of democracy just topsoil.

STRONGMAN
Aspiration Gets into Politics

There are moments that shape the political outlook of a generation, and sometimes its moral compass as well. Had my parents been Americans, theirs might have been the Montgomery bus boycott of 1955. For me, growing up in the United States, it was the struggle against apartheid in South Africa, culminating with Nelson Mandela's release from jail in 1990. For many of my contemporaries in India, it was the Ram Janmabhoomi movement, culminating in 1992 with the destruction of a sixteenth-century mosque by a group of militant Hindus. If you were my age and growing up in India, chances are the Ram Janmabhoomi movement shaped what kind of future you imagined for your country. It was your fork in the road.

At the crux of this movement was an item of faith. Since independence, a Hindu militant group that called itself the Rashtriya Swayamsevak Sangh had agitated for the right to erect a Hindu temple on the grounds of the mosque, known as the Babri Masjid, in the city of Ayodhya.[1] They believed that India's first Mughal emperor, Babur, had erected that mosque on the very site that marked the birthplace of Ram, the protagonist of the epic *Ramayana* and one of the most revered gods of the Hindu pantheon. They wished to build a temple to mark it (the name of their campaign, the Ram Janmabhoomi movement, referred literally to the birthplace of Ram). It had proved to be a potent organizing issue for the Sangh for more than half a century.

The first flashpoint in independent India came one night in 1949. Small statues, including one that represented the infant Ram, mysteriously appeared inside the Babri Masjid complex. Hindu supporters called it a miracle; Muslims were chagrined.

No wonder. It was a symbolic, emotionally charged issue for a country born out of a spasm of Hindu–Muslim violence, and it turned the Babri Masjid into something akin to the disputed Temple Mount in the old city of Jerusalem. Hindus are by far the majority faith in India, but since its birth, India had promised to be a secular nation and protect its minorities; Muslims are its largest religious minority.

The Ram temple movement reached its peak in the winter of 1992. Supporters of the Sangh marched thousands of miles, from the south to the north, chanting Ram's name. On the morning of December 6, they arrived in Ayodhya. As politicians gave fiery speeches, their foot soldiers climbed on top of the Babri Masjid domes, pounding with hammers and bare hands, until pieces of it came tumbling down.

When the news trickled out, as an Indian, either you were horrified (How could they destroy a house of worship in a country that had been founded on the principle of respect for all faiths?) or you felt your chest rise (No longer did Hindus have to make concessions to minority Muslims). After December 6, 1992, it was permissible to talk openly about a Hindu nation. A contemporary of mine, growing up in Delhi, remembered it as the first time she heard otherwise polite Hindus maligning Muslims in public conversation.

Shashi was eighteen years old then, a college student at home in Hyderabad for winter break. That day was as seminal for him as it would have been for me, had I grown up in India. Shashi and I belong to roughly the same generation; we are equally interested in the generation that follows.

Shashi's upbringing was different from mine. His father was a lifelong activist with the Rashtriya Swayamsevak Sangh. He was raised on the Sangh's convictions, which regarded Hindu civilization to have been beaten down for centuries by Islam and Christianity and, more recently, corrupted by Western modernity. The Sangh was keen to groom young Hindu men to defend it from onslaught. Shashi attended its training camps from a young age.[2]

What relief, Shashi remembers thinking when he heard that the Sangh's followers had finally begun to chip away at the Babri Masjid—but also feeling a sense of dread at the Hindu–Muslim violence that followed in cities across the land. Not least, he found himself wondering: Now what? How would the Hindu nationalists that his family championed actually build the country?

The storming of the Babri Masjid would be a watershed for the Sangh. Its political affiliate, the Bharatiya Janata Party, would use the Ram temple movement as its principal campaign issue and, with it, win state and national elections throughout the 1990s.

It would be a crucial moment too in Shashi's political coming-of-age. He would soon graduate from the IIT campus in Mumbai, get a job in India's nascent technology industry, and move to Texas like so many Indian techies. But he would not abandon the Sangh. He would return home twenty years later to advance the ambitions of a man who had helped organize that 1992 march for the Ram temple and then proceeded to ascend the ladders of the Sangh to become one of India's most successful—and certainly most polarizing—politician: Narendra Modi, or NaMo to his fans.

The value of India's youth bulge was not lost to either of them. By 2014, nearly half of the electorate was under the age of thirty-five. They had come of age in the period since the economy creaked open in the early 1990s. They were hungry and impatient.

For this generation, Modi reckoned, the temple was no more the political lodestar. Religion mattered to them, but it wasn't quite the flashpoint it had been once. This generation, Modi was convinced, wanted politicians who could deliver. They wanted jobs. They wanted prosperity.

They wanted a tough, muscular India. Shashi began to refer to them as "aspirational Indians," and he knew he was in a position to help Modi win their votes.

And so, in 2012, a full two years before the next national election, in a nondescript office above a lunch counter that served crispy, fresh-off-the-griddle *dosas* in Bangalore, Shashi and a half-dozen Modi backers launched a political start-up the likes of which had never before been tried in India. It was privately funded. It was independent of the political party to which Modi belonged. Its goal was to use the power of the Internet to make Modi the next prime minister of India—and to do so by retooling the grievances and wants of political Hinduism for an impatient, aspirational generation.

Modi turned the narrative of aspiration into the dominant political meme of the 2014 election. And it led to a historic victory. His Bharatiya Janata Party, the BJP, scooped up an absolute majority in the 543-seat lower house of parliament, which meant that for the first time in decades, one single party could form a government without having to link arms with smaller regional and caste-based political parties. Modi needed no coalition partners, which also meant that he needed to make fewer political compromises than his predecessors.

"Mind-blowing," Shashi said the morning after the election results were announced.

Shashi is not one of noonday's children, but like me, he too had been looking over his shoulder to study them and to win them over, fully aware of how important they were to lifting his candidate to power—and also, how demanding. He understood that his efforts would not be aimed at winning one election to a five-year term. He understood that he would have to be in the long game, because his man, NaMo, was determined to be in the long game—to be in charge for a decade, or more.

And yet, to turn his country's demographic shift into a meaningful political dividend, Shashi also knew he had to keep his eyes squarely on an entirely different kind of political storm—one that captured the imagination of millions of young Indians who were not so sold on Modi, who had found their own voice (mainly on the Internet), and who imagined a new politics for their country. One of those scrappy idealists was a slight, stubborn young man from Bihar named Ankit: a child of noonday. More on him soon.

On November 25, 1949, just months before the Indian constitution went into effect, Bhimrao Ambedkar, the Constitution's principal architect and a future law minister, delivered his last speech to the Constituent Assembly. The historian Ramachandra Guha says the speech contained "prophetic warnings" about what could happen to India's experiment in democracy unless radical reforms were made fast. India would face a dangerous contradiction: Its citizens would enjoy political equality—one person, one vote—even as they remained intensely unequal in everyday affairs.

"How long shall we continue to deny equality in our social and economic life?" Ambedkar asked. "If we continue to deny it for long, we will do so only by putting our political democracy in peril. We must remove this contradiction at the earliest possible moment or else those who suffer from inequality will blow up the structure of political democracy which this Assembly has so laboriously built up."[3]

Remarkably for a country so deeply unequal, the Constitution promised everyone the right to vote, regardless of caste, creed, or gender. It made it illegal to practice the custom of untouchability. To redress centuries of subjugation, it set aside government jobs for Dalits and *adivasis*—quotas that were extended later to intermediary castes officially called "backward." In other words, the promise of free India was to radically transform a poor and stratified society into one where all its citizens, regardless of their station at birth, could have a shot at improving their lot. This was to be the end of karma; no more would the deeds of your past life dictate who you could be.

For generations of India's lawmakers, the challenge has been to do this through a democratic system, which by definition resists radical transformation.

When Indira Gandhi, the daughter of Jawaharlal Nehru, took over as prime minister in 1966, she immediately recognized the political utility of social transformation. She courted the rural poor, who at the time made up the lion's share of voters. She announced ambitious land reforms, nationalized banks, and ordered financial institutions to serve in remote, underserved areas. She kneecapped the maharajahs, with a constitutional amendment that declared monarchy to be "incompatible with an egalitarian social order."[4]

Her grandson Rahul Gandhi was a baby when she won reelection in 1971 on a campaign manifesto of "*Garibi Hatao*" (Remove Poverty), along with the latest ambitious five-year plan to accelerate economic growth. Reality quickly got in the way. The rains didn't come in 1972. The drought forced India to import thirty-three thousand metric tons of food aid from the United States, after the Agency for International Development concluded that "millions of people were faced with near famine conditions."[5] The drought was all the more crippling for the humiliation it heaped on a nation that had promised its people self-reliance.

Mrs. Gandhi's troubles worsened. By 1974, inflation soared to nearly 30 percent. Cooking oil fell in short supply. The commercial capital, Bombay, erupted in industrial unrest. The middle class that my parents were a part of started to feel the pinch (this is when Baba got tired of hustling for cooking gas and Horlicks). For the first time in Calcutta, you thought twice about staying out late. You worried about street crime as well as political violence. Federal police rumbled down the streets in open-air trucks, guarding against unruly demonstrations. Reports of corruption fueled public anger. Opposition to Mrs. Gandhi's regime mounted across the country, as new political opponents from the socialist left joined her longtime right-wing rivals from the Sangh. Both sides sought to oust Congress, which had ruled India since independence, and in particular Mrs. Gandhi.[6]

At the height of the summer of 1975 came a devastating blow to her dominion. A court concluded that she had employed illegal tactics to get herself reelected in the parliamentary election—and ordered her to give up her seat. She had no intention of doing so. On June 25, 1975,

Mrs. Gandhi persuaded a pliant president, Fakhruddin Ali Ahmed, to issue a declaration of emergency, citing "internal disturbance." It was understood then—and still is—that this was Mrs. Gandhi's fiat. The president was carrying out her wishes.

That summer, my parents began to pack for our departure from Calcutta. The piano was put up for sale; a teak cabinet moved to my grandmother's house; a silver tea set locked up, as well as a set of lime-green custard bowls and stacks of cotton saris, which would serve no use in Canada. My parents, improbably it seems in hindsight, said they intended to come back.

Mrs. Gandhi claimed she had little choice but to declare emergency rule. In her view, the stability of the country was at stake. "The state of emergency was proclaimed because the threat of disruption was clear and imminent," she told the *Saturday Review* in a remarkable interview in August 1975. She called the Sangh "sinister."[7]

"I do not believe that a democratic society cannot take strong measures to deal with its foes, from within or without," she went on.

Mrs. Gandhi banned the Sangh. Shashi's father, a lifelong Sangh activist but also an employee of a state-owned company, burned Sangh literature in the boiler of their home. To have it lying around at home was to risk being arrested. At the time, Modi was a full-time organizer with the Sangh; he went underground to evade arrest. Several of Mrs. Gandhi's political rivals were picked up and detained under the Maintenance of Internal Security Act. Civil servants were told to meet sterilization targets to check what was considered a perilous population boom. Those who appreciated Mrs. Gandhi's iron hand pointed out that government workers began showing up to work on time.

My aunt in Delhi made sure to hang a black-and-white portrait of Mrs. G. in the living room. Her husband worked for the government, and the prime minister's portrait was visible from the front gate.

Censorship laws were promulgated. In defiance, some newspaper editors left blank spaces on the front pages of their publications to signal the news that had been gagged. The *Washington Post*'s resident correspondent in India was expelled.[8] The *New York Times* resident correspondent

deftly took over the lease of the *Post*'s sprawling bungalow, the same one
that I would come to occupy thirty years later.

The emergency did not serve Mrs. Gandhi well. In 1977, when she
lifted it and India held fresh elections, she and her Congress party
were crushed.

Morarji Desai—he who had boasted of urine-drinking on *60 Minutes* during my California childhood—became prime minister. In
a burst of populism, he forced Coca-Cola to pull out of India and drew
the Indian state into the soda business. The resulting Indian cola was
called Double Seven, in homage to '77, the year democracy returned.
The news came to us on a gossamer blue, thrice-folded aerogram.

The Sangh could once more print its books. It could reopen its
shakhas, and so Shashi's father made sure the boy went to those morning
camps before he was old enough to go to school. Shashi dressed in the
requisite khaki shorts and white short-sleeved, button-down shirt. He
learned to march, military style. He sang Hindu *bhajans*. He learned
about that mosque in Ayodhya, where Ram was born, and why Hindus should build a temple there. The Sangh believed in the grandeur
of Hindu civilization and that all Indians, even if they were Muslims or
Christian, were really Hindus at heart. The Sangh believed that Hindus
had not been strong enough to protect their nation. The Sangh considered their country—they preferred the Sanskrit name Bharat over
India—to extend to the countries we now know as South Asia, including India's neighbors. *"Bharat Mata ki Jai,"* they chanted. Victory to
Mother India.

There is no holy book in Hinduism, as there is in the Abrahamic
faiths. So there is no opportunity for a literal, or fundamental, reading
of a religious text, as there is among, say, Christian or Muslim funda-
mentalists. The Sangh has a distinctly political philosophy. It deploys
religion to mobilize its ranks. Among its chief convictions is the notion
that Hinduism has been under assault for centuries in part because Hindus have been too pliant—and that since independence, the Congress

party (the Sangh's political nemesis) has made too many concessions to religious minorities. If Nehru saw India as a modern republic, proud of its many cultures and beliefs, the Sangh sought to restore what it saw as an ancient Hindu nation. It sought to abolish beef eating and revise school textbooks to reflect its view of history. It made a push into the *adivasi* belt, where many people, like Mani, had embraced Christianity long ago; Sangh supporters wanted them to convert to Hinduism. There was a spate of attacks on churches.

The march for a Ram temple at the Babri Masjid site proved to be a powerful organizing tool for the Sangh, enabling its affiliated Bharatiya Janata Party to lead a coalition government for a six-year period starting in 1998.

Like others of my generation, Shashi was not shaped just by the Ram temple movement. He was also shaped by the political campaign to extend affirmative action quotas to people who were classified as "backward" (like Anupam and his family). Upper-caste Indians—Shashi was born to a Brahmin family, the highest perch on the Hindu caste ladder—were generally revolted by the idea that a greater number of seats would be set aside on the basis of caste. It meant a shrinking share of spots for "forward" caste students in government universities and jobs. Shashi threw himself into those protests. He and his college friends once hijacked a truck in Mumbai and went around the city shutting down campuses. "We were crazy" is how he recalled it many years later.

In college, he says, he recognized how hard some of the "quota" students had worked to get to where they were. He became friends with some of them. Eventually, he dropped his identifiably Brahmin surname, at least when it came to his political activities. There, it didn't help to flaunt Brahmin credentials. In politics, the upper castes no longer ruled.

Modi was among midnight's later children, born in 1950, shortly after my own parents and just three years after independence, to a small-town Gujarati family of modest means, on the lower rungs of the caste ladder, one of hundreds of communities categorized as "backward." His father ran a tea stall.

Modi went to government schools, but his real education came from the camps run by the Sangh. He became one of its full-time organizers before going on to become a BJP politician.

The world learned his name just months after he was elected chief minister of his native state, when early one morning in February 2002, the smell of burning flesh came from a train station in a small Gujarat town, called Godhra.

A train carrying members of the Sangh was engulfed in flames when it stopped at Godhra. Inside, fifty people were burned alive. The next day, their charred corpses were displayed in public. It enraged Hindus across the state.

Over the next few days, an estimated one thousand people were killed in retaliation, most of them Muslims. A Muslim-occupied apartment complex in the middle of a Hindu enclave was set on fire, incinerating those inside. Muslim-owned businesses, including vegetarian restaurants that catered to Hindus, were destroyed. Women were raped in daylight. Not a single person was arrested from among the thousands who rampaged through Muslim neighborhoods on the first day after the train fire. A Gujarati police official told my colleagues with *The New York Times* that Chief Minister Modi had directed law enforcement to go easy on Hindu protesters rampaging through the streets. One police officer called it "a state-sponsored pogrom."[9]

Human Rights Watch concluded that the Modi administration had not only failed to conduct serious investigations but also intimidated activists seeking accountability and protected perpetrators of the violence.[10]

Over the next decade, after painstaking probes by special investigators appointed by India's Supreme Court, several dozen people were convicted for the massacre of Muslims. One of Modi's top lieutenants, Maya Kodnani, was convicted of murder, arson, and conspiracy and sentenced to twenty-eight years in prison.[11]

When the violence broke out, Shashi was living in Dallas, on assignment for an Indian company hired to solve the IT problems of American firms. That was his day job. In the evenings, he had another mission. He was a blogger by the name of "Offstumped," a cricket term, and the Gujarat violence and its aftermath offered him plenty of material. Shashi was infuriated by what he saw as the liberal media's biased coverage of the unrest, and especially of Modi's role. "The media was making it look like something really bad had happened," he said.

In fact, he said, what happened in Gujarat in 2002 was not uncommon. India was prone to violent eruptions, he said. He gave the example of incidents during his childhood in Hyderabad. When there was political trouble, his math teacher, who was a Muslim man, did not leave his Muslim neighborhood in the old walled city. Math class was canceled. When the troubles died down, the teacher returned. Math class resumed.

"Political violence is something we grew up with," Shashi told me.

It was one of the few times I felt truly like a foreigner in India. Here was a man of my generation, smart and worldly. The way he explained his country rattled me. Murderous rage was described as normal, something to grow up with.

Over the years, India has allowed chauvinists of all stripes to carry on with impunity. Even the Hindu–Muslim violence that marked India's birth, at midnight, on August 15, 1947, has never been accounted for.

Likewise, in 1984, after Indira Gandhi was assassinated by her two Sikh bodyguards, many of her supporters went on a killing spree against minority Sikhs, notably in Delhi, the nation's capital. The anti-Sikh pogrom left an official death toll of three thousand. Repeated government commissions were appointed to investigate. Some of them pointed to the likely involvement of Congress party leaders. None were convicted, and many rose politically for the next twenty years.[12]

Then came the carnage of Gujarat.

In 2005, the government of the United States, in a most unusual step, barred Modi from visiting the United States in connection to his role in the Gujarat violence.[13]

The visa ban had no impact on Modi's political fate. He was easily reelected as Gujarat's chief minister. As I wrote in the *Times* in 2007, it seemed as though his "charismatic, often pugnacious," style of politicking would be "a force to be reckoned with in the future."[14]

I trailed him again eighteen months later, when he was campaigning for his party in the 2009 national parliamentary elections. His supporters had gathered on a sports field, and hundreds of them had covered their faces in Modi masks. It was as though Modi were every man, everywhere.

Modi electrified audiences. He spoke without notes. He was brash and confident. His jokes could be snide. At one rally, he compared the ruling Congress party, the nation's oldest political group, to an aging woman. At another, he mocked Manmohan Singh, the incumbent prime minister, for reaching out to the American president for help in staunching terrorist networks that operated in next-door Pakistan.

"O-baaaa-maaa," Modi shouted, in a whining child's voice. "O-baaa-maaa. Our neighbor has come and attacked us. Do something!"

The crowd laughed and hollered. Soon, the entire field of supporters was crying, "O-baaa-maa." All bearing Modi's face over their own.[15]

Shashi is of medium build and medium height. He wears stern black-rimmed glasses. Where Modi is a powerful orator who speaks with arms outstretched, Shashi talks so sparingly one gets the impression that he doesn't much like to talk.

Shashi found his voice not on the campaign stump but on the Internet, as Offstumped became well-known among Sangh followers in the Indian diaspora and, soon, among BJP politicians. He railed against the Congress party and its leader, Indira Gandhi's Italian-born daughter-in-law, Sonia. He was aghast when Congress defeated the BJP in 2004—and again in 2009.

By 2011, he became part of a small, obscure group of Modi backers that quietly explored the prospects of a NaMo prime ministerial bid in 2014.

If Modi had the instinct for politics, Shashi, a quarter century his junior, had the skills to leverage him to a big, young audience. Shashi was steeped in the language of twenty-first-century American-style elections. He had the technology chops to put the latest data-mining tools to work. He also understood how to link Modi's political fortunes to young Indians' hope for their own fortunes—all by bypassing the journalists and intellectuals who had dominated Delhi's political circles for years. Shashi referred to the views of Modi's liberal critics as "elitist secular extremism."[16]

In October 2011, Shashi was coming home for a family wedding in Hyderabad when an invitation came from the Gujarat chief minister's office: Would he like to come meet Modi?

Shashi brought a gift to that first meeting: news clippings that he had collected from the 1893 visit of Swami Vivekananda to the United States. Vivekananda was a Hindu monk who had charmed America with his tall orange turbans and his lectures on ancient Hindu philosophy. He was the first modern Hindu evangelist—and one of Modi's heroes.

Shashi recognized a fellow introvert in Modi. They sat facing each other for several minutes in awkward silence—the controversial chief minister and his digital defender from Texas. Two generations of Sangh loyalists.

The Vivekananda clippings helped break the ice. Slowly, Modi began to open up, offering Shashi an early glimpse into his ambitions. By then, the BJP had lost two consecutive parliamentary elections. If it was to have a chance in the next one, Modi said, it would need a national leader, someone who could rouse a mass audience. It would also need to find an issue beyond identity politics, Modi averred; the party could no longer rely on the Ram temple movement to rally the electorate, certainly not the youth.

The meeting lasted thirty minutes, Shashi recalled. He left Modi's office energized. "It was clear there was something going on in his mind," Shashi said. He was thinking big. He had national ambitions.

This was a critical time in Indian politics. By late 2011, India was beginning to feel the effects of the global financial crisis. The booming optimism of just a few years ago plummeted. The Congress-led coalition government was flailing. It had not pushed through the economic reforms that foreign investors sought. Its leaders were blasted by one corruption scandal after another. Tens of thousands of people were demonstrating in the streets.

Modi's star was rising. At the end of 2012, he won his third consecutive term as chief minister of Gujarat.

This is when Shashi made the leap. He had recently moved back to Bangalore with his wife and their two children. He now quit his day job. He threw himself into launching the political start-up, dedicated to advancing Modi's national bid. It was bankrolled by a Modi supporter. It was independent of the party machine. That way, Shashi said, it could be more agile. He once described the model as something between an American Super PAC and an Al Qaeda cell.[17]

Early on, Modi told Shashi that it was imperative to laser-focus their efforts on young voters, including those who would otherwise have no interest in the party, or even in politics. "His whole thought process was 'We need to have a direct connect with the young generation,'" Shashi said.

In the past, age had been a relatively unimportant factor in shaping how Indians voted; it mattered much less than, say, what caste they belonged to, or whether they lived in city or country. In the 2014 race, the demands of young voters began to shape the political agenda—and the medium through which politicians sought to reach them.

The narrative of aspiration would be at the heart of the 2014 election. For the first time, candidates would vie to be seen as ordinary.

This would doom Rahul Gandhi, the great-grandson of India's founding prime minister, Nehru; the grandson of Indira Gandhi; and the son of her son and successor, Rajiv Gandhi and his widow, Sonia, who led the party. By 2014, it was a burning hot liability to be seen as having been born to lead. It didn't help that Rahul, Congress's presumed prime ministerial candidate, displayed little acumen for politics. And even though he was forty-three years old at the time of the election, he did little to address the ambitions of the young. His party had presided over nearly ten years of galloping economic growth but could not boast of having created the jobs that India's young electorate clamored for; graft was endemic in the Congress-led coalition government; and when young people took to the streets to protest a ruthless gang-rape in Delhi, in the winter of 2012, Rahul did not seize on it to express solidarity with his country's young. Critics said he was politically tone-deaf. Modi referred to Rahul as *shehzada*—prince. It dripped with deprecation.

Meanwhile, NaMo cast himself as the very avatar of aspiration, a mirror to the aspirations of Indian youth. He branded himself as an ordinary man, a *chai-wallah* seeking to vanquish the Nehru–Gandhi dynasty. His campaign made it known that he was a friend to business and strict with bureaucrats, and that he had a wide chest (fifty-six inches). He promised a muscular India: safe, strong, and prosperous. "Good days are ahead" was his slogan.

His campaign deftly turned the election from what it actually was—a race to fill 543 seats in the lower house of parliament—to a referendum to elect NaMo. Never mind that many in his coterie, including those who were elected to parliament, were old BJP hands, many of them with criminal records or linked to graft. (At one point, Modi let it slip that God had chosen him to do God's work.)

Modi repeatedly reminded voters that he was self-made, unlike Rahul Gandhi. He eschewed the Indian politician's standard white *kurta* and pajamas, choosing instead to campaign in stylishly long *kurtas* of many colors and show off his Movado watch. The message was clear: You too can rise. You too can have this. He projected himself as a pro business leader who alone could usher in double-digit economic growth and put Indians to work. His record in Gujarat sent a message that he would guard the interests of the Hindu majority.

The Congress symbol is the upheld palm of a hand. You could see it as a hand that gives blessing or a hand that says, "Stop." The BJP symbol is an open-petaled lotus, on which Lakshmi, the Hindu goddess of wealth, traditionally appears.

Lifting a page from the Obama playbook, Modi used social media to target those who had not been traditionally engaged in politics—young, urban people. Shashi helped Modi crowd-source ideas for his first big speeches, enabling him to tell his supporters what they wanted to hear. Throughout the campaign, Modi spoke repeatedly about issues that would resonate with the young: job skills, jobs, prosperity.

Ankit was precisely the sort of voter whom Shashi was trying to win over. Young. Hindu. Upper caste. His parents had long backed the Bharatiya Janata Party. His brother loved NaMo. Ankit himself distrusted politicians. He had never voted before the 2014 election. He didn't see the point.

Ankit grew up in Patna, just like Anupam, the math prodigy who made it to the IIT, though Anupam's gritty working-class *mohalla* was not the sort of place Ankit would dare venture into after dark. Ankit grew up comfortable, went to private schools, moved to Delhi, and became a software programmer. He planned to go to America for graduate school, and then return home to take care of his parents. His path was conventional, much like Shashi's had been.

Until a strong wind came and blew those plans away.

It was called the Aam Aadmi Party, a rambunctious new force that sprang from the zeitgeist of Ankit's impatient generation and upset the political narrative of his age—at least for a moment. The Aam Aadmi movement sought to speak to those who had become revolted by the established order—most of all, by corruption. Politicians were thieves, went the Aam Aadmi mantra. They kept none of their hifalutin promises; they fattened their pockets; they needed to be booted out.

Aam Aadmi branded itself as an alternative to the two dominant poles of Indian politics: a left-leaning Congress tied to the Nehru–Gandhi dynasty and a conservative Hindu nationalist BJP. It was an upstart. Still, Shashi knew he had to keep an eye on Aam Aadmi. It instinctively knew how to appeal to young, urban voters.

The party had no deep-pocketed backers. It had no established political organization. It had no track record. Its rallying cry was to rid the body politic of corruption.

Its logo embodied exasperation with the political order, which also happened to be the starkest caste mark of all: the sweeper's broom.

All this was central to both its rise and fall.

Ankit was twenty-seven years old when this movement swept him up. It forced him to look at his own destiny and the destiny of his country with new eyes. It led him to squander his career plans—and eventually, his parents' blessings. Ankit dropped everything to direct the Aam Aadmi's social media push, which for a brand-new organization with no money and no organization was hugely important.

Before this, Ankit hadn't been just uninterested in politics. He had been revolted by it. And this stemmed from the stories he had heard since childhood. Ankit's father, Atul, had been an activist when he was a young man. He had joined the anti–Indira Gandhi agitation of the 1970s, when public anger escalated over unemployment, rising prices, and graft. "Total revolution," that agitation had promised, only to be met with Mrs. Gandhi's emergency rule.

His father's political activism turned out to be useful. He founded a company that supplied security guards to a variety of organizations in Bihar and its neighboring state of Uttar Pradesh, including to government offices. His business partner was a BJP legislator in the Bihar state assembly. He also became something of a consigliere to local politicians, which meant that Ankit had a crucial backstage view of political deal making.

Over the years, in the family drawing room, Dad and his friends conferred over who should be fielded for which seat, which caste constituencies could be lured with whom, which rivals could be defeated. There, Ankit heard about who stole ballot boxes and how dummy candidates could be used. He had a pretty good idea of how much cash and liquor was disbursed before election day. In Bihar, as elsewhere in India, accused and convicted criminals were sometimes elected to office. Some wielded power from jail.

Politics was a part of the morality tale of Ankit's childhood. His father had been steeped in it. And he wanted his son to have no part in it, which was fine by Ankit. He thought of politics as foul. "It was one of those things I hated," Ankit said.

Then, in the summer of 2011, as he was studying for the GREs, Ankit heard about thousands of people gathering day after day at Jantar Mantar, Delhi's protest mecca. Ankit was not much of a protest goer. But these protests hit home. They were about the one thing that affected the life of every Indian: corruption. Every day in the papers, Ankit was reading about spectacular cases. One politician was accused of pocketing huge sums of money from building contracts during the preparations for the 2010 Commonwealth Games. Another was accused of selling mobile-phone-spectrum licenses at low prices in exchange for kickbacks. Few political parties seemed immune to graft. In the southern state of Karnataka, an anticorruption board concluded that the chief minister, a BJP man, had granted illegal iron-ore-mining contracts.

All of these scandals magnified the corruption that ordinary citizens faced all the time. Once, when Ankit went to file a police report for a stolen phone, the only way to avoid a bribe was to name-drop a politician friend of his father. Even the destitute people of Jharkhand, where there was nothing to eat if the rains were late, were not immune. Mani came home from her maid's job in Gurgaon one summer to learn that her mother had to share a portion of her widow's pension with a local bank official. In Gurgaon, a traffic cop once suggested to Mani's boss, Supriya, that she could give him a bit of cash instead of paying a costlier speeding ticket. Corruption had so seeped into the marrow of public life that it led a group of disgruntled citizens to create a website—called, simply, www.ipaidabribe.com—to document their encounters with crooked civil servants.[18]

Ankit was captivated by the anticorruption protests at Jantar Mantar. Dad warned him. Sure, go for a few days, he told Ankit, but don't let yourself be pulled in. Don't let politics ruin your plans.

But Ankit kept going back for more. Day after day. He started volunteering full-time. And when an acceptance letter came from the New Jersey Institute of Technology, he didn't turn to his father for advice.

He didn't even tell his parents. He went to the protest leader whom he had come to idolize: a skinny, bottlebrush-mustachioed activist named Arvind Kejriwal.

"What do you want to go to America for—to make money?" Kejriwal asked.

"No. Not the money really. The experience," Ankit replied.

"Experience you want? Then stay with me," he recalled Kejriwal telling him. "You'll get the experience of a lifetime."

Ankit was already smitten. "He was very sharp, very to the point. He talked data. He talked evidence," Ankit said.

Kejriwal's invitation was all Ankit needed to chuck his grad school plans. This would not be his karma. He would not follow the path his parents had in mind. He would make his own.

Anyway, the political activists of Dad's generation had left so much unfinished business. Money had come to rule politics. "Had the issue of corruption been solved by my father's generation we wouldn't be fighting today," Ankit said.

The protests at Jantar Mantar turned Ankit's life around in other ways too. It was there that he met Prerna, a journalist with a passion for politics, who was four years younger than he, just as impetuous, big-mouthed, and stubborn. They could talk for hours about politics, about what the country needed, about whether their anticorruption movement was truly democratic or not.

There was one gulf between them. She belonged to a "backward" caste, he to a "forward" caste. And while their families didn't forbid them from marrying, there was clearly some unease. Both sides advised them to wait. What's the rush, they asked. Give it some time.

Neither Ankit nor Prerna had time for such counsel. Avatars of the new, they were defiant. They decided on a Friday they would get married that Sunday. They cobbled together what little money they had. They bought new clothes worthy of going to temple in. They put down the first and last month's rent on a tiny, decrepit apartment.

They were in love. They were young. They were also a bit afraid.

Prerna said: "We wanted to live with each other."

Ankit said: "I had a fear maybe they would brainwash her, convince her you'll find a better guy."

The wedding took place where most cross-caste weddings take place: at a Hindu temple of the reformist Arya Samaj sect not far from Jantar Mantar. In her father's place, Kejriwal gave away the bride.

The anticorruption protests spawned the political party that came to be known as the Aam Aadmi Party—literally the commoners' party. And Ankit, as its social media chief, forced Shashi to pay attention.

B y the time he was campaigning for the prime minister's job, Modi had spent more than a decade flatly refusing to discuss what happened in his state in 2002. Once he even walked out of a television interview when the host asked him about it.

He broke his silence in 2013. When journalists from Reuters asked whether he felt regret, he compared himself to a passenger in a car that has accidentally run over a dog. He said that if "someone else is driving a car and we're sitting behind, even then if a puppy comes under the wheel, will it be painful or not? Of course it is. If I'm a chief minister or not, I'm a human being. If something bad happens anywhere, it is natural to be sad."[19]

By that time, a court had cleared him of wrongdoing. He said after the verdict that the entire episode had caused him "pain."

It helped his cause when his political opponents mocked his lack of pedigree: What could a tea seller's son possibly know about running a country, some of them chided. Modi instantly turned that to his favor. He proposed public meetings at one thousand tea stalls around the country.

Modi's digital strategist in Bangalore, Shashi, played to the frustrations of India's young. In a dig at Aam Aadmi, he tweeted: "'the broom' at best is about basic hygiene, 'chaai' on the other hand is inspirational and aspirational."

Even if Modi avoided references to 2002, it stuck to him—and often in his favor. One young party strategist told me that the episode had forever sealed Modi's image as a protector of Hindus. As chief minister of Gujarat, Modi had let Hindus avenge the killings of Hindus on the train at Godhra—and for that, this young man believed, Hindus would be grateful. For Modi, that was "an asset, not a liability," he said. "He taught the Muslims a lesson."

Elections are often about reinvention. In 2014, the parliamentary election in the world's most populous democracy was in no small part about how the state enabled its people to reinvent themselves—to break free of the past. By now, democracy was no more just top dressing on Indian soil.

Shashi knew that, unlike the Sangh enthusiasts of his father's era, their children and grandchildren did not have either the time or patience to go door-to-door rallying voters. They would not waste hours waiting to hear Modi speak at a campaign rally. They would not bother to go to mass meetings. The Internet was how they would join politics.

On Shashi's flagship website, www.india272.com, young Sangh sympathizers were invited to share information on who they were, where they lived, how they could help. Their Facebook "likes" and retweets told Shashi's team exactly which slogans and which speeches worked. Shashi's team could collect email addresses, Facebook user names, mobile phone numbers: all incredibly rich pieces of data that could be used to reach voters on election day—this year and in years to come.[20]

Shashi wanted to build what he called NaMo's "youth army." They would be the "firewall," as he called them, against Modi's opponents in the public conversation online. Indeed, they pounced on journalists, bloggers, and anyone else who dared criticize him. "Internet Hindus" is what his opponents called them.[21]

Shashi's most ambitious venture was to digitize India's mammoth voter roll—all 800 million names. He collected information on every voting booth; there are about one thousand voters per booth. He tracked how each booth, the smallest unit of the electorate, had voted in the last election. This gave him a reasonable approximation of its political leanings.

He digitized whatever nuggets of information he could find on every voter in every state: names, ages, voter identification numbers, whether they lived in a Muslim enclave or a gated community dominated by Brahmin surnames. It took a year to gather it into a database that could then be automatically analyzed. The website drew even more information from potential Modi supporters, including their Facebook friends and their mobile phone numbers.

No doubt, it was the biggest exercise in political data mining in the world. The effort allowed party workers to zero in on the tiniest voting blocs, getting a handle on exactly where party workers should focus their efforts. This deep vat of data was aimed at the future. It would help to mobilize voters in polls to come. "We'll know people better. We can target them better," Shashi said. He declined to give details on how much all this cost.

Shashi was looking over his shoulder the whole time—and looking at what the kids over at Aam Aadmi were up to.

They had zeroed in on the rage of an important constituency: young, urban Indians, many of them, like Ankit, angry and impatient with the political class. Their volunteers had grown up with social media. Many had never before bothered to vote.

I met Ankit in April 2014, in Varanasi, a city in Uttar Pradesh, India's most populous state, in the weeks just before the last round of voting, when his team was scrambling to collect the names and phone numbers of voters in the city's sixteen hundred polling booths.

While Shashi's voter database—covering the entire country—was ready months in advance, Ankit was starting from scratch, for Varanasi alone. The party's campaign office had been hastily set up in a former rooming house for college students. Chemistry homework was still taped to the walls. Ankit was sitting on the floor, battling a virus on his laptop. There were no tables or chairs in the social media team office yet. (They came only later that day.) Nor had anyone yet found a broom to sweep the floor. None of this seemed to bother Ankit. He juggled a pair of mobile phones. He goaded his greenhorn volunteers to post videos faster on Facebook. He pushed out hashtags on Twitter. He checked for trolls; one of his main convictions was that Aam Aadmi volunteers not be abusive to their critics online.

His social media team was made up entirely of digital natives like him, mostly men in their twenties, most of whom had never before even registered to vote. Everything was DIY: campaign videos, Facebook posts. One of their most eye-popping innovations was to blast a fund-raising appeal on Twitter, and then post on their website exactly who gave how much. This was unheard of in India: politicians never declare where they get their money from.

Ankit looked like he was subsisting on air. He was so small and slight I suspected one of Varanasi's notorious monkeys could knock him out. He wore a red-and-white peasant's *gamcha* around his neck, like his hero Kejriwal

Ankit was working around the clock. And he was tilting at windmills. Varanasi is Hinduism's holiest city. It had been a BJP stronghold for fifteen years.

Aam Aadmi sought to cast itself as something of a postideological party—and in some ways, this reminded me of Obama's early efforts to blur the traditional left-right divide. It was never really clear what Aam Aadmi would do if it were elected, other than denounce corruption.

One evening, at the tail end of the campaign season, Ankit and his teammates decided to take a break from their computer screens and head down to the banks of the holy Ganga. They put on their heads the Aam Aadmi's signature boat-shaped Gandhi *topis* and wandered down to the *ghats*. This enraged the BJP workers who had already decamped there. An argument erupted. It got out of hand. Men got in one another's faces. It was the peak of the hot season. The sun burned their heads. Someone threatened Ankit, to which he remembers asking incredulously. "What, you're really going to beat us up?"

Sure enough, a BJP campaigner slapped Ankit on the ear. His head spun. He had to be rushed to the emergency room.

From this encounter, Ankit drew two important lessons. First, that getting beat up was probably not the best way to make political change. Second, that his fellow Indians could be brutally intolerant. "We need to be more receptive to what others want to say," he rued. "We are not willing to listen."

On election day, noonday's children weren't very receptive to Aam Aadmi either. The party won only 4 out of 543 seats. Once mighty Congress won 44. Modi's BJP won a solid majority.

Modi had a measurable edge among voters under the age of thirty-five, according to exit polls by the Center for the Study of Developing Societies. Separately, an analysis by the news website IndiaSpend suggested that the BJP did especially well in the five states with the largest share of young, first-time voters.[22]

Modi declared on Twitter: "Conquest of India. Good days are ahead." It was retweeted more than seventy thousand times, making it one of the most widely amplified posts by any world leader, a global survey found.[23]

His brand campaign had worked. Those surveyed by the Center for the Study of Developing Societies said they wouldn't have voted for the BJP had it not been for the promise of Modi as prime minister.

Young though the electorate was, the parliament they elected was not. Nearly half of them were over the age of fifty-five.[24] The share of lawmakers under age forty, which had fallen since independence, reached a record low of 13 percent.

For all his heat on the Nehru–Gandhi dynasty, Modi's party was also stuffed with dynasty. Several BJP parliamentarians were sons and daughters of BJP politicians.

Anupam sent me an email from Mumbai the day after election results were announced. Anupam was sorry not to have been able to vote; he hadn't lived in Mumbai long enough to register on the rolls. He was relieved that Modi had won, because Modi alone seemed capable of reviving the economy and creating jobs. Still, he felt a twinge of regret. He hadn't completely bought the Modi rhetoric.

"These elections are also a bit disappointing as it has moved AAP to the backfoot," he wrote, referring to the Aam Aadmi Party. "AAP could have been in a better position in fighting against corruption if it had a handful of MPs elected. I hope the AAP movement would not fade in the midst of Modi Wave and would sustain the long journey of its fight for an Aam Aadmi (common man)."

Modi immediately let it be known who was in charge of the government. He kept a tight leash on bureaucrats, on one occasion letting one of them know when he was inappropriately dressed—and then letting that story spread through the political chatterati in Delhi. He made it clear that he distrusted journalists, whom he saw as part of the Delhi establishment (many of them had been on his back over the violence in Gujarat in 2002). He appointed his loyalists to key posts, including compatriots from the Sangh. His government aggressively went after Greenpeace, which had tirelessly campaigned against the environmental degradation brought on by several big industrial projects. It went as far as stopping Priya Pillai, a Greenpeace advocate and Indian citizen, from leaving the country to speak to British parliamentarians in January 2015; later in the year the government revoked the group's ability to receive donations from abroad, saying it had "prejudicially affected the economic interest of the state." Several other nongovernmental organizations came under government scrutiny, including the Ford Foundation, which had backed several scrappy civil society groups and which the government accused of working against "national interest and security," among other things.

Noonday's children had chosen a strongman. Not since Indira Gandhi had Indians elected such an iron-fisted leader.

Ankit was crestfallen by the election results. "Our overall messaging wasn't clear," he said.

The campaign had been a time of profound personal discovery for him. He had tossed his plans to go to graduate school in America. He did not think he would be happy ever again in a conventional office job. His wife remained sympathetic to the party but returned to a day job. They needed to pay the bills. Ankit could not turn to his parents for help. He had defied their wishes and chosen a life in politics.

One of his uncles scolded him. "He was like, 'Man you've just screwed it up,'" Ankit recalled.

Ankit shot right back. It upset him that Indians did not appreciate a sense of civic duty, without which, he was convinced, democracy could not prosper.

"I said, 'No, the path I've chosen is what I wanted to do. If someone was doing the same thing in America, they would be revered. Why not in India?'"

Modi stormed America in the fall of 2014. The U.S. visa ban melted away. There was no way the United States could—or wanted to—keep out the democratically elected leader of the world's most populous democracy. The White House took pains to say it wanted improved relations with India. The United States was keen to drum up American investment in India and to increase strategic cooperation with this young, ambitious nation next to China.

Modi curated the trip with an eye to every detail: where he went, whom he was seen with, what he wore. He wore starched white cotton—white is the Hindu color of mourning—for his visit to the 9/11 Memorial in New York City, signaling that he could be an ally in the U.S.-led war against terrorism. He invoked ancient Hindu traditions in an address to the United Nations, going as far as to suggest that a yogic lifestyle was an antidote to climate change.

He made sure to be photographed scattering flower petals at a statue of Mohandas Gandhi in Washington; it was left unsaid that Gandhi was no icon for the Sangh.

He met not only with President Obama. He made sure to get face time with some of the 2016 presidential hopefuls too, along with some two dozen members of the U.S. Congress and the chief executives of some of the biggest American companies, ranging from Boeing to Google.

And he famously appeared before thousands of his Indian-American fans at an event in New York's Madison Square Garden, not least to show American lawmakers that he had the support of an increasingly influential political constituency. This was also a vital constituency for Modi. His N.R.I fans could drum up investments for India. They could lobby members of the U.S. Congress. To this audience, Modi spoke of India's "ancient heritage." He wore a saffron yellow *kurta* and matching orange vest. He spoke with arms in the air, telling jokes, rousing the crowd.

Modi played the N.R.I.s like a fiddle. Many of them were from his native Gujarat. Many belonged to Hindu nationalist groups in the United States. He said they had "glorified the honor of India."

Throughout his trip, there was one key message: he was selling a young India. By 2020, the world will be old, Modi observed, but India will be young. He said: "We will be the world's workforce."

He did not specify how he would prepare young Indians for that role. He did not mention that most kids came out of school unable to read or do basic arithmetic. Or how he would create 10 million jobs a year.

Shortly after his return home to Delhi, his Bharatiya Janata Party came in for a bit of rude awakening. In the Delhi state elections in early 2015, the BJP was routed by the Aam Aadmi Party.

Modi had stoked aspiration, which made his challenge as India's leader all the more urgent. His Movado watch seemed to scream it. You too deserve this, even if you are a tea seller's son. You too can have it.

In his first few months in office, Modi made it clear he was keenly aware of the demands of a young electorate. He goaded businesses to start manufacturing in the country. He created a new ministry with a mandate to provide job training to young Indians. He seized, rhetorically at least, on the issue of women's safety that had so energized young Indians, scolding parents for keeping a tight leash on girls and not on their wayward boys. (His government announced a new initiative to prevent female feticide, but it was unclear whether it could do any better than the many well-meaning programs that had come before—and achieved little.)

He promised to improve the country's dreadful sanitation system, which researchers increasingly said was a big factor behind childhood disease and malnutrition. But it wasn't clear how his initiative to construct toilets would persuade Indians to actually use toilets, rather than relieve themselves in an open field.[25]

He pledged to increase childhood immunization rates to 90 percent by 2020; however, in his first national budget, he did not allocate more money toward either health or education, which are central to young people realizing their ambitions.

He got a thumbs-up from the business community for getting rid of expensive subsidies for diesel; raising limits on foreign investment in key sectors, such as defense; and announcing ambitious targets, like the construction of thirty kilometers of roads every day through 2017. But even his supporters said they were disappointed that he didn't do more to push through unpopular reforms—for instance, to make it easier to acquire land, which is extremely contentious because it can step on the toes of politically powerful farmers.[26]

Modi's first year in office also brought rewards for the Hindu right. He gave Sangh loyalists important posts in his administration and in his party. His education minister said at one point that schools should remain open on Christmas day. His home minister proposed to ban the eating of beef, and the state government in Maharashtra, controlled by Modi's party, made the trading and even possession of beef punishable by law, which, as critics pointed out, left many unemployed. The government-appointed head of the Indian Council of Historical Research said he regarded the *Ramayana* as a historical account—not mythology.[27]

Meanwhile, the Rashtriya Swayamsevak Sangh mounted a campaign to convert Christians and Buddhists. The head of the Sangh, Mohan Bhagwat, railed against the late Mother Teresa.[28]

Prime Minister Modi's backers argued that he could not possibly maintain law and order in every corner of the country, which is the responsibility of state authorities anyway. Still, while Modi occasionally spoke out for religious harmony, he did not act to rein in the excesses of his hard-right supporters, including when they turned to violence.

It not only sent chills through the country's religious minority communities; it prompted warnings from unlikely quarters, including in late 2015 the governor of the Central Bank, Raghuram Rajan, who warned of the economic consequences of intolerance. "India's tradition of debate and an open spirit of inquiry is critical for its economic progress," he said in a widely covered speech in late October at the Indian Institute of Technology. He went on to say that it was important for India to protect "the right to behave differently so long as it does not hurt others seriously."[29]

By this time, three Indians had been murdered on suspicion of having eaten beef or having slaughtered or stolen cows; a fourth would be killed shortly thereafter.

For Modi, the political costs began to pile up. By November 2015, his party had lost a crucial assembly election in the big, bellwether state of Bihar. The BJP had branded the opposition as being pro-Muslim and of insulting cows. This backfired badly. The party won fewer than half the seats of a new political coalition made up of Lalu Prasad Yadav—who ruled Bihar during Anupam's childhood—and his former rival Nitish Kumar—who had tossed Yadav from power in 2005.

The surprise machine of Indian politics had revived Yadav's career once more, and in a coalition with the man who had accused him of running the state into the ground! In an email just days after the election news, Anupam called the victory "unprecedented." But he worried that the "whims and fancies of Lalu Yadav," whom he disliked, would prevail, and that this would prevent the new coalition from keeping its promises—roads, electricity, vocational training for youth.

Modi's biggest challenge confronted Shashi every morning as he left home to go to work. He lived in a gated community on the edge of Bangalore very much like the one that Surpriya called her "bubble" in Gurgaon. Shashi once described his complex as "America inside—India outside." Every day, as he drove out of its gates, he saw the long line of young men, a generation younger than him, queuing up at the hiring line of a Coca-Cola bottling plant nearby. (Coca-Cola had returned to India in 1993, after the economy opened up.)

They would be there all day, those young men who hoped to get a factory job. They were so close to the good life that they could almost lick it. And so very far away.

Some nights, when he came home, Shashi heard of drivers being robbed just near his gates. Crime was not yet a potent political issue, but it could become one, he sensed. Anger would have to be dammed. It was not lost on him that one million Indians would turn eighteen every month from now until 2030. They could be turned into Modi's army at election time, sure, but Shashi knew they could also pose the greatest challenge to his government.

His own generation, he said, was different: They were willing to wait for democracy to deliver. "This generation wants it right now."

As Modi completed a year in power, Shashi counseled patience. He said Modi was focused on trying to create jobs. He rued that Indians were living in "an era of instant gratification." He said social media was partly to blame.

"Public Memory is woefully short these days with the News and Social Media outrage cycles shifting by the hour," he wrote on the Niti Central website. Once devoted to the election campaign, it was now devoted to promoting pro-Modi messages.[30]

FACEBOOK GIRLS
Speaking Up,
Testing Democracy's Conscience

O n the third Sunday of November 2012, a dead man in sunglasses brings hustling, bustling, no-elbow-room Mumbai to a standstill. More than a million people line the streets for the funeral cavalcade of the city's most influential and most controversial politician, a right-wing party boss by the name of Bal Thackeray, who even en route to cremation wears his trademark black shades.

His supporters weep, chant, and wave party flags, which are orange and bear the image of a roaring lion. Most everyone else stays indoors.

About two hours up the coast, in Palghar, one of Mumbai's far-flung commuter towns, a twenty-year-old college student named Rinu stays indoors too. That evening, while her parents go to temple, Rinu goes on the Internet. On her laptop, she bounces between three open tabs. On one, she chats with a friend in the United States; on another, she fiddles with a music-recording program; on the third, she scrolls through her Facebook page, clicking "like" as indiscriminately as only a twenty-year-old can.

She has heard about Thackeray's demise. Who hasn't? At eighty-six, Thackeray was among the most feared political bosses in contemporary

India—a chauvinist, according to his critics, who over the years encouraged his followers to beat up migrants from other parts of India, then Communists, then Muslims, as well as to destroy gift shops that carried Valentine cards, because he considered Valentine's Day to be a corrupting Western export. The writer Suketu Mehta once described Thackeray as "the one man most directly responsible for ruining the city I grew up in."[1]

Rinu has zero interest in politics, and therefore spends next to no time pondering Thackeray's death. Her passion is music—specifically, pop songs, and not those arduous Hindustani classical scales her mother forces her to learn. Rinu is into Bruno Mars at the moment. She listens to his hits again and again. She plays his videos on YouTube repeatedly too, until she gets the words, the feel, the drawl exactly right. She records herself singing his songs—his "It Will Rain" is one of the songs she is presently working on—and if she is pleased with her own rendition, she posts it on Facebook. She posts a lot of stuff on Facebook, including pictures of her gorgeous curls, pictures of dogs, and a whole lot of minutiae about her daily life:

"Made capcicum bhaji. Delicious!"

"6 billion people and I'm still single."

"Off to sleep! *Feels like a ninja!* :D."

That Sunday night, Rinu thrusts herself into something bigger and scarier than she could ever have imagined. With a couple of off-the-cuff clicks and comments, she finds herself inside a police station and charged with a crime—for the first time in her life. Without meaning to, she also prompts a high-stakes national debate over the right to free expression for Indians in the networked age.

Rinu is arrested that evening under one section of a federal law, the Information Technology Act of 2008, designed to prevent posts online from sparking lawlessness offline. Her college friend, Shaheen, is arrested too, making them among the first to be charged under the provisions of the new measure—and certainly the most famous. News of their ordeal spreads instantly on social media, incenses their peers, and unleashes so much public outrage that within days, government officials promise to review the rules restricting online speech.

The right to free expression becomes one of democratic India's increasingly delicate pillars, but it is one that Rinu's generation takes as a given. By 2012, the year of the girls' arrest, India is home to one of the largest concentrations of Facebook users in the world, and nearly half of them are estimated to be between the ages of eighteen and twenty-four.[2]

So, quite by accident, Rinu and Shaheen come to symbolize the demands of their generation. No matter how forcefully the state tries to tie their tongues, they holler back. They spur an intense legal and political battle, between a state machinery nervous about the nonsense that flows through the pipes of the Internet and a generation of digital natives for whom it is like air. In turn, they reveal an important fault line in the world's most populous democracy. On a global index of free expression, compiled in 2014 by an American group called Freedom House, India ranks only as "partly free," alongside Myanmar and Belarus.[3]

India has wrestled with freedom of expression since independence.

The preamble to the Constitution, which came into effect on January 26, 1950, enshrines "LIBERTY of thought, expression, belief, faith and worship." Among the "fundamental rights" of Indian citizens, article 19 of the Constitution is unequivocal in its support for this idea: "All citizens shall have the right to freedom of speech and expression."[4]

Free expression is a celebrated legacy. From India's creative ferment has come an extraordinarily rich mix of music, dance, theater, and literature—not to mention the world's most prolific film industry.

India has never had the gulags of Solzhenitsyn's Soviet Union. It has never forced its citizens into reeducation camps as China did under Mao. Even Mrs. Gandhi's emergency era was mild by the standards of modern totalitarianism.

And yet, since independence, India has been ambivalent about any speech that can inflame emotions and disturb the public order—all the more so because the state has had to pay attention to the sentiments of so many castes and creeds. India has had to weigh the cultural and religious sensitivities of all its people against the values of a secular, plural republic. That has been a delicate balance to strike, and the scales have often tipped in favor of order; Indian authorities have very often opted to squelch expression, giving the nation an improbably rich record of banned books and movies.

Nothing exemplified independent India's anxieties about civil liberties more plainly than two cases that reached its Supreme Court shortly after the passage of the Constitution.

The first case was brought by a leftist magazine called *Cross Roads* after a state government banned it, on the grounds that it threatened public order. Its publisher, Romesh Thapar, argued that his constitutional right to free speech had been violated.

The second case was brought by a magazine published by Rashtriya Swamsevak Sangh, the same Hindu organization where India's future prime minister Narendra Modi received his political education. The Sangh went to court after it was ordered to have its publication prescreened by government authorities. The group was already a grievous thorn in the side of Prime Minister Nehru's government. In court, the state's attorneys contended that the Sangh magazine could endanger public order.

In both cases—one from the government's leftist critics, the other from the right—the Supreme Court was skeptical of the state's argument. The judges said that a threat to public order alone was not enough to override the constitutionally guaranteed right to free speech, unless the state could prove that the published material specifically threatened the security of the state or sought its overthrow. The court ruled against the state.

These twin rulings unsettled Nehru. He assembled his cabinet and proposed that the Constitution be amended. His ministers vigorously debated. They weighed the perils of squelching dissent versus allowing radicals, whether right or left, to threaten the stability of the new nation.

The language they finally came up with seems now extraordinarily broad. They agreed on a constitutional amendment to limit the right to free speech if it was "in the interests of the security of the State, friendly relations with foreign States, public order, decency, or morality or in relation to contempt of court, defamation, or incitement to an offence."

The amendment empowered the government to impose "reasonable restrictions" on speech; Bhimrao Ambedkar, law minister at the time, had insisted on the insertion of that "reasonable."

Nehru made his case to the nation's parliament. He said that like other democracies, India could not afford to protect speech that allowed someone to advocate "crimes of violence."

India's First Amendment passed on June 18, 1951—"the first major crisis of the nation state," a law scholar named Lawrence Liang called it.

"It exposed the inherent tensions between balancing freedom of speech and expression and the promotion of national security and sovereignty," he continued.

"It also posed the question as to who the guardians of the Constitution were. Finally it set in motion a debate which would haunt Indian democracy for the next fifty years, viz. the exercise of a democratic right as a threat to the larger, abstract ideal of a democratic state."[5]

When it was born, at midnight, on August 15, 1947, India was a most unlikely nation. It contained a multiplicity of faiths, languages, and races. There was no obvious glue to bind its people, only an idea that was radical for its time: that a poor, populous, incredibly diverse people could live together as a modern, secular republic. Its closest cousin among nations was the United States.

By and large, in the first two decades of independence, what the state banned revealed the prickliness of a new nation. Racist tracts were not welcome. Prohibited too were writings that preached secession for Kashmir—the Himalayan territory that both India and Pakistan claimed.

There were other sensitivities. In 1956, the state banned *Rama Retold*, a cheeky retelling of the *Ramayana* written by the Indian-English satirist Aubrey Menen. In 1960, it banned Arthur Koestler's collection of essays *The Lotus and the Robot*, which was skeptical about India's ability to nurture democracy.

In the coming decades, India outlawed films that state authorities thought might engender violence. The 1984 Hollywood film *Indiana Jones and the Temple of Doom* could not be screened in India because it suggested that Indians ate chilled monkey brain for dessert. (We did not, not chilled anyway, as I assured my sixteenth-birthday party guests in California that year.)

The most notorious ban came four years later, when Rajiv Gandhi's administration banned the importation of *The Satanic Verses*, published in the United States. This was even before Ayatollah Khomeini of Iran put a price on Salman Rushdie's head.

Mahesh Bhatt's 1998 film about Hindu–Muslim strife, *Zakhm* (the Hindi word for "wound"), could be screened only after it erased references to a Hindu extremist group. (Its members could not be shown waving orange flags, which is the color of Thackeray's Shiv Sena party. Bhatt agreed to turn them into gray.)

No one party or ideology has held a monopoly on squelching free expression. The Congress Party called for a ban of Katherine Frank's 2001 biography of Indira Gandhi, which suggested that Mrs. Gandhi had had an active sex life. In 2003 the Communists who ruled my home state of West Bengal banned an autobiographical novel by Taslima Nasreen, a Bangladeshi feminist who had angered some Muslim clerics. (Perhaps only in India can Communists be so concerned about offending clerics that they order police to confiscate all copies of a book.)

Sometimes, it's the fear of hooligans that squelches free expression. *Parzania*, a film based on the true story of a family that lost a son during the 2002 violence against Muslims in Gujarat, could not be shown in that state. Gujarat's movie theater owners refused to screen it; they said they feared vandals, and the state authorities said nothing to reassure them.[6]

I find it a bit strange that India's leaders are still so anxious about free expression. The nation is no more as fragile as it may have been in 1951, when the First Amendment was passed. Yet, the anxiety about civil liberties has held on. It has arguably become more intense. Indian authorities are quick to squelch any utterance that might offend.

To my mind, it is a measure of the state's inability to guarantee law and order. That is to say, if you can't protect your citizens from troublemakers on the street, you might as well squash anything that can upset the troublemakers—an offensive Facebook post, say, that might offend one community or another.

India has done this repeatedly. One aggrieved group after another says it is offended by something someone has written, painted, uttered, clicked. The authorities respond by quashing the potentially offending utterance itself. Pratap Bhanu Mehta, a political analyst, once described it to me as "offense mongering."

The most egregious example of offense mongering came over a handful of modernist works by Maqbool Fida Husain, India's most famous painter. He attracted the ire of Hindu radicals with two nude, abstract figures of the Hindu deities Durga and Saraswati, as well as a painting that showed the figure of a female nude superimposed on the map of India.

Mobs attacked galleries that displayed his work. They were not punished. Instead, there were long, live debates on television about nudity in Hindu iconography. A lawsuit, filed on behalf of Hindu nationalist groups, accused the artist of promoting religious "enmity." It was eventually thrown out by the Supreme Court. Still, fear of attacks kept other galleries from displaying his work. Husain fled, living abroad for nearly nine years, in Dubai and London. He said he did not feel safe in his home country.

Husain, inspired equally by European cubism and Bollywood, was an iconoclast, and he did not always make himself welcome among his fellow Muslims. One of his paintings portrayed a donkey at Mecca, prompting howls of protests. Husain called the animal a symbol of nonviolence, just as he described his choice of nudity as a metaphor for purity.

I met Husain in 2008, in his home in Dubai. At ninety-three, he was still full of joy and flamboyance, still walking around barefooted as he had for much of his life. By this time, the Supreme Court had thrown out the case against him. But he feared that hard-liners would pounce on him if they could, and that the government, led at the time by Congress, would be unable to protect him. He chose to remain in Dubai, far from everyone and everything he cared about.

To me, his exile came to represent the growing intolerance for cultural expression, just as it represented the state's inability to protect its citizens—in this case, its most famous painter—from thugs.

"The State fails to send a signal about protecting the boundaries of free speech," Mehta told me. "If we want social stability we need a consensus on what our freedoms are."

Husain shrugged when I asked if he ever felt angry. He told me he bore no malice, not even at the government that, he said, was too weak to protect him. So I can't go to Bombay. I can still paint, he said. His eyes lit up. Why don't we take a ride in my Ferrari? he proposed. He sat in the passenger's seat, shoeless, squealing like a child at his chauffeur, pleading that he drive a bit faster.

Three years later, in June 2011, Husain died in London.[7]

The demands of digital natives sharpen India's dilemma over free expression. It is hard to suppress content on the Internet, unless you're China. India is not China and cannot be perceived as being China.[8]

India's predicament is further complicated by the fact that the companies that run Internet platforms have their own rules about what they allow on their sites—their own jurisprudence, if you will, which complicates matters for governments that want to censor digital speech.

Compared with rich countries, like the United States and much of Western Europe, a still-small share of Indians have access to the Internet—about one in ten, according to 2011 figures—but that number is growing exponentially, making India one of the fastest-expanding Internet markets in the world. Three out of four Internet users in India are under the age of thirty-five, like Rinu.[9]

Like young people everywhere, young Indians have rushed online to read, listen, watch, troll, organize, fall in love, and express them-selves. Most Indians access the Internet on their phones, which occa-sionally prompts village elders to call for restrictions against women's cell phone use. Indians listen to music on their phones, check cricket scores, review astrological forecasts. Farmers look up crop prices. Vot-ers listen to rousing political speeches at election time. Shubrangshu Choudhary, a friend of mine, has designed a platform for villagers in remote hamlets of central India to send text messages about news in their areas—much of it is about droughts, floods, road conditions, prob-lems getting rations, and the like. And of course, Indians spend hours on Facebook. In conservative hamlets where teenagers are not allowed to meet members of the opposite sex face-to-face, they strike up what are known as Facebook romances.

Neither Rinu nor Shaheen know quite where freedom on Facebook begins or ends.

On that balmy Sunday in Palghar, Rinu's friend Shaheen is also at home, on her computer, scrolling through Facebook. It is about seven o'clock. There is still a bit of light in the sky. A sea breeze comes in through an open window.

Her Facebook newsfeed is peppered with mentions of the death of Thackeray, the political party boss, and of his followers thronging the streets of Mumbai for his funeral. They have called for a *bandh*, effec-tively shutting down the city.

That Shaheen finds excessive. And she says so, on Facebook. "With all respect, every day, thousands of people die, but still the world moves on," Shaheen writes. "Just due to one politician died a natural death, everyone just goes bonkers."

Shaheen is shy in person, but expansive online. So on Facebook, she goes on to suggest that it would be better for Indians to devote their energies to commemorating the achievements of those who fought for the country's independence. She cites one popular antiimperialist hero, Bhagat Singh, "because of whom we r free living Indians."

Shaheen's post floats up in Rinu's newsfeed shortly after seven. "Wow!!!" Rinu writes.

Shaheen and Rinu aren't super close. Students at the same local college, they are what Rinu describes as "hi-bye friends." Shaheen studies management science. Rinu majors in biology. They live a short distance from each other. And their circumstances are similar. Both their families settled in Palghar because Mumbai, which is a two-and-a-half-hour ride away, in a stinky, flesh-packed commuter train, has become way too expensive for middle-class families like theirs. Rinu's father, who comes from Kerala, in the south, worked on merchant ships. Shaheen's father, who moved here from the state of Chhattisgarh, in central India, sells bolts of cloth. Both Rinu's and Shaheen's mothers are homemakers. Neither Rinu nor Shaheen plan to be homemakers. Rinu imagines running her own recording studio; Shaheen plans to work at a bank. They spend hours on their computers at home. Facebook is a big part of how they pass the time.

Shaheen's opinion resonates with Rinu. After an initial "wow," she clicks "like" under Shaheen's post, just as she clicks "like" a bunch of times every day on a bunch of things. That little blue thumbs-up.

A boy named Akaash soon weighs in, furious. "Just mind your own busyness," he writes, as a response to Rinu's post.

Rinu clatters out a rebuttal: "We agree that he has done a lot of good things, we respect him also, it doesn't make any sense to shut down everything! Respect can be shown in many other ways! Even his soul might be like 'Why so much?'"

Around 7:15 P.M., Shaheen's cell phone rings. A stranger, a man, barks at her: "Was it right to say that about the *bandh*?" She hangs up. She is rattled. So she clicks "delete" next to her post.

It is too late. Her father gets a call too. He comes into the bedroom.

"What is this about?" he asks her.

His face turns ashen when she tells him what she wrote. Her face turns wet with tears. "He was a little bit shocked. He didn't say anything," Shaheen recalls. "I was crying and crying."

Ten minutes later comes a knock on their door. Police stand in the stairwell—maybe three or four, she doesn't remember. They tell Shaheen there are some very angry people at the police station, and that she will need to come and apologize.

Shaheen throws a *dupatta* over her shoulders, puts on her sandals. She is terrified of what awaits her. She has never been to a police station before. "Totally frozen," she says.

A bit later, across town, Rinu's phone also rings. A friend calls to tell her that the cops have picked up Shaheen and that there's a big crowd of Shiv Sena followers outside the police station.

Rinu doesn't believe it at first. Can't be true, she thinks. But what if it is? She too deletes her "like" on Facebook—and then she deactivates her account. Gone. Vanished. Except not really. Her posts have already spread. They live elsewhere, on other people's Facebook pages.

Her friend calls again. He says the crowd at the police station demands an apology from both of them, that she should go and join Shaheen. "I was so much panicked and afraid," Rinu says.

She calls her father. "Come fast" is all she needs to say on the phone. "I didn't even explain. He figured out I was really panicked."

Her father, P. A. Srinivasan, a fifty-nine-year-old former naval officer, asks no questions. He immediately senses the panic in his daughter's voice. He immediately gets that she needs him. So he hops on his scooter and races home. As soon as he walks in the door, Rinu makes a most improbable demand. Take me to the police station, she says without explanation. Again, he asks nothing. All he knows is that he needs to stand by her.

"I was really confused," Srinivasan says. "I thought she had done something really wrong that she couldn't be pardoned for. I didn't even know it was a Facebook post."

The scene at the police headquarters in Palghar shocks father and daughter both. It is dark by then, close to eight o'clock. At the gates of the station is a loud angry mob. People are shouting, waving their fists. One woman, a complete stranger, walks up and slaps Rinu in the face.

Dad blurts out: "Forgive her." For what, he still has no idea. To make matters worse, the police say Rinu will have to go inside the station by herself, to be interrogated without her father.

"It was all of a sudden," Rinu says. "Fifteen minutes back, I'm at home relaxing. Then I was at the police station and people were very, very violent. They were shouting. Very aggressive."

Shaheen is already in a back room at the station by the time Rinu gets there. Together, they try to explain to a pair of policewomen what they wrote. They said they meant no harm. They were just expressing their opinion about something, just as they would about a movie they had seen.

The policewomen have no idea what they are talking about. What is this Facebook? they want to know. What is a "status update"? they ask. Rinu says it would have been funny were it not so terrifying. Shaheen starts weeping. Her uncle's medical clinic has been vandalized, apparently by a group of Shiv Sainiks, as party loyalists are called. It doesn't help that Shaheen's family is Muslim. The Shiv Sena is not known to be fond of Muslims.

Finally, at midnight, comes an assistant superintendent of police who knows what Facebook is. He urges Rinu and Shaheen to compose an apology, which they do. "I'm sorry for offending Shiv Sainiks," they each write by hand, like schoolgirls made to compose notes of contrition. They are scared out of their wits.

Close to midnight, once the crowd outside has dispersed, the girls are allowed to go home. But their ordeal is not over. The next morning, Palghar police announce that they will file criminal charges against Shaheen and Rinu for "promoting enmity," among communities, and for sending electronic communications that cause "annoyance or inconvenience." The two young women walk into the police station once more. They are arrested under Section 66A of the Information Technology Act and punishable by up to three years in jail.

Their images flash across television screens throughout the day. Rinu covers her face with a pale handkerchief. Shaheen uses her *dupatta*.

The Internet had given them a way to express themselves and, in a flash, taught them how dangerous expressing themselves could be. "I was totally shattered," Rinu recalls.

T he Indian state has been confounded by the power of the Internet. India has not erected a firewall, to keep out forbidden content, as China has. To do so would be to fly in the face of everything that a secular, democratic republic stands for. It wouldn't work.

Like many other nations, both autocratic and democratic, India keeps a close eye on what its citizens do online, generally with the help of surveillance technologies available on the open market.[10]

It is unusually aggressive in monitoring who says what on popular web platforms. India was number two on the list of governments asking Google to disclose information on its users in 2014, second only to requests from the United States. Its requests ranged from the names of Gmail users and their Internet Protocol addresses to who posted which YouTube videos. In a majority of cases, Google provided what the government asked for.[11]

Likewise, from Facebook: India sought information on more than 7000 users in the second half of 2014, second only to the United States.[12]

As for gagging expression, India has had mixed success.

In the spring of 2011, the Congress-led coalition government put into place a set of regulations to restrict web content based on a vague set of criteria. Known as the Information Technology (Intermediaries Guidelines) Rules, 2011, they required Internet companies that run platforms like YouTube and Facebook to take down within thirty-six hours any material that, among other things, the government considered "harassing," "disparaging," or "hateful."[13]

By this time, it was impossible for Silicon Valley tech companies to ignore the Indian market: a billion people, so many of them young, and 90 percent of them yet to be connected to the Internet. At the same time, it was becoming extremely hard to do business in a country that had such a muddled policy on what users could and could not post on their platforms.

To operate in India, of course, means that the web companies must abide by India's own laws. And so they must take down content when government authorities order them to. On this score, Indian authorities have been unusually aggressive too.

In 2014, Facebook removed 5832 pieces of content at the request of the Indian government, more than in any other country in the world.[14] Facebook, for instance, said that content was restricted specifically inside India because it violated Indian law "including anti-religious content and hate speech that could cause unrest and disharmony."

In the summer of 2012 came a new crisis. A localized Hindu–Muslim clash in northeastern Assam spread swiftly across the country. As attacks against ethnic northeastern migrants intensified, turning fatal in many places, the government blamed the Internet. It ordered a host of Internet companies, including service providers, to block more than three hundred websites. Twitter was blamed for flaming communal tensions. The government told the company to shut down more than a dozen accounts.

In a compromise, Twitter agreed to suspend about a half-dozen accounts that, it concluded, had violated the company's terms of service (a bit like its own constitution) by impersonating Indian government officials. Twitter bucked the government's request to take down several obvious parody accounts, including one that mocked Prime Minister Manmohan Singh with the Twitter handle @YumYumSingh.

Government authorities seemed to grow ever more incensed by posts, pictures, and cartoons circulating online. In April 2012, police in Calcutta arrested a middle-aged chemistry professor for emailing a cartoon that mocked the chief minister of the state. That October, a businessman in the southern city of Pondicherry was arrested for a tweet that criticized another businessman, who happened to be the son of India's finance minister.

Then, in November, Shaheen and Rinu were hauled into the Palghar police station for speaking up. Nothing enraged India's Internet generation quite like it. They revolted.

All these arrests were made under Section 66A of the Information Technology Act. That section, vague and heavy-handed, imposed up to three years in jail on anyone found to "transmit a) any information that is grossly offensive or has menacing character; or b) any information which he knows to be false, but for the purpose of causing annoyance, inconvenience, danger, obstruction, insult, injury, criminal intimidation, enmity, hatred, or ill will, persistently by making use of such computer resource or a communication device." The legal bar was mind-bogglingly low: you could be jailed for "annoyance."

The cover of *India Today*, a newsweekly, summed up the zeitgeist this way: "The Paranoid State," read the headline, illustrated by a handcuffed fist pointing its thumb downward, the opposite of a Facebook "like." It was a pie in the face of the government, which had vastly underestimated how unpopular its new rules would be in a country so young.

Kapil Sibal, the government's technology minister at the time, made sure to tell the press he was "deeply saddened" by the arrests. "It is just their point of view, and enforcement of these laws are not to ban people from expressing their views," he said in a television interview.

Within weeks, police dropped the charges against the two young women.

The government also swiftly agreed to tweak the controversial section of the law. A beat cop was no longer allowed to make a decision to arrest someone based on that law. A senior police officer—holding the rank of at least a deputy commissioner—would have to sign off before a case could be filed under that statute.

However, young Indians were not content with such a cosmetic fix. Before the end of 2012, just weeks after watching television images of Rinu and Shaheen being paraded to the police station, a young Delhi woman named Shreya Singhal went to court to challenge the law. She told reporters later that she had been outraged by it, and that her mom, a lawyer, suggested that if she cared so much about free speech she should file a petition with the Supreme Court. Singhal was twenty-two years old. She called the law "a gag on the Internet."

In March 2015, the Supreme Court agreed with her. It struck down several provisions of the Information Technology Act, including Section 66A. The judges concluded that it was vague and unconstitutional. The court also cited the case brought before the Supreme Court in 1950 by the publisher of *Cross Roads* magazine, one of the two lawsuits that led to India's First Amendment.

The judges wrote: "The Preamble of the Constitution of India *inter alia* speaks of liberty of thought, expression, belief, faith and worship. It also says that India is a sovereign democratic republic. It cannot be over-emphasized that when it comes to democracy, liberty of thought and expression is a cardinal value that is of paramount significance under our constitutional scheme."[15]

The judges went on to say that under the law "no distinction is made between mere discussion or advocacy of a particular point of view which may be annoying or inconvenient or grossly offensive to some and *incitement* by which such words lead to an imminent causal connection with public disorder." The italics are mine.

*   *   *

India is not alone among modern secular democracies in having to balance free speech and public order.

The rise of Islamist extremism has made this an urgent challenge for many Western governments. In March 2015, just as India was throwing out the controversial law under which Rinu and Shaheen were arrested, a court in France ruled against a Facebook post by a comic named Dieudonné M'bala M'bala. In the aftermath of the brutal attacks on the satirical newspaper *Charlie Hebdo* and a Jewish supermarket that January, M'bala M'bala declared on Facebook that he felt like "Charlie Coulibaly." It was a blend of the popular rallying cry "Je Suis Charlie," the slogan championing the free speech rights of the newspaper, and the name of one of the gunmen, Amedy Coulibaly, who killed four people at the supermarket. A court found M'bala M'bala guilty of condoning terrorism. Critics said the verdict showed French selectivity in enforcing the right to free speech. France, like other European countries, has long banned anti-Semitic speech.

Private companies that run social media platforms have also been forced to scrutinize what amounts to their own jurisprudence. Twitter, for instance, had come under intense criticism for letting the Islamic State spew violence on its site, including by posting pictures of executions. In April 2015, it announced new rules for users of its service, threatening suspension for those who promote violence against others.[16]

The debates over free expression online are nowhere more challenging, in my view, than they are in India. The country has a horrific legacy of sectarian strife. Tempers can be riled easily. The damage can be grave.

It makes it all the more remarkable that Indians have insisted on their right to speak their minds rather than trade it away for a sterile, but peaceful, model of authoritarianism. This is by no means a done deal. How much can be said, sung, filmed, or written is still very much being negotiated—and it is Rinu and Shaheen's generation that is pushing the envelope.

In some ways, India at noonday is clearly more modern, more open than the nation had been at midnight. But it is also less so. There's no telling who will be offended next, and how they will react. And so it's hard to know what you can write or how you can paint, let alone what you can "like" on Facebook. Tolerance is in short supply.

Kailash Satyarthi, the child rights advocate and Nobel Peace Prize winner, drove home this point when I met him in the spring of 2015, as I was wrapping up the writing of this book. I asked him what he worries about most when he thinks about the future of his country's young.

He said he worried about two things. One of them, he said, was a lack of tolerance.

"We are not able to inculcate the value of tolerance, of listening to each other" is how he put it. "Intolerance is going to result in irreparable violence if we cannot control it now."

He said he was keen to speak to the nation's prime minister about this. (The other thing he worries about, he said, is that young people seem more interested in competing with each other than in cooperating.)

The trespass of the Facebook girls, the outrage of their peers, and the subsequent judgment by the Supreme Court of India were in many ways an emblem of the pressures that India's digital generation is putting on its elders. These negotiations are likely to continue for some time, as India's leaders seek to placate the sensitivities of its many constituencies, while also allowing its citizens to express themselves as they demand. The Supreme Court ruling on Section 66A also made it slightly more onerous on the government to demand that websites and Internet service providers block content. It made sure that those service providers—and the users whose speech was being contested—could be heard in court, and it insisted that any restrictions on speech be "reasonable." That was the term that Ambedkar had insisted on adding to India's First Amendment.

This may not be so easy for Prime Minister Narendra Modi. Some of his fellow travelers in the Hindu nationalist movement have been notoriously intolerant of their critics. To wit, Wendy Doniger, a scholar at the University of Chicago, found herself at the mercy of a Hindu right-wing gadfly who went to court to argue that her book *The Hindus: An Alternative History* had run afoul of a section of the Indian Penal Code that prohibits "deliberate and malicious acts intended to outrage religious feelings" of Indian citizens. Her publisher, Penguin India, after fighting the lawsuit for four years, agreed in a 2014 out-of-court settlement to destroy the remaining copies of the book in India.

In late August 2015, as this book was going to print, M. M. Kalburgi, a rationalist critic of the Hindu right and a member of the government-funded Sahitya Akademi, the National Academy of Letters, was gunned down in his home in the southern state of Karnataka. In October, right-wing Hindu activists smeared black paint on the face of a political analyst, Sudheendra Kulkarni; they were objecting to his hosting a talk with a former Pakistani minister. Incidents like these prompted an outcry, leading dozens of India's leading writers to return the awards they had received from the Akademi.

In 2015, Mr. Modi's government unexpectedly banned hundreds of porn sites online, only to reverse itself in days, following public outcry. Not surprising, perhaps. India at noonday is a thriving market for Internet porn.

I visit Rinu and Shaheen in Palghar, three weeks after their arrests.

Shaheen, who has recently finished her bachelor's in management science at a local college, is waiting to hear back from a bank, where she has applied for a job. She used to log in to Facebook five, six times a day, posting little snippets, looking at pictures her friends had posted. "Actually I am addicted to Facebook," Shaheen confesses. She has acute withdrawals after deactivating her account on the day of her arrest. She watches television to make up for it. "I'm quite bored," she says.

Shaheen's Facebook fast lasts about a month. Conveniently for her, Facebook doesn't actually delete the contents of her account just because she deactivated it. As a matter of policy, Facebook stores everything— every picture, every status update, lists of friends, every blithe "like" for several months. It's all there, in a data center somewhere in the world, in case someone changes her mind about quitting Facebook and, like Shaheen, becomes "quite bored."

By January 2013, Shaheen is back on the social network, though with a promise to her parents to be more circumspect about her political opinions. "I should be more careful," she says. "I will think twice about what I'll be posting."

Since then, I notice, she sticks to commenting on movies and liking her friends' pictures. She likes a lot of pictures. In 2013, she announces her engagement, and in 2014, her wedding. She posts some vacation pictures, a few jokes.

Then, on March 24, 2015, she lets out this uncharacteristic yelp: "Supreme court quashed section 66 A.. LANDMARK VICTORY.. Thanks media for ur support..—☺ feeling proud."

Rinu reactivates her Facebook account faster than Shaheen. She doesn't seem to mind the fame that this Facebook kerfuffle yields. Rinu still dreams of being the next Miley Cyrus. And if her singing career doesn't quite take off, she plans to run her own recording studio.

In 2014, she takes a course in audio engineering, and is on her way to do an internship at a recording studio in Chennai. She doesn't get to vote in the 2014 general election, because on Election Day she is away from her polling booth in Palghar. She is shocked by the election results. She had been rooting for Aam Aadmi. She is no Modi fan. But in our Facebook chat, she quickly puts a positive spin on it. "If he can do something for this country. I'll be happy," she writes. She records a song for a film produced in Kerala. She teaches herself to play guitar. She posts a lot of dog photos on Facebook.

Her father is her biggest defender. He says Shiv Sena supporters should not have been so upset by a young woman's personal opinion, expressed on Facebook. She meant no disrespect to their leader, he says. She merely pointed out that a shutdown of the city meant that people couldn't work. He is pleased that his daughter speaks up for what she believes in. "I'm proud of her. It's putting your mind out and feeling for poor people," he says.

Rinu and her dad are close. She describes him on Facebook as "the only Superman I know."

APOSTATES
When They Dared to Love

From the corner of her eye, Monica spies him looking at her. She is on a cycle-rickshaw on her way to college. He is on a motorcycle. They stop at a red light at the same time.

Monica allows herself to look back and notice how handsome he is, how stylish. In time, she allows herself to give him her cell phone number, to whisper when no one is in earshot, to fall in love. Finally, on a rainy night in July, she allows herself to run away with him, sit cross-legged on the floor at an Arya Samaj temple far from home, and exchange garlands.

Monica is twenty, the carefully guarded daughter of a Gujjar family on the northern outskirts of Delhi. The handsome man is Kuldeep, a year older, the younger of two sons from a Rajput family, who lives around the bend. Exchanging garlands, they vow to be together for the rest of their lives.

This turns out to be a fatal indiscretion. In Monica's community, a girl was not to step across the line like that. She was not supposed to want a man like that, certainly not to choose him. Monica had trespassed further by falling in love with a man from a rival caste, from the same neighborhood.

Both the Gujjars and Rajputs wield power in the area. They both own plenty of real estate, which makes them equally well off. Never, ever have there been cross-caste marriages. Or so everyone is told growing up.

The neighborhood, known as Wazirpur, is an in-between place, suspended between modern and medieval, between day and night, unsure which it would rather be: city or *gaon*. If there was a soundtrack to this state of being, it would be in the *raga multaani*, the melodic scale meant to be played in the late afternoon, not quite in the fullness of the day, but well before dark, in a state of unbelonging.

At independence time, Wazirpur was a village on the outskirts of small, sleepy Delhi. The Gujjars and Rajputs had land. They grew wheat and mustard; in their kitchen gardens they cultivated vegetables. The Gujjars, traditional herdsmen, had an additional asset: they kept cows and buffalo in their yards.

After independence, as Delhi swelled with refugees fleeing bloodshed on the country's new western border with Pakistan, Wazirpur's fortunes changed. The city authorities needed more land, so they acquired plot after plot of farmland. Delhi began to stretch its arms around Wazirpur, as if to say, You might think of yourself as a village. But your children will be smitten by the city. You'll see.

Wheat fields disappeared. Up came factories and office buildings. The landowners, both Gujjars and Rajputs, got money in their pockets, but they had no more land to till. They were rich and fallow.

Under city code, Wazirpur remained one of several incorporated villages within Delhi. In truth, it was just one of the many dingy neighborhoods in the capital. Starting in the early 1990s, as India began to open its economy, Wazirpur's fortunes changed once more. Land values shot up. Their squat village houses, with cows in the courtyards, turned into skinny, higgledy-piggledy apartments. Migrants from all over the country flocked to Delhi for work. They needed a roof over their heads. They squeezed into these one- and two-room flats. Rents spiked. Shops opened: tailors, grocers, doctors, cell phone top-up booths, cybercafés.

The Wazirpur boom embodied the transformation of Delhi, as its population doubled between 1990 and 2015, to more than 25 million, well on its way to becoming the world's second most populous city, after Tokyo.[1]

All this meant that Wazirpur's homeowners grew ever more prosperous. They tacked on more rental units to their buildings. They installed air conditioners, then satellite dishes. First came motorcycles, then cars.

Cows still roamed the narrow alleys, but now the houses were so tall and so tightly pressed against one another that the sun couldn't enter. Wazirpur was dark even at high noon.

Another Wazirpur generation—children raised in the years of economic liberalization—did not have to work, whether they were Rajput or Gujjar. They didn't need an education. They didn't need anything close to Anupam's fire in the belly or Mani's courage. They lived off of rents from their family's real estate. They were certainly not poor. They had opportunities. But there were plenty of men who whiled their days away on the corner, jumped on their motorcycles for joyrides at night.

Kuldeep and his older brother, Amit, were different. They too could afford to live off of the family property. Their father owned two buildings. Plenty of rent money came in. They didn't have to work, but they wanted to. The aspiration bug had rubbed off on them. "Working and earning money improves a person," Amit said.

Amit was the shorter, squatter, more traditional of the two. He found a good job in the garment industry, and he rose up the ranks to manage a factory that stitched women's clothes for export to Europe. He was dedicated to his job. The factory was all the way across Delhi, so his daily commute was a two-hour drive.

Amit was the low-key one of the two. He didn't care much about brand-name fashion. He rarely went out for dinner. He had never been to a nightclub. His favorite drink was fresh milk. He let his parents choose a bride for him, one who was from the same Rajput caste but a different *gotra*, as was the norm. His wife was pretty and quiet-spoken. She dressed in simple *salwar* suits and came to live in the family house in Wazirpur.

His brother, Kuldeep, three years younger, shared many of his aspirations. He worked in a call center. He had risen up the ranks too, to become a team leader, and he wanted to rise further, which is why he took advantage of the management courses that his company offered on-site. But Kuldeep was the bon vivant that his older brother was not: he dressed well, ate out, and once he married Monica, took her out to the mall. "I can say he was like a brand ambassador for Benetton," Amit said of his brother's sense of style, which was also his way of saying how different they were.

Kuldeep loved going out. His friends were "hi-fi" kids who grew up across the main road, in a neighborhood known as Ashok Vihar and who considered Wazirpur's fly-choked lanes to be *ganda*. Kuldeep knew early on he wanted out. Amit had never considered it.

Amit knew Kuldeep had a thing for Monica. He even warned his brother not to take it too far. He figured it would pass, a brief romance. Not in his wildest imagination did Amit envision that love would drive Kuldeep to risk everything.

In fact, Amit didn't know anyone who had fallen in love. "We never knew what is love marriage" is how he put it. "It never happened in our family."

But then it did. During the rains in 2007.

Amit is the first to get a call that night from Monica's infuriated father. His daughter hasn't come home, he says. He accuses Kuldeep of kidnapping her. Amit tries to put him at ease. Don't worry, Uncle, he says. We will find them. Amit searches for Kuldeep everywhere. He goes to the gym where Kuldeep usually works out. He goes to the pool hall where he sometimes meets friends. He calls and calls Kuldeep's cell phone; it is turned off.

This is when Amit starts to get a sinking feeling. He knows Kuldeep can't have kidnapped Monica. He wonders: Could they have eloped?

The rains have just broken over Delhi. Heat rises from the black tar.

Tin roofs turn into drum sets. Amit doesn't sleep that night. No one in his house sleeps that night.

The next morning, Amit's apprehensions turn out to be correct. He gets a call from the courthouse a few miles away from home. There he finds Kuldeep and Monica. After exchanging garlands at the temple the previous evening, they have come to court to register their marriage with a judge. They are both over eighteen. Adults. The judge makes it clear that they have the right to choose to marry each other. In the eyes of the law, no one can take that away.

Amit doesn't have it in him to be angry at his little brother. What can he do but give his blessings? His parents too embrace Monica. Welcome to our family, they say, but please don't live in Wazirpur. Find yourself somewhere safe, far away from her people.

"*Beta*, they'll kill you both," Kuldeep's mother says.

Monica is no rebel. She obeys the rules. She dresses in a *salwar kameez* when she visits her in-laws. She wears jeans—which has, strangely, become a metonym for the loose woman—when she goes to the movies or to the mall, which she does only with her husband. She complies with her husband's wish that she not work outside the home. She is devoted to him: if Kuldeep is on a night shift at the call center where he works, she stays awake until he comes home.

Monica asserts herself in one notable way: she chooses to love him. She chooses to love.

After living on the other side of the city for the first couple of years of marriage, Monica makes peace with her parents. Monica and Kuldeep return to be closer to both their families. Not to Wazirpur—but the more modern, more pukka Ashok Vihar, the next neighborhood over. In Ashok Vihar, there is no cow dung to step over on the way home. Most people have cars and office jobs. They go for morning walks. They dress well. Monica and Kuldeep rent a second-floor apartment that overlooks a shady neighborhood park. Monica speaks to her sister-in-law, Amit's wife,

Reshu, on the phone almost every day. She visits her mother regularly. She is no longer afraid of her people. To Reshu, Monica seems happy.

Things take a turn when two other daughters of Wazirpur stray. Sisters named Shobha and Khushboo, they live along the same alley as Monica's family. They are known in the neighborhood as dancers. What sort of dancer, no one can quite tell me, but just to be known in this community as a dancer means having a shady reputation. One woman tells me she heard they were models— also considered shady.

Shobha and Khushboo have a domineering brother: Mandeep, a high school dropout and an occasional used car salesman who mostly cruises around on his motorcycle and lords over his sisters.

Khushboo later tells the police that he was on the girls' backs all the time. If she or her sister went out with friends, they faced his wrath at home. He yelled at them. He slapped them. Once, according to Khushboo's written testimony to police, he threatened to kill her.

The girls can't take it anymore. One day at the end of May, at the peak of the hot season, in 2010, they run away.

The lanes of Wazirpur immediately start buzzing with talk. How could these girls dare to run away? If they ran away, who else would run away? Ah, remember that girl who ran away before?

The memory of Monica's misdeeds is resurrected. And it circles back to Monica's brother, Ankit (not to be confused with Ankit, the political activist you met earlier in these pages).[2]

The boys of Wazirpur sneer. Perhaps they lean against their motorbikes, as boys do to while away the stifling summer evenings, and cluck their tongues. See, they might say, your sister Monica started this.

"I was demeaned by my friends," Ankit later says in his written testimony to police. "I was stressed."

Ankit is a Class 9 dropout. He has a motorcycle and no job. His father has plenty of money, earning rent from the grocer who operates out of the ground floor of their property. He is the eldest son, and perhaps when the sneering starts, he begins to see himself as the enforcer of the rules his sister broke.

Shobha and Khushboo's brother Mandeep also feels demeaned on the street. "Torture" is how his older brother recalls it.

Who among the boys first suggests that they avenge their family's honor? It's not clear.

Police suspect that Ankit and Mandeep are egged on by their peers. "Maybe because of these things they were conscious of prestige and what people were saying," N. S. Bundela, the police official in charge of North West Delhi, tells me.

I suggest the obvious: "These are boys born and bred in the city."

Yes, of course, he says. But they have "village" attitudes, he says.

Police say it falls on the two boys whose sisters had erred to take action. They recruit friends, among them a Class 7 dropout named Nakul, who lives in the neighborhood and who sometimes sells milk. His family warns him when they hear him talk about the runaway girls. They're not our daughters, they tell him. Stay out of it.

Nakul doesn't listen. On the night of June 20, 2010, according to police, the boys procure a pistol and borrow a car.

First they lure Shobha into the car, according to the suspects' written testimonies to the police. They make her sit in the passenger's seat. Her brother, Mandeep, sits just behind and shoots her in the head. They park the car in front of a local electricity supply office. Police find Shobha's corpse inside.

Next, according to the suspects' testimonies, Ankit calls his brother-in-law, Kuldeep, on the pretext of needing a ride. His cell phone records show Ankit's is the last call he received.

Police find the car parked around the corner from the couple's apartment. Kuldeep's body is slumped over the steering wheel. Ankit is accused of shooting him in the head at point-blank range.

Then, police say, they go up to see Monica. She has just made mango juice for Kuldeep, as she often does during mango season, because that's what he likes to drink when he comes home from work.

Police find two glasses of mango juice standing, untouched, on the kitchen counter—and her corpse on the floor.

Ankit is accused of shooting her in the head.

Police arrest the suspects in a matter of days. They are charged with murder.

The day of the arrests, television news stations dispatch reporters to Wazirpur to collect vox pop reactions. Several older men appear on camera and praise the killers. It had to be done, they say. The men on camera show no remorse.[3]

When Kuldeep's older brother, Amit, sees them on television, something inside him snaps. These are the men he has grown up with. These are the values he has grown up with too—and now his brother is dead. This is when he resolves to pursue justice for his Kuldeep and Monica's death. He persuades his parents to cooperate with the authorities. Hold strong, he tells them, do not cave in to pressures from anyone in the neighborhood.

Amit's most immediate fear is graft. "We prayed to God for an honest judge," he says.

As I write this, five years after the triple murders, none of the accused has been convicted of a crime. They have been in custody since their arrests, pending trial. I have pieced together a chronology of what is alleged to have happened on the day of the murders on the basis of interviews with police, family members, and the suspects' written testimonies to police. Those testimonies may or may not be allowed in court, depending on whether the defense can show that they were obtained under coercion.

One of the most widely shared Hindu parables about love and loyalty comes from the epic tale the *Ramayana*. Ram, the protagonist, is a popular royal, who, as part of an internecine power struggle in the court of Ayodhya, is banished by his father, the king, to the forest. His wife, Sita, and his brother, Lakshman, join him in exile in the wilderness.

One day, Sita is left in their forest home alone, with strict instructions not to stray. A line is drawn in the dirt, encircling their hut. Do not cross this line, Lakshman tells her, and you will be safe.

Sita, the good wife, agrees to stay within her bounds. Except that soon she forgets. Perhaps she disobeys—we don't know for sure. Sita strays. A hungry, wandering Brahmin approaches the hut. She steps across the line to give him food. And just then, the monk changes shape and turns into the demon that he really is. He whisks her away across an ocean to his own kingdom, and proceeds to seduce her. Sita, we learn, is a loyal wife; she rebuffs the demon. She prays that her husband will find her.

Sita's abduction paves the way for a long, bloody battle, and eventually her rescue. But her story does not end happily there.

Ram forces her to prove her purity in a trial by fire, which she does. For a while, their marriage is fine, but Ram is again plagued by suspicions about his wife. He banishes her back to the forest. The *Ramayana* tells us she eventually melts back into the earth.

There are many readings of this great epic, and some readers will inevitably dispute mine.

But no matter how you assess Ram and Sita's conduct in the *Ramayana*, theirs is a powerful fable about love and trust, devotion and disobedience. It is also very much about a woman's place. It is all the more powerful for how popular it remains, how ubiquitous. As a child, I learned about Sita from the comic book version of the *Ramayana*. My sister, who studied Kathak, the sixteenth-century classical Indian dance form, learned of Sita during her classes: *Sita Haran* is one of the most popular fables to be dramatized in dance. It is only a matter of time until my daughter learns the story of Sita and her boundaries.

I never met Kuldeep and Monica. I reconstructed the story of how they fell in love, when they married, and how they were killed from interviews with relatives, neighbors, schoolteachers, and police as well as from the documents the authorities shared with me.

I was drawn to their story for two reasons. First, like others in their generation, Kuldeep and Monica did not set out to upset the status quo. Survey after survey show that in social terms, young Indians tend to be pretty traditional. Especially when it comes to marriage, they are more likely to defer to their families than defy them. In a 2012 survey, for instance, married women in their twenties said their parents were to some degree involved in their choice of husband; only 5 percent said they had married across caste lines.[4]

It is one of the paradoxes of this generation. Noonday's children push for a more genuine freedom, certainly. But on the whole, they can be very conventional.

The second thing I found remarkable was that their suspected killers were not illiterate old men living in a medieval village, fuming at the thought of a modern girl acting on her own desire. The suspects included Monica's own brother, two years her junior, born and raised in the same prospering, fast-modernizing neighborhood of Delhi. This was not a straightforward clash of old and new, or even old versus young. It was a case of young men in New India defending traditional rules of power—and in so doing, punishing a young woman, also in New India, for stepping across the line.

Perhaps it was born of confusion. Clearly it came from fury.

"Accident *ho gaya*," said Mandeep's older brother. "An accident has happened" is how he put it, using the passive voice. He did not want to be named. He did not really want to talk.

The June 2010 murders of Kuldeep and Monica, in a fast-churning corner of sprawling Delhi, came amid a rash of widely publicized so-called honor killings across north India. The victims were all young heterosexual couples who had chosen each other in contravention of caste diktats. Police said their killers had sought to restore family honor. They were often sanctioned by elders in their communities, in the form of verdicts rendered by extrajudicial all-male tribunals, known as *khap panchayats*. They brought into sharp relief the impotence of law enforcement officials in the face of these informal authorities, which operated with impunity.

The Indian Express counted thirty-four reported honor killings in one North Indian state alone, Punjab, in the previous two and a half years leading up to the murder of Kuldeep and Monica, or roughly one each month.

In one of the most gruesome cases, in a village in the state of Haryana, next to Delhi, a couple was dragged off of a bus even after a local judge had ordered police to keep a watch over them. The young man was tied to the back of a car and dragged along a road until his body was reduced to pulp. The young woman's corpse was found in a ditch. The people of that village could rattle off several recent examples of honor killings nearby. In one hamlet, I was told, a man used a tractor to run over a daughter who had eloped, then strung her body from a tree so that it would serve as a lesson to others. *Khap panchayat* leaders sometimes blamed cell phones for encouraging unsanctioned romance. Also Facebook.

During that season of killings, which were covered widely by the Indian and foreign press, politicians by and large ducked for cover. The local elders who reigned over the *khap panchayats* could deliver votes at election time. Few lawmakers seemed to want to rein them in.

L et this be clear: I am not telling you this story of honor killing because I am keen to draw attention to the dreadful things that happen in India. That gives me no pleasure.

In my own Indian family, most people have chosen whom they married. My parents chose each other, and so did half of their siblings—some of them across caste lines. Some of my cousins, living in India, have had arranged marriages; some have not. The vast majority of my friends in India, gay and straight, have chosen their partners, though my gay friends cannot marry by law, even if they wanted to.

Across India today, honor killings are relatively rare.

More often than not, families accept intercaste marriages, rare as they are. For instance, Ankit and Prerna, the political activists who fell in love amid the anticorruption protests in Delhi, also married across caste lines, and also at an Arya Samaj temple, where so many of these defiant unions are consecrated. Neither of their families was thrilled about their decision, and both sides wanted the couple to wait a while before tying the knot. But in the end both families came around. They were not willing to lose their children forever.

I am telling you the story of Kuldeep and Monica's murders because they embody both desire and fury. They represent a power struggle, between those who pry open the old rules of blood and sex, and those who violently defend them.

I tell you their story because I am haunted by it. Kuldeep and Monica loved each other so openly. Their love changed those who loved them, in unexpected ways.

Honor killings, it seems to me, are part of a continuum of contempt against girls who try to control a piece of their destiny—and the men who collaborate with them. They happen not just in the Indian back of beyond. They happen in places of transition, among young people struggling to figure out who they are and who they can become.

It complicates our notion of what happens when a traditional society modernizes. Even those who become more prosperous, growing up in a modern, dynamic city, cling to some of the old norms. In so doing, they preserve the old pecking order.

It is an extreme example of how the most basic freedom is thwarted in my daughter's India: the freedom to love who you want.

If they are gay, the law is certainly not on their side.

One of the sharpest collisions on love came over a British-era law banning homosexuality. A clause in the Indian Penal Code, known as Section 377, made it a criminal offense to engage in "carnal intercourse against the order of nature." It was largely used to harass and humiliate gay men. For this reason, an HIV/AIDS advocacy group, the Delhi-based Naz Foundation, sought to overturn the law. Criminalizing homosexuality impeded AIDS prevention, the group argued in its lawsuit. It also violated a central tenet of the Constitution, it argued—the right to personal liberty.[5]

The lawsuit led to an extraordinary judicial ruling in 2009. A Delhi

High Court panel of judges rendered a portion of Section 377 unconstitutional, concluding that outlawing consensual sex among adults in private was indeed a violation of the fundamental right to liberty and equality.

The ruling riled religious conservatives. In an exceptional show of unity, a Christian evangelical group, an Islamic clerical lobby, a Hindu astrologer, and a self-described yogi filed a challenge in the Supreme Court. In the Supreme Court, these petitioners argued that any change in law regarding homosexuality must be made by the legislature, that it was too serious a matter to be handled by a court of law.

The Supreme Court judges deliberated over what could constitute "carnal" or "unnatural." acts. They discussed the legal ramifications of a man inserting his penis into the nose of a bullock, as well as a gynecologist inserting a hand into the vagina of a pregnant woman to ascertain the condition of the fetus. One of the Supreme Court judges mused aloud that he had never met a gay person.[6]

At the end of 2013, the Supreme Court overruled the lower court decision to overturn Section 377, effectively reinstating the ban on homosexuality. The judges averred that the matter would have to be taken up by the nation's lawmakers.

The leadership of the Bharatiya Janata Party at the time cheered the Supreme Court decision, calling homosexuality "unnatural." Narendra Modi, who was the party's candidate for prime minister at the time, said nothing about the verdict. I read that as strategic silence; he couldn't afford to alienate either his socially conservative foot soldiers in the Sangh or the young urban voters who might have been more libertarian.

The Congress party boss, Sonia Gandhi, said she was disappointed and suggested legislative redress.

The Aam Aadmi Party made the most explicit overture to the sentiments of a young, urban electorate. Indians who are "born with" or who "choose a different sexual orientation" should not be hounded by the law, the Aam Aadmi statement read. "This not only violates the human rights of such individuals," it went on to say, "but goes against the liberal values of our Constitution, *and the spirit of our times*" (my italics).

India is among seventy-six countries around the world that continue to criminalize consensual same-sex sexual conduct among adults, or have other laws on the books that allow their courts to prosecute gay and lesbian citizens.[7] It shares that distinction with countries of the Arab world and much of sub-Saharan Africa. Russia overturned its Soviet-era ban on homosexuality in 1993, but in 2014 a new law banned what it vaguely called "propaganda about nontraditional relationships."

A league of seven countries, including Iran and its regional rival, Saudi Arabia, considers same-sex sexual conduct to be punishable by death.

Gay rights seem to have little to do with a country's prosperity or even the trappings of modernity. It has to do with the limits of freedom, arguably the ultimate freedom—to choose who you are and who you love.

In May 2015, Ireland made history, when a majority of Irish voters passed a referendum allowing gay people to marry, signaling defeat for the Catholic Church, which had lobbied vigorously against it.

That same week, an Indian mom tried to place a matrimonial ad for her son. It read: "Seeking 25–40, Well Placed, Animal-Loving Vegetarian GROOM for my SON (36 5'11") who works with an NGO. Caste No Bar (Though IYER preferred)."[8]

The Times of India described it as the first gay matrimonial ad, which its own advertising department had rejected "for legal reasons," without citing specifics. Homosexuality was illegal, although no provision in the law barred marriage ads for a gay son. Another Bombay paper, called *Mid-Day*, ended up carrying the ad.

The woman who placed the ad, Padma Iyer, said that she wanted her son, Harish, to "settle down."

On the last Friday of June, the U.S. Supreme Court gave a nod to same-sex marriage, calling it a right guaranteed by the U.S. Constitution. "No longer may this liberty be denied," Justice Anthony M. Kennedy wrote as part of the majority opinion.

If my parents ever considered setting me up for an arranged marriage, with someone from my caste or my Bengali-speaking Hindu tribe, they never told me. I was not raised to be a good wife. Neither my mother nor father told me I had to learn to cook or iron shirts or stay at home to raise children.

I was expected to do well in school, to go to a good college (but not too far from home, where they couldn't keep an eye on me), and get a respectable job (becoming a foreign correspondent wasn't what they had in mind, certainly not one who would end up in faraway war zones). They assumed I would get married, "be settled," as Harish Iyer's mother put it, and inevitably, bear children.

My own worries were not really about settling down or finding a member of my tribe. I belong to a generation of extremely privileged women who can plan our destinies—or at least so I thought. I could choose my own career—it wasn't prescribed by my caste, though clearly I enjoyed a legacy of caste privileges, not least the right to learn. I could choose my lovers. I could choose whether and when to have children. The women's movement assured that women of my generation had access to contraception—and crucially to safe, legal abortions starting in 1973 (a full two years after India enshrined the right to abortion).

My own worries were about how to make it as a journalist, how to write about the world on my own terms.

For much of my twenties, I worried about whether I was responsible enough to raise a child, whether I had money enough to raise a child, whether the man I was with would be an asshole or a decent father. I worried whether a child would pinch my hard-won freedom. In my thirties, I worried that I would have to pay the mommy fine at work—that is to say, get paid less and promoted less often if I bore children. I started collecting information about how to adopt a child from India; I discovered the file folder many years later in a storage box.

At the time, I worried a lot, about a lot of things. I wanted no one to think that I was less able, less serious, less ready to hit the road and chase any story that was asked of me. Also, I loved my freedom.

It was never the right time to bear a child. I deferred. I never felt entitled.

Instead, I wrote about children. I never really intended to. I was just drawn to their stories. In Manhattan, I wrote about mothers and fathers who marched into a courtroom and signed over their troubled teenagers to the state. In Iraq, I wrote about teenaged girls whose lives were turned upside down after the U.S. invasion. In Congo, I wrote about a boy whose parents were dead and whose legs had been chewed up by shrapnel. I still remember his name. Jean de Dieu. John of God. I stood with him in front of a makeshift hospital on the day members of the United Nations Security Council came to visit. I wrote in *The New York Times*, "He especially liked watching the French soldiers who led the way, standing stiff in their jeeps with stylish sunglasses and menacing machine guns. Watching them, he said, took away his worries for a little while."[9]

For a moment I thought about taking Jean de Dieu home. It was an absurd idea. At the time, I traveled on average three weeks out of every month, covering godless wars like his. When I met him, I was sleeping in an abandoned convent around the corner from his hospital. The convent was deserted, except for a dozen journalists and an assortment of children who washed our clothes, swept our floor, and fetched bananas and soap from the market. "One dollar," they demanded for every chore I assigned.

It was never the right time. I never felt entitled.

By the time I chose a husband, I was already in my midthirties. I knew that my reproductive years were limited. But it still wasn't the right time. I was the first Indian-American in the bureau chief's job in New Delhi. I wanted no one to think I didn't take it seriously. So again, I deferred. Again, I wrote about children. The boy who blew out his ear in a Maoist guerrilla camp; the malnourished babies who resembled monkeys; a boy orphaned by the tsunami in Sri Lanka. (I wrote about him in the *Times*: "Baby No. 81's awful burden is not in being unwanted, but in being wanted too much.")

It's possible that the urge to be a mother was made more acute by living in India. A woman without a child is an oddity, a confounding creature and also everyone's business.

A pedicurist might look up at you in casual conversation and say, "Madam, no children? Why?"

The shopkeeper might probe casually. "Is it Sir who has the problem or you?"

The gynecologist might shout across the packed waiting room with your chart in her hands: "Still ovulating, no?"

By the time my India assignment was coming to an end, so were the excuses to defer. By this time I was forty. My husband was a year older. We signed up to adopt. In October 2009, we were given the most remarkable gift: a headstrong little girl whom we brought home from an orphanage; she was eighteen months old.

As my friend from Bombay reminds me, sometimes you have to accept your destiny. Not a day goes by that I don't thank my lucky stars.

The only grace that Kuldeep's father, Ajit, could see in the murder of his son and daughter-in-law—he referred to them once as "my children"—was that they were both gone. "If only one of them had been killed, the other would go mad," Ajit said.

The killings changed Kuldeep's family in ways that they could barely imagine at the time. They braced themselves for the consequences of a trial. A police officer was assigned to keep watch over them, in case the families of the accused tried to intimidate them—or do something worse—for cooperating with the prosecution.

The first time I went to visit the family, a few days after the murders, what caught my eye was a framed photo of Monica and Kuldeep hanging on the wall. It was taken at a studio shortly after they married. And in it, they posed shoulder to shoulder. His blue shirt matched her *dupatta*. Their eyes were on me this time.

Kuldeep's killing had the biggest impact on his brother, Amit—not least because he had just become a father for the first time.

It wasn't only for his brother's sake that Amit said he needed justice. It was also for his daughter. She was born just a month before the murders. Kuldeep had chosen her name—Harika—after scouring the Internet.

Fatherhood changed Amit. He began to question many of the rules he grew up with, including the ones on love and marriage. He became convinced that these rules would have to disappear in the world his daughter would inherit—and he seemed to know exactly when.

Arranged marriage, he predicted, would be history in five years. Caste, he said, would vanish in ten, maximum fifteen years. His daughter would live in a different kind of country. "Tradition has changed. The new generation wants to live the way they are," he said.

It was hard not to be moved by Amit's convictions. Becoming Harika's father, he said, had changed his perspective. He was seeing the traditions he had grown up with through her eyes. And he didn't like all of what he saw.

I asked him if he imagined an arranged marriage for his daughter. Amit offered a bashful smile. Ideally, he said, he would like to find a good husband for her—but it would be fine with him if she chose for herself.

By the time Harika was two and a half, Amit's principal obsession was to find a good school for her. "I dream she becomes a big personality of the nation," he said. "An icon. In any field. It's her life."

By then, Harika was already ruling the household. This afternoon, she ran circles around her father, as we sat in the one air-conditioned room in the house. He on the bed, me on a plastic chair rolled out for guests. Harika wanted her father's full attention. She demanded that he play with her. She stuffed cookies into her mouth. Amit's wife, Reshu, was busy in the kitchen. She was pregnant with their second child.

I asked Amit whether he wanted a boy or a girl next. He insisted that he did not care one bit. He said that he would not subject his wife to an ultrasound to check the sex of the fetus. And anyway, after this child, there would be no more. Two were enough. "In the present day, I don't feel there's a difference between a son and a daughter," he said gamely.

His wife had a different perspective. Reshu said that her father-in-law had made it clear he wanted a male heir. And so this is what she prayed for too.

You know how some lovers are. They think there's no one else on earth. They whisper to each other on the phone, as if no one's listening. They glow from head to toe and pretend like no one notices. They look at each other and forget there is such a thing as death.

Kuldeep and Monica were lovers like that. Reshu was struck by their intensity. They couldn't bear to be without each other. If Monica went to her mother's house for a *puja*, she would soon call and ask him to come and join her. Once, when Monica broke a nail, Kuldeep rushed home from work to comfort her. Who ever heard of such a thing? Reshu giggled at the memory.

Together, they could look like movie stars. Stylish. Going places. Happier than they were supposed to be.

In Reshu's eyes, Monica was a modern girl. She wore lipstick even when she was just at home. She had a way of hiking her sunglasses above her head like a celebrity. She wore jeans and capris—but also, like a good wife, a *mangalsutra* around her neck, to let the world know she belonged to someone. Monica had once wanted to teach in a preschool, but Kuldeep didn't like that idea. So she didn't push it. She stayed at home.

Reshu and Monica spoke to each other on the phone every day. What are you cooking? Reshu would ask. Why don't you trim your hair? Monica would suggest. Don't wear so many bangles. Be a little modern, which Reshu admits she is not. Reshu doesn't even walk to the market by herself. If she needs something, she asks a neighbor to walk to the store with her, usually an older woman. Or her husband takes her where she wants to go.

I asked Reshu about love marriage. She thought about it for a second. She said she considered her own marriage to be sort of a love marriage. The families arranged the union. But she was allowed to speak to Amit on the phone after the elders had decided on the match. Then, she said, she fell in love.

In January 2013, Reshu gave birth to their second child. Amit sent me an email. "God has blessed me with a baby boy," he wrote.

I went to Monica's family house twice. The first time, right after the killings, in the summer of 2010; no one answered the door, though I could hear voices inside. The second time, two and a half years later, I was greeted by Monica's youngest brother, nicknamed Shanky, who was lolling around at home at three in the afternoon. He was a student at a spiffy private school nearby. His teacher described him as restless, a boy who was uninterested in class, disruptive, often a bully who sought to be the center of attention.

Shanky let me into their home. He wasn't interested in talking. I can't say I blamed him. It was he who discovered her body on the night of her murder, lying in a pool of blood. His older brother was in jail for her murder. The family was ruined.

As for the other two suspects. I picked up few details about their lives. Both of them had attended school, though neither had distinguished himself academically. Neither had a full-time job. Their families owned property. They could afford to eat well, drink well. They could buy jeans, cell phones, and motorcycles of their own. They didn't have to eke out a living on the fields as their grandfathers had once. They didn't have to break their backs on a factory floor like their tenants did. Or drive auto-rickshaws. Or mop floors. They didn't even have to roll chapatis: that was their mothers' work, their sisters' work.

They lived comfortably by Wazirpur standards. They lived by Wazir-pur rules too. They saw themselves as the guardians of Wazirpur's rules, when it came to their sisters at least, when *their* aspirations became too much.

Five years after the killings, they were still in jail, pending trial. Amit wanted them to hang.

Amit considered moving out of Wazirpur once the verdict was finally delivered. He feared there could be trouble if the boys were convicted.

But moving would not be easy. Delhi had become a very expensive city. Anyway, Wazirpur was home. For generations the family had been on this land. Would it be good to be here when Harika would come of age? Amit wasn't sure.

"The mind-set of this village is very old," he said.

CURSE
A Father's Fears,
a Daughter's Dreams

Saturday night, suburban Gurgaon. The sky turns from blue to black, the burnt-toast smell of fireworks blows across the ravine, and tall, broad-shouldered Varsha hauls a hot-coal iron over the shimmering finery of others.

Quietly, quickly, she presses the wrinkles out of a brushed pink chiffon *salwar-kameez*, another the color of *nimboo-pani*, followed by three button-down white dress shirts. Her cell phone trills. "Yes, *didi*. It's almost ready. Send your driver in ten minutes."

Didi is a customer with a wedding to attend, perhaps several, since it is wedding season, and many *didis* around town have many weddings to attend. Firecrackers begin to boom-snap in the distance. They will go on past midnight. It is Varsha's job to make sure *didis* don't show up to their parties all rumpled.

And so she presses their clothes, places them on hangers, one after the other, *futt-a-futt*, racing against the clock. Left hand on cloth, right hand on iron, she removes every crease, every wrinkle. If only she could press away her worries this way, I think.

Varsha is seventeen, every bit the dreamer, like the IIT-striving

Anupam. She too is born to a family of modest means. She too wants to rise. The difference is that Varsha is a girl, and she doesn't have a mother like his Sudha, willing to move mountains for her.

And so Varsha tries to move mountains herself. She aspires to go to college and to one day be financially independent. She dreams of being a cop, gold stars on her shoulders, capable of protecting herself from the louts out there who harass and abuse girls. This conviction becomes all the more urgent after her country is roiled by the gang-rape of a young woman in late 2012.

Varsha finds beauty in Kathak. For a while, she fantasizes about learning to play guitar. In her head, day and night, she hears a hot, impatient voice: I am not bound by my past. I make me.

She is one among many.

Varsha's ambitions alternately bemuse her father and make him sick with worry. There is no question of her becoming a cop, as far as he is concerned. By the time she is twenty, he intends to find her a husband— from a good family, of course from the same caste, with a capacity to earn and protect his child. If the in-laws allow, she can work. Kathak lessons are out of the question. Likewise, guitar. It will not improve her marriage prospects.

Varsha regards her papa as her ally, but he is also her obstacle. He loves her but he also sabotages her. He too wants her to break free of her past—but not too much. She keeps pushing the bounds, and he has to figure out how far to let her go.

Varsha is born to a community of *dhobis*, whose ritual occupation is to clean other people's dirty clothes. The advent of washing machines has tweaked the caste norms. *Dhobis* have become press-*wallahs*. They take rumpled piles of machine-washed clothes, press them, fold them, and return them to their owners.

Varsha's father, Madan Mohan, is a pioneer in Gurgaon. He moves to the new city in 1998. Varsha is a baby then, and Gurgaon is too. The very first suburban villas come up. A smattering of gated communities are under construction.

In the pressing business, location is everything. And being first in this emerging suburb gives Madan Mohan a chance to corner the market early. He establishes a press stand, which is no more than a flat piece of tin held up by four sturdy bamboo trunks. Under the tin roof stands a cement platform with a smooth piece of marble on top, courtesy of Varsha's uncle, who has moved up the ladder from the *dhobi* line and into construction. The family erects their press stand at the intersection of two dead-end streets, on the edge of a ravine of *neem* and acacia. In those early days, you can see straight across the valley all the way to sunset. Antelopes slink out of the bush to explore. Varsha is just learning to walk.

Soon, all around the press stand, villas and high-rises spring up—and with them come customers with piles of cottons and silks to be pressed. Varsha's parents work the press stand in the early days. As soon as she can find her way around the neighborhood, Varsha starts going house to house to pick up and deliver. When her sisters learn to walk, she takes them along on her rounds. The girls become a fixture on these blocks. They march up and down the streets with bundles on their heads—tidy, warm stacks, neatly contained in old bedsheets: button-down shirts, linen trousers, *salwars*, saris. Sometimes, men even send old *chaddis* to be pressed. Varsha giggles at the thought that a man would want hot, pressed underwear.

Varsha grows up in the press stand. She learns how to load coal into the heavy iron. She learns how to haul it across cloth. Once Papa accidentally brushes a hot iron against her hand. It leaves a permanent black scar.

In time, her father gets a gig washing towels for a neighborhood beauty parlor. He buys a secondhand washing machine. He props it up on a pair of bricks behind the press stand, and plugs it into a jerry-rigged power cord that looks like it bursts out of the bush, until city authorities get wind of it and crack down. They accuse him of encroaching on public land, eventually letting him continue to press clothes, but snipping the water and electricity connections. The washing machine has to be moved into the family's tiny two-room apartment. Varsha has to wash the salon towels at home. Her sisters have to spread them out on an empty field to dry—and guard against pooping crows.

By the time Varsha is three, Papa saves up enough money to diversify the family business. He buys an auto-rickshaw, packing as many passengers into the puttering three-wheeler as he can. A few years later, he buys a second, which he rents out to a driver who hasn't yet saved up enough to buy his own. Gurgaon's population is burgeoning by this time, there are hardly any public buses, and auto-rickshaws are in high demand. The auto business provides the family a solid, steady income, but not enough to discard the pressing business altogether, which Varsha's mother runs. Each daughter pitches in. I never see Varsha's brother, Badal, being put to work.

Madan Mohan is sure of one thing about the *dhobi* business. He wants none of his children to inherit it. Nor does he want his daughters to marry into it. A *dhobi*'s wife must work all day, standing over a hot iron, which means that by the time she gets home, she is too tired to do much housework. A woman is better off staying in the house, in his view, looking after the children. And anyway, a *dhobi*'s work is neither easy nor valued. You work outside all day—in the heat, in the rain, in the cold. And at the end of it, he says, a greedy developer can come and toss you out.

When Varsha is six, he finds a school for her. It is ideal for his purposes. It is nearby. It costs nothing. And classes are held in afternoons, which means Varsha can help her mother in the mornings and then go to school.

What a boon it turns out to be for Varsha. The school is run by a charity. And the reason it holds classes in the afternoons is that it borrows space from one of the posh private schools serving Gurgaon's privileged—or what Varsha will one day call "the elite sections of society," including, a few years later, Supriya's sheltered daughter. In the morning come the children of bankers and ad executives. In the afternoon stream in the children of *dhobis* and drivers. The school is blessed with all the things that the neighborhood government-run school lacks: tables and chairs, educational posters on the walls, teachers who show up. Classes are conducted in English.

Varsha loves it.

She absorbs everything the school offers: math, songs, history. And then she runs back to the press stand to help Mummy.

Shubha, one of the first homeowners on the block, remembers seeing Varsha march up and down these streets, one hand balancing a bundle of clothes on her head, the other gripping her little sister's wrist. She must have been seven at the time.

Shubha observes her closely. The girl is unusual. No wallflower, this one. Quite the opposite. She is inquisitive and impatient, even pushy at times. When Varsha brings her stacks of pressed clothes, Shubha lets her linger in her house and read books from her own library. Soon, Varsha is barging through her gates and demanding help with homework. Eventually, she is allowed to settle herself in front of the family computer. By the time Varsha is in Class 9, she has enlisted Shubha's entire family into service. The daughter helps with English, the son tutors her in physics. I am just getting to know Varsha around this time, and Shubha warns me: Varsha can be in your face, she says, not impolite exactly, just unrestrained. Shubha is struck by her intensity.

"My own children," Shubha says, "don't have the aspiration that she has."

Fire in the belly is what I call it. Like Anupam. Except that Anupam had his mother's prayers to float on. And Varsha—she has her mother's demons to contend with.

What exactly her mother, Santosh, suffers from is not quite clear. Its first signs emerge after the birth of Varsha's sister, Neetu, two years younger. Mummy screams. Mummy doesn't get out of bed. She does not breast-feed. There are other times of trouble that Varsha recalls. Mummy wakes up screaming at night, or she stays in bed for days at a time. Whatever ails her, it is Varsha who learns that Papa needs her help to hold the family together. Childhood vanishes as quickly as it begins.

Varsha is in Class 6 when Mummy has another episode, which costs her four weeks of school. In Class 9, Papa lands in hospital with dengue fever; Varsha misses her year-end exams. Where she lives, there are dirty puddles in the streets, and they are lush, hot vats of mosquitoes and disease. Later that same year, Varsha herself comes down with chikungunya. Another three weeks of school gone. Many girls would drop out; me too if I were in her shoes. Varsha does not. School is her refuge. It is where she can prove her mettle. It is where she finds beauty, in song and dance and poetry. School is to be her exit ticket from the press stand.

Papa agrees to let her finish high school, but mainly to improve her marriage prospects. He knows only louts will marry a girl without a high school degree nowadays.

By the time she is fourteen, which is when I first meet her, in the winter of 2010, she and her mother do most of the pressing. Her younger sisters, Neetu and Megha, pick up and deliver. Badal, the first son in the family, born after three daughters, mostly plays. The baby suckles at his mummy's breast.

Varsha juggles the pressing among her many other obligations. It falls on her to roll chapatis every evening, dozens of them, one after the other—and so many do they all eat, her family of seven, that by the time she is done, she has little energy left for homework. She worries about exams. She worries about the useless government school where Badal and Megha are enrolled. She worries about a useless boy she likes, who has no ambition to speak of, but whom she talks to quietly on her cell phone every night. She worries that if she keeps on with it, there will be terrible consequences. "Papa will kill me," she says.

Varsha's father takes his responsibilities seriously. He tries to protect her from harm. At the same time, he is the chief enforcer of the very traditions that circumscribe her dreams. He keeps putting up fences around her. He keeps stopping her from becoming who she can be.

"I have been pressing clothes all my life," he says once. "The main thing I want for my children is that they do something better."

It is a bland answer to a bland question about his hopes for Varsha, but it fills Varsha's eyes with tears to hear her father speak this way. She turns around and buries her head on his shoulder, which catches him by surprise. He awkwardly pats her on the back.

He is pleased with her progress at school, but not always. He worries she is becoming too independent. "She is growing wings," he once complains to her school principal. "She's talking back."

Varsha pushes the limits, finds herself pushed back, pushes some more. She is a child in an impossible situation. She has gulped the Kool-Aid of aspirational India. Deep inside, she believes she can make something of herself. She is convinced school is her best exit strategy. And so she has risen to all its demands: studied, scored well on the critical exams, become captain of the girls volleyball team. She has risen to the demands of family too: hung towels to dry, helped with dinner, made sure her siblings do their homework, made sure Mummy takes her medicines, and smoothed out crease after crease after crease. Not a child and still a child.

I get Varsha. She is like so many girls I have known. Obedient and dutiful, we keep our heads down and do as we're told. We mostly follow the rules, but we dream of escape. Despair catches us when we least expect it, and we wonder why.

Violence against girls seems to preoccupy Varsha's papa. He hears terrifying stories about what happens to girls who are in the wrong place at the wrong time. He tells me about a barber's daughter, no more than five years old, who had gone to temple for a free meal, only to be abducted by a man, raped, and dumped at a traffic circle nearby. Every time he drives by that traffic circle, and usually it is several times a day, it makes him shudder to think of a girl raped and dumped like that.

He is exceptionally protective. He doesn't let Varsha walk home from the press stand after dark. Even in the middle of the afternoon, when Varsha gets out of school, he doesn't let her go anywhere—neither to a friend's house, nor to a neighborhood study hall. Nowhere but straight to the press stand. He demands that she call him as soon as she gets there, and that better be by 2:20 P.M., which is exactly how long it takes her to walk from school. The streets are not safe, he says. They are especially not safe for Varsha, who is by now tall and curvy, as full of adventure and desire as only a teenaged girl can be.

Varsha grows into a young woman at a time when the safety of women and girls takes center stage in the public life of her country. It fills her father with foreboding, and he tries to rein her in even more. And it makes her all the more determined to become a cop.

It suits her personality, she tells me. "I'm like a boy at school," she says, by which she means that unlike other girls, she never asks boys to help her, say, lift a heavy chair in the classroom. She is usually the one helping others. "I'm independent. I can do my work. My nickname at school is 'Proactive.'"

It's true. She's bossy—in a really good way. A girl born to more privilege might be described as a leader. Fearless and tough.

Varsha was sixteen when a young woman, just a few years older, was gang-raped not far from Varsha's home, on the southern edge of Delhi. The woman was not so different from Varsha: ambitious, smart, hardworking, studying to be a physiotherapist, and poised to leap from a life of working-with-hands to working-with-head.

It happened on December 16, 2012, when the city shivered from a cold spell and the smell of coal fires hung low in the night air. The woman was home from college for the holidays that Sunday. She had met a friend, a young man who worked as an IT specialist. They had gone to the mall, to see a movie that everyone was talking about, *Life of Pi*. On the way home, she was assaulted by five men, plus a juvenile, who had been joyriding all night on a private bus. They jammed a steel rod inside her, which perforated her intestines. They beat her male friend. They threw them both on the road, naked.

I was in Delhi the morning that the news of the gang-rape broke. I learned of it when a friend with whom I was staying burst into the guest room with the day's papers. "Gang-rape nation," she spat. She was furious. She insisted that I not raise my daughter in India.

The news uncorked grief and rage across the country. Every day came a new revelation that infuriated people even more. It was revealed that the woman's assailants had earlier that evening robbed and assaulted a day laborer, dumped him on the side of a road too, and assumed—correctly, as it turned out—that he wouldn't have bothered to file a police complaint. In news reports, it emerged that the couple had languished on the side of a busy road for close to an hour that night before police came, and even after they came, police debated for a while about which police district was responsible for handling the investigation. The woman bled.

Two nights after the gang-rape, as I was getting ready to fly home to the United States, four of my friends gathered for a meal. We couldn't talk about anything else. It seemed no one could. My friends, all Indian, ranged in age from their thirties to their fifties. They were all women who had been raised to think of themselves as no less than men. They were all smart, kind, funny, and accomplished in their fields—precisely the women I wanted my daughter to grow up around.

Each of them had a story of degradation.

The oldest among them, a lawyer in her early fifties, recalled that some years ago, someone kept scrawling lewd messages on her car window while it was parked in the basement garage of her office building in the commercial center of Delhi. It rattled her. It took her weeks to get to the bottom of it, only to discover that it had been the handiwork of the parking attendant.

"Just the idea of a woman driving to work was too much for him," my friend surmised. It left her so freaked out that for a while she was afraid of going down to the parking lot by herself late at night. She was compelled to ask a male colleague to walk with her. This humiliated her doubly.

The youngest among them, a lawyer, recalled sitting in a Delhi courtroom, listening to the case of a woman who had eloped with her boyfriend. The girl's parents, who were present, had accused the boyfriend of having kidnapped their daughter; and now they were willing to drop the charges and accept the marriage. The judge was no naïf. "If your daughter comes to any harm," the judge warned them, "you will be punished." It was a reference to what had happened to countless girls who had married against the wishes of their families: they were killed, by their own families.

This woman's brother, barely a man himself, leaned over to their mother and said, loud enough for everyone to hear: "Having a girl is your punishment."

I thought of Monica, across town in Wazirpur, and her brother, charged with her murder.

The woman on the bus lived long enough to tell her entire story to the police. Two weeks later, she suffered massive organ failure and died. By then, protests had broken out in city after city. Day after day, women and men, most of them young, braved the cold to come out into the streets of Delhi and sometimes also brave the water cannons of riot police. "*Azaadi,*" they chanted, which is the word for "freedom" in Hindi. "Freedom at day. Freedom at night." The rape and its aftermath were covered widely in the Indian and international media. I have pieced together her story from those news reports.

Certainly, there had been other widely publicized sexual assaults before.[1]

Still, the December 2012 gang-rape resonated widely because the woman on the bus was so much like so many of her generation—the very portrait of aspiration. She was raised in a working-class warren in Delhi. Her father worked as a baggage handler at the airport. In newspaper accounts, neighbors described her as a studious child, the family's hope, the one who was on her way to getting out of the ghetto and making something of herself. Her parents believed in her. They sold a patch of land back in their village to pay her college fees. One of her college professors described her as "punctual and hardworking." I made a note of this. I thought about Varsha.

It wasn't just the woman on the bus who was emblematic of her generation. So too were her rapists. They lived in a tin-roof ghetto in the center of Delhi, encircled by five-star hotels. They were mostly in their twenties. They had all come from the countryside for a better life in the city. They were all uneducated and marginally employed. The man who drove the bus drove that same bus to ferry children to and from school. His brother, who was a co-conspirator, sometimes drove a taxi. With them was a fruit seller, a young man who worked part-time at a local gym, and a seventeen-year-old who somehow made ends meet by washing dishes at roadside lunch counters. "There was nothing very extraordinary about them," *The Guardian* pointed out in a richly reported portrait of these men.[2]

Police arrested the six almost immediately. There were angry calls for them to be hanged. One was found dead in a Delhi jail cell. Four were sentenced to death; they are appealing. The juvenile among them was sentenced to a maximum jail term of three years.

The protests that sprang from the rape seem to catch politicians completely off guard. Prime Minister Manmohan Singh, the father of three accomplished daughters, didn't speak out for the first several days, nor did the head of the ruling Congress party, Sonia Gandhi. The depth of outrage, especially among the young, seemed lost on them.

Several other politicians, when they did speak out, showed themselves to be woefully out of touch with the sentiments of a generation. One member of parliament, who was also the son of the Indian president, said on national television that the women protesting did not appear to be young but rather "dented and painted," which is a term used to describe old cars that are patched up with copious coats of paint.

A politician in Rajasthan, where Varsha's people are from, proposed that skirts be outlawed as part of school uniforms.

A Hindu religious leader suggested that the victim was to blame too, because she didn't sufficiently implore her attackers to stop. Penetration, he asserted, requires the actions of two individuals. "Can one hand clap? I don't think so," he was quoted as saying.

With public anger boiling, the government appointed a committee of retired jurists to recommend how to address violence against women.

The committee produced a remarkable report. It called out political and religious leaders for "gender bias"; it faulted police and courts for failing to protect women from harassment and assault; and it recommended overhauling laws dealing with rape and sexual harassment.

It went on to remind India's leaders of the promise made at independence and listed all the ways in which women had been cheated, concluding bluntly: "de facto equality guaranteed by the Constitution has not become a reality for them."

The report was released in January 2013, on the eve of Republic Day, as India marked the birth of its constitution. In the face of persistent protests, the parliament quickly passed a batch of new laws to stiffen penalties for assaults against women.

The protests drew attention to campaigns by women's groups to make Indian cities safer by doing simple things: installing better streetlights near bus stops and subway entrances, repairing sidewalks, making sure public toilets are clean. And the protesters called for women cops—many, many more women cops.[3]

The streets of Delhi, the country's capital, are notoriously unfriendly for women. A 2010 study by an advocacy group called Jagori found that two out of three women in New Delhi said they were subjected to sexual harassment between two and five times during the past year.[4] Surveys of men's attitudes were equally revealing. For instance, a poll conducted in late 2012 by the *Hindustan Times* found that half of all Indian men between the ages of eighteen and twenty-five said a woman in a short skirt was inviting trouble.[5]

Varsha's father seemed to have a good read on those sentiments. By the time she was seventeen, he did not like her wearing a skirt as part of her school uniform.

Ever since the 2012 gang-rape, I have been asked repeatedly: Are women more likely to be raped in India than in other countries around the world?

No. There is no data to suggest that's the case. It is pretty much impossible to get sound data on the incidence of rape and other forms of violence against women—in India and in many, many other countries. Stigma runs high. Reporting remains low. Police and prosecutors can be ignorant or insensitive or both.

What we do know is that the reported rates of violence against women in India roughly mirror the rates of violence that women face world-wide. The World Health Organization, which looked at survey data from around the world, found that roughly one in three women—35 percent—said that in their lifetimes, they had experienced "intimate partner violence and/or non-partner sexual violence." One in ten girls under the age of eighteen was forced to have sex, a separate study found.[6]

The corollary to this question, which rightly rankles defenders of Indian women's rights, is this: Is there something about Indian culture or the mind-set of its men that makes them so brutal? So much attention has the December 2012 gang-rape drawn to India that Kavita Krishnan, a prominent feminist activist, says she has started to school foreigners on how not to talk about rape in India.[7]

What *is* true about rape in India is also true about rape elsewhere. First, rape survivors are not always keen to file a crime report. And second, their assaulters are usually men they know—friends, neighbors, or family members.

What is notable about India is that rape in particular—and violence against women in general—has seized the public imagination like never before. Girls and women are refusing to keep quiet about it anymore. They are pouring into the streets to protest, sometimes braving water cannons. And many more of them are filing police reports.

In Delhi alone, there were 1493 rapes reported to police in the first eleven months of 2013, more than double the number reported in the same period of 2012. Complaints of sexual harassment went up sharply too.

Nationally, there was already a steady uptick in reported crimes against women. Between 2006 and 2010, the total number of reported crimes against women, including rape, increased by 29.6 percent, according to national crime records.[8] That did not necessarily mean that incidents of rape had gone up. It likely signaled that women reported them more often. It's worth noting that conviction rates for rape remain lower than for other violent crimes.

All of which is to say, a once hidden problem—particularly in the countryside, where rape has long been a way for upper-caste men to subjugate lower-caste women—was becoming less hidden.

The December 2012 gang-rape seemed to have emboldened survivors. In June 2013, a thirty-seven-year-old Calcutta woman appeared on television and described how she had been gang-raped over a year ago, and how she had only now felt brave enough to speak about it.

In August, a photojournalist in Mumbai went to police to report that she was gang-raped by five men at an abandoned industrial building. A receptionist came forward and said she had been assaulted by the same men earlier, but hadn't filed a report out of shame. (The men in court said they were innocent.) Three months later, a lawyer accused a retired Supreme Court judge of having sexually harassed her when she worked for him as an intern. A journalist accused her boss of assaulting her in a hotel elevator. Equally important, the woman told her friends that very night there was no question she would keep quiet about it. The man she accused was jailed, pending trial.

My friend the writer and editor Priya Ramani wrote pointedly in the financial paper *Mint*: "This will be known as the year rapists, sexual molesters, perverts, predators and assorted other Indian creeps realized they can no longer count on that one big assumption that makes them so brazen; Indian women don't like sharing horror stories."[9]

The Constitution of India, which went into effect in 1950, enshrined equal franchise for men and women. This was an extraordinary edict for a society where women like my grandmother ate only after the men of the family—and then the children—had had their fill. Many women still do.

Equally extraordinary, since then, India's lawmakers have passed specific measures designed to redress the marginalization of women in life and politics. The most radical of these was a 1993 constitutional amendment that set aside seats for women in village governance councils. The law required that in every village, one in three council members would have to be a woman. It further stipulated quotas for Dalit women, those considered "untouchable" on the caste ladder and traditionally the most powerless.

Critics said the quota system was misguided: women sat on these councils in name only, while their husbands and sons remained the real decision makers. This may have been true in certain cases. But women's participation also brought tangible changes to their communities. Councils that were led by women, showed one study, were more likely to invest public funds in things that women considered more valuable—like building and repairing drinking-water wells.[10]

One wonders how federal government funds would be spent if India's parliament was also required by law to have one-third representation by women. One can keep wondering. A bill to extend the women's quota to the national legislature has languished for years. Parliament remains a predominantly male province: about 12 percent of the 543 elected members of the lower house are women. (Women's representation is far higher in many other parliamentary democracies worldwide.)

The women's quota in village councils coincided with a series of other events that irreversibly changed women's lives. The economic reforms that began in 1991 created new private-sector job opportunities, for men and women both, and with it, new social norms. Education was the most obvious example. Illiterate mothers began to send their girls to school, knowing that only an education could improve the girls' chances of getting a job and also getting a husband with a job.

Between 2000 and 2010, more women than men became literate, though female literacy overall remains lower than male. By 2013, female enrollment in primary school peaked at close to 100 percent. Women started marrying slightly later in life, though by global standards, they remained among the youngest to marry: on average, around age twenty-one. One government survey, carried out in 2013–2014, found that among women aged twenty to twenty-four, nearly one in three was married before turning eighteen.[11]

The opening of the economy created new kinds of jobs. As private airlines sprouted, women could work as pilots as well as flight attendants. They could legally work as bartenders, after the Supreme Court in 2007 overturned a colonial-era law that had prohibited women in the capital, New Delhi, from mixing drinks. Armies of women went to work at call centers. But social norms around women working outside the home were oddly slow to change. While girls' education soared and the economy grew rapidly, women's participation in the labor force actually went down. Less than 30 percent of women worked for a living in 2011, placing India near the bottom among 131 countries with available data.[12]

When I posted, on Facebook, an essay about how this would hold back India's economic advance, Varsha quietly clicked "Like."

For every story that testified to improvements, there was another that spoke of degradation.

In 2006, shortly after I had moved to India, dozens of little bones were found at the bottom of a well behind a private clinic near Patiala, a prosperous city in Punjab state. Police said the doctor there had conducted ultrasound tests to determine the sex of the unborn children and had then aborted unwanted females for a fee. The following year female fetuses were discovered in Gurgaon. Stories like this came at a regular clip. A government-appointed committee, in a 2012 report to the prime minister, warned of "a silent demographic disaster in the making."

A study published in *The Lancet*, an international public-health journal, estimated that between 1990 and 2005, up to 12 million female fetuses were aborted. That was the period when ultrasound machines became increasingly accessible, enabling many more parents to learn the sex of the fetus. Sex determination tests are illegal, but this law, like so many others, seems to have been flouted routinely.[13]

India has one of the most skewed sex ratios of any country in the world. Among children under the age of fifteen, there are 1.13 boys for every girl. Only China is worse. Thanks to its one-child policy, by 2011, there were 1.17 boys for every girl in the same age cohort. They came to be known in Chinese as "bare branches," who would eventually have to care for their elderly parents and who would inevitably, one day, find it hard to marry. (For sake of comparison, the male-to-female ratio in the United States is 1.05 boys for every girl.) The numbers tend to be worse in cities, because that is where maternity clinics are more likely to have ultrasound machines.[14]

Relatedly, girls are far more likely to be abandoned and put up for adoption. In 2013, there were nearly 3000 girls in the formal adoption system, compared with 1800 boys.[15]

A girl's chances of surviving her fifth birthday are slimmer than a boy's. That could be because she is not fed as well, or not as likely to be taken to the doctor when she falls sick. By their teenage years, half of all Indian girls are anemic, a condition that makes them feel tired, weak, and sometimes unable to produce enough breast milk for their own babies. Fewer than half of all pregnant women get prenatal care. One in 70 women risks dying in childbirth; by comparison, in Vietnam, which is not nearly as wealthy a country as India, that figure is one in 280.

One study found recently that the money that a family invests in a pregnant woman falls off noticeably after she bears a son. Apparently she is more valuable if there's a chance that she is carrying a boy in her womb.[16]

I find it hard to be hopeful about whether this attitude will turn around by the time my girl grows up. Valerie Hudson and Andrea Den Boer, two academics who study gender issues worldwide, conclude that the status of women and girls in India reflects "the profound devaluation of female life."[17]

Scholars are increasingly beginning to wonder whether gender balance also has something to do with gender violence. That is to say, could an unnatural surplus of young men in a given society be a symptom of violence against women—and simultaneously, a cause?

In China, one study found that as the sex ratio of a province grew more imbalanced, so too was there a measurable increase in violent crime between 1988 and 2004. The authors looked at data from province to province, homing in on the period when the one-child policy was enforced, resulting in a corresponding rise of men in the population. They concluded that where there was a 0.01 increase in the sex ratio, violent crimes and property crimes went up by 3 percent. The suspects were largely men between age sixteen and twenty-five. The authors surmised that "the increasing maleness of the young adult population" offered at least a partial explanation for the rise in overall crime.[18]

I am not persuaded that a skewed sex ratio *causes* more violence against women. A correlation between those two things is not enough to prove that one causes the other.

Guy Standing, a University of London economist, has coined the term "precariat." A play on the notion of proletariat, he uses the term to refer to men who are by-products of globalization, "living and working precariously, usually in a series of short-term jobs, without recourse to stable occupational identities, social protection or protective regulations."

There are many of them loping about in my daughter's India. They find themselves at knife's edge, without enough land to live on in the countryside and without enough skills to get a good job in the city. What they do have—or they think they have—is just enough power to kick the women and girls around them.

I find Varsha walking home from school with her friends one afternoon, past an empty field strewn with garbage, then through a gated community, whose guards let the schoolkids through, because it's a shortcut, then across the rushing river of traffic of the Mehrauli–Gurgaon Road. The sky turns orange-gray, a harbinger of the hot dust that will blow in from the Rajasthan desert, farther west. Then the sky turns purple. Skyscraper lights come on, and construction debris and sand and waste rise and swirl through the air. On days like this, it doesn't seem like a bad idea to shield your face with a *dupatta*.

Varsha is now fifteen. She is straight-backed and loud-mouthed and prone to boxing a schoolboy on the ears if she needs to. She is a popular kid, a joker and the one among her friends least afraid to step out and cross the street, braving cars that may or may not stop for a gaggle of schoolgirls with plaited hair and gray *salwar-kameez* uniforms and over-stuffed knapsacks.

A gaggle of skinny young men, not in school uniforms, are leaning against a fence and making catcalls as Varsha and her friends pass by. The girls don't even look up. It is so routine. This is why Papa doesn't want her walking around by herself.

Varsha signs up for everything that school offers: volleyball, debate team, something called the English Olympiad, Kathak dance class. It means she has less time to help with chores, less time for pressing. It becomes a source of domestic strife. On one occasion, Papa wants her to attend a family wedding; Varsha refuses, because it means missing a full week of school. Another time, Varsha wants to attend a school-run dance competition that would take her out of state; Papa refuses. He races over to the school, parks his auto-rickshaw at the gates, and marches up the stairs to the office to stare down the principal, Raji Nambissan, from across her wide wooden desk. Not in a million years will Varsha go to a dance competition out of state, he says.

He also tells the principal what happened to his own niece who got too much schooling, went off to college, and fell in love with a boy from another caste. The girl ran away and eloped with him. It caused a scandal in the family.

This is also when he tells Nambissan that he doesn't like Varsha growing wings.

Nambissan, an unflappable woman with nearly three decades of experience in dealing with parents of many varieties, tells me there is little she can do to change the minds of men like Varsha's father. Education is a double-edged sword for men like him, she says. They want their girls to be educated, but they don't want their girls to think for themselves. Nambissan takes pains to point out that this applies not just to Varsha's class of poor people. It is also true of her own more privileged social class.

"*Choop raho ghar-pay.* That's the attitude," she says. It literally means "Be quiet at home." Which also means: Do not defy.

"I call it a civilized way of slavery," the principal continues. "They're ready to give exposure to education. But there's a limit. They don't want them to argue."

Varsha is fifteen when she overhears relatives talk about finding a groom for her. This only stiffens her resolve. She vows to herself that she will score so high on her school exams that Papa will be forced to stave off marriage talk.

The ones who come to Nambissan's school are the children of Gurgaon's worker bees. They are all one generation away from the village. They grow up with their noses pressed against Gurgaon's high-rise air-conditioned condos, like the one Supriya and her family occupy. They grow up in the one- or two-room flats squeezed in between those high-rises, amid the drunken brawls of their neighbors and the dengue that strikes postmonsoon, and the neon promise of noonday.

The school eventually raises enough money to move out of the posh kids' schoolhouse that Supriya's children go to and into a building of its own, at the end of a narrow road, next to a ramshackle spread of tarp and tin, as though to remind every child, all through the day, of the perils of getting stuck here.

Nambissan's students are survivors. One is an orphan who lives with an abusive uncle. Another suffered second-degree burns when a kerosene tank exploded and sent ripples of flames through her narrow lane. Just before the Commonwealth Games began in 2010, police swept through the slums and chased away those without valid identification, which meant that many of Nambissan's students vanished for a few months.

For most of her wards, school is a refuge. There is order here, as well as flush toilets and grown-ups who are better fed and better dressed than anyone in their *mohallas*, and who, for the most part, care about what happens to them.

Nambissan is not starry eyed. This is what I most like about her.

She says the school tries its best to arm its students with basic skills to survive in the modern economy—chiefly, the ability to communicate in English. Most of these kids want to graduate from college, but Nambissan knows they will need much more. A college degree is no guarantee of a steady paycheck for most Indians of Varsha's generation. Nambissan is convinced they will need to learn a marketable trade, which is not part of the formal school curriculum. A few of them, perhaps a handful of the truly gifted kids, will triumph academically, she says. Not many.

So what about Varsha? I ask.

Nambissan is blunt. Varsha is a hard worker, she tells me, but she is not intellectually exceptional. She is a leader, but also a hothead, quick to blow a fuse. In the end, Nambissan says, her fate depends on what her father has in store—and how hard she pushes back.

Nambissan's school does not nurture idle dreams. So when Varsha first tells her teachers she wants to be a psychologist, as a way to help women like her mother, she is not encouraged. In fact, her teachers discourage her. Too much math, they warn, too much studying. You won't be able to manage, they say.

For a while, Varsha wants to be a dancer. "My heart's dream is to be a dancer" is how she puts it. "I forget that dream. My father won't allow it."

It becomes a pattern. A burst of ambition. A splash of cold water. A new burst of ambition. Kindly adjust. Tamp down your dreams.

"First Papa said no to college," she says quietly. "Then my feelings also changed."

The policewoman idea is scaled into her brain after she and Papa listen to a speech by one of Gurgaon's assistant police commissioners, a woman who describes growing up in a mud house in a village, studying hard for the police service exam, rising up the ranks. Varsha is charged up by this. She thinks: If she can do it, why can't I? She looks over at Papa. She sees that he is applauding enthusiastically when the policewoman finishes speaking. He is beaming.

But when she broaches the idea of taking the Indian Police Service examination, Papa is the opposite of beaming. No way, he tells her. How would he find a husband for her? Imagine. A daughter-in-law packing a pistol! No respectable family would allow that of a *bahu*.

*   *   *

Varsha and I share a birthday. A Virgo, she is stubborn like me. She has trouble keeping her thoughts to herself. She mouths off when she shouldn't. She falls in love easily. She despairs sometimes.

I go to see Varsha on a Tuesday afternoon in winter, a few months before the critical Class 10 exams that will determine whether she can continue her studies and at what kind of school. Her mother is on her haunches, filling the iron with hot coals. She looks up when I ask after Varsha. Her mouth is packed with the blood of a betel nut. "She said she'd be gone only ten minutes for some tuition. But look what time it is. She's still not back," she says. She points her chin in the direction of three bundles of clothes that still need pressing.

If Varsha can imagine another life, I reckon her mother cannot. Santosh is a *dhobi*'s daughter and a *dhobi*'s wife. She seems incapable of seeing beyond the piles of clothes that need pressing. Or the child that needs her breast. I have a hard time seeing the world through her eyes. At first, it seems to me that she treats her daughter like a beast of burden. Only later does it occur to me that maybe she isn't just being mean to Varsha. Maybe she sees it as her duty to teach this girl to make herself useful—to be able to work like a mule. For what good is a girl who can't work like a mule?

I meet Varsha at the front gate of her neighborhood benefactor, Shubha. Varsha has been head down in physics homework. Her face lights up when she sees me. She says she is glad I have come. She needs to talk. We walk aimlessly around the neighborhood. A litany of grievances pours out.

"I have a lot of problems. At school. At home. Everywhere," she says. She is flustered. I knew this already because she has sent me several text messages throughout the day, demanding to know where I am, how much longer I would take. This is vintage Varsha. Pushy. Anxious.

I learn today that Varsha's troubles stem not just from her father's traditional views on a girl's ambitions. There's also that boy she likes—and he seems to have a caveman's view of a girl's ambitions.

"*Didi*, don't mind, but can I ask you one thing?" Varsha ventures while we walk. "Before marriage, was there any boy you liked very much?"

"Many," I reply, which cracks her up. "Why? Is there someone you like very much?"

"Not very much," she says. "A little."

The object of her affection turns out to be a ne'er-do-well who lives in the neighborhood. He tells her he loves her. He calls her on the phone whenever he thinks she is alone. "Have you eaten anything today?" he asks, which she takes as a sign of his affection.

He belongs to the Jat caste of landowning peasants, old-time Gurgaon folks who sold their land to real estate developers and made small fortunes.

The boy is as uninterested in his own remaking as she is obsessed with hers. He has dropped out of school, and he tells her he sees no reason to study. His family has money. He has a motorcycle, a phone, and a house. He tells her he will never have to work a day in his life. When she nudges him to take the high school matriculation exam, he snaps at her. "I don't want to discuss this business of studying with you," he says.

It's unclear what she sees in the boy. She admits he is neither handsome nor smart. He seems to be fiercely possessive. He appoints one of his cousins to spy on her at school and report back on whom she talks to. He gets on her case about talking to boys. He tells her she shouldn't wear jeans and T-shirts, which he apparently sees as symbols of immodesty. Still, she speaks to him nearly every night on the phone; sometimes she falls asleep with his voice in her ear.

They are on the phone late one night, when everyone else is sleeping. Come run away with me, he says.

It is an excruciating night. She stays up for hours in the darkness, thinking. She feels so torn.

There are moments when it feels like she can't live without him. But running away with him? That is different.

She thinks and thinks. Sleep doesn't come at all. She can hear her sisters' breath rise and fall in the bed next to hers.

By dawn, she has her answer. To run away with him would mean being cast out of her family forever, and this thought she can't bear. Her family is everything to her. No matter how much they frustrate her, they are her world: Papa, Mummy, her sisters and brothers. Without them, who would she be? Unmoored, truly alone.

She knows also that the boy would inevitably pull her down.

"He's not doing anything with his life, and I have so many dreams" is how she explains it. "If my future will be with him, I'll be sitting in the house and crying every day."

Her eyes fill with tears. She is trying not to talk to him at all. But it's not easy. She is sixteen, after all. "I love him. But I know I won't be happy if I have a future with him," she says.

Varsha adjusts her *dupatta*, wiping her tears. Mummy now makes her cover her breast with a *dupatta* whenever she steps out of the press stand. Her phone rings. Papa is on the line. He wants to know exactly where she is and with whom. "I'm coming back now," she says. She blinks back tears and begins walking back to the tin-roofed shed.

I am struck by how carefully she has weighed her choices. Her decision reflects not just that she is her father's daughter—she will submit to Papa's choice of a husband for her—but also by how determined she is to make her own path in the world. Her father, if he finds out about the boy, will inevitably be very, very angry. I hope he will also be proud.

A few months later, in May 2013, Varsha nails her Class 10 exams, earning the second highest score in her class. Papa agrees to let her enroll in a local high school, but insists that she wear only trousers and not a skirt. He softens that stance after a few months, but keeps a tight leash on her nonetheless. No going to the library after school. No going to a friend's house, not even to do homework together. I sense he suspects something about the boy.

Varsha does not stop goading Papa to let her take the police service exams. There are practical upsides, she tells him. Women are in high demand in the police force since the December 2012 gang-rape. The Delhi government alone promises to hire thousands of female cops, so each police station in the city can be staffed by at least a dozen policewomen.

It is hard to imagine another profession in which a grown-up Varsha would feel safer.

Varsha makes this case to Papa too. He is not convinced. No daughter of his is going to become a cop.

It is not that he doesn't love her. He loves her fiercely. He wants her to have a good life. He wants no harm to come to her, which is precisely why he cannot let her pursue this foolishness. He tells her he will find a husband for her by the time she is twenty. If the in-laws let her work—say, at a bank—she can work.

She pleads with Papa to let her take a dance class. He says no; it won't even fetch a job. She wants to learn to play guitar. Waste of time, he tells her. Varsha seeks beauty. Papa is consumed by fear.

That evening, during wedding season, when the burnt-toast smell of fireworks lingers in the air, she seems more dejected than I have ever seen her.

"Now I've changed my dreams. In my heart it's still there: can I become a police officer?" she said. "But when I see my family situation my confidence gets down."

Darkness falls. Varsha leans into the glowing-red iron. Someone lights a pile of garbage and dead brush on fire. A man approaches, shouting. Who lit this fire? he wants to know. He pets the mangy dogs that follow him. Varsha tells me later that he is an environmentalist. Madan Mohan says the man has gone mad. "Sometimes you study too much and this happens," he concludes. He is only half-joking, the half-contempt of a man who works with his hands for a man who works with his head, or who is comfortable enough not to work at all.

From next door come two young women who are about Varsha's age. They are flight attendants in training for one of the new private airlines. They are staying at a new bed-and-breakfast on the block. They want to go to a club at Gurgaon's largest mall. They are wearing skinny jeans and shimmer on the eyes, going out well past dark on a Saturday night.

Varsha has been pressing clothes since midafternoon. When the work is done, she will ride home in Papa's auto-rickshaw to roll chapatis.

Varsha is not yet eighteen when the 2014 elections come around, so she is unable to vote. She says the one thing she wants the new government to focus on is women's safety. "I want that girls should be able to walk on the road at any time" is how she puts it.

I could tell you about the many girls in India who are so anemic, hungry, or beaten down—or all of the above—that they can't even imagine studying psychology or learning to dance or enforcing the law. I tell you about Varsha because she does imagine it. She imagines it vividly.

I think about Anupam. True, he was an extraordinarily gifted child. But he was also blessed with an extraordinarily loyal mother. She didn't laugh when he told her he wanted to explore the prospect of life in outer space. She simply said, "*Beta*, perhaps when you're old enough, you can see if there is."

The contrast with Varsha is inescapable. Bright and headstrong, she is every bit as ambitious as Anupam. Her ambitions are repeatedly doused. Her resilience is repeatedly tested. She has had to rewrite her dreams, again and again, all because it would be unthinkable for her to cross the line, to defy her papa.

I try to be sympathetic to her father but find it difficult. He knows she is special, that she is smarter and more driven than all his other children. He relies on her to help run the household. He guards her. He also thwarts her at every turn. He is a product of the very traditions that she is trying to outrun. School isn't enough of an exit strategy.

Reluctantly, Varsha signs up to take business and economics classes in Class 11. Papa has it in his mind that bank jobs are good jobs for young women. A teacher mentions there are jobs in accounting. So she signs up for an accounting class. It is a breeze for her. It is also boring. Every hour spent on accounting homework, she begins to see as an hour away from preparing for her police service exams.

I briefly consider printing out a police application for Varsha—and then decide against it. It is her life. This is her father.

She tells me she intends to finish Class 12 and look for a job as soon as possible. She intends to enjoy a year or two of freedom before her father marries her off. Maybe, just maybe, she can persuade her would-be in-laws to let her continue to work. That way, she could at least stand on her own two feet. That will have to be her escape.

Ah, but stubborn, smart Varsha.

At the end of May 2015, she nails her final exams, scoring well above the 80th percentile, which nudges her papa to let her chase her dreams a bit further. He says she can go to a university in Delhi! This is unexpectedly good news, and they are discussing the details of her commute. She is trying to allay his fears about when and how she will walk back home from the metro station.

In the back of her mind, she is still plotting to be able to take the Indian Police Service exam, still pushing Papa every step of the way.

Epilogue

W hile my parents clung to the idea of the country they left, India was busy reinventing itself. The old houses near Gariahat Market became six-story apartment blocks. A spa opened on the ground floor of Jasoda Bhavan, where my father's father had once persuaded residents to make room for Partition refugees in 1947; there are no signs of the communal kitchen that once fed refugee families, but you can get a tummy tuck.

My parents and their Calcutta friends in California deftly improvised home. Can't slaughter a goat to supplicate Ma Kali in the suburbs? No problem. Slaughter an overgrown zucchini instead for the goddess. No Ganges holy water to sprinkle at the altar? No big. Tap water from the California aqueduct will do. (It's cleaner anyway than Hinduism's holiest river, I want to tell them. But I keep quiet.)[1]

Some of the certainties of twentieth-century India have dissolved. These include a belief in the idea of a state-led economy and state institutions that protect the poor, though in fact India's poor never really had anything like a safety net and still do not. They include the conviction that the state should deliver water and electricity to all of its people, as well as basic services like education and health. Those certainties have vanished, as the state proved incapable of providing basic services and those who can afford it managed to buy them privately. My father was educated in government schools. None of my friends or cousins in India would even contemplate sending their children to government schools. Private companies still complain of the state's heavy hand in putting up obstacles to business, which sometimes require bribes to remove. For more than twenty years, there have been demands for labor reforms, although in fact, only a fraction of India's workforce is employed in the formal sector, where labor laws apply; the rest are in the informal sector, with no protections, and most workers are in what the International Labour Organisation considers vulnerable jobs.[2]

There are new certainties. By 2022, India is poised to become the most populous country in the world. Also its youngest.

Noonday's generation is not like the generations that have come before it. These young Indians expect democracy to deliver something—for them. The idea of democracy is no longer just topsoil, to invoke Bhimrao Ambedkar, India's first law minister. It has become very much part of the undersoil. Millions of Indians coming of age in the last two decades take it for granted that they ought to be able to make their own fate. They are hardly going to bottle their aspirations forever. They may not give their elders much time. They can be pushy.

Mani, the young woman who once looked after Supriya's children, in her own quiet, introverted way, refuses to accept the lot of a girl born in a drought-prone *adivasi* village, just like she refuses to be cheated by a man.

Anupam, a child of remarkable grit, pushes his way through a tiny hole in the fence to the other side, where the hi-fi people are. Varsha has even a smaller hole in the fence open to her. Whether her papa will let her get anywhere close to the fence is not yet known, although, clearly, Papa is already a changed man because of her.

Rinu, on the other hand, is as outgoing and outspoken as she is because her father has her back. He believes in her completely. I hope she becomes the next Miley Cyrus of India and that Shaheen, having done her part to strengthen free speech laws in India, is never again afraid to express herself—on Facebook or anywhere else.

Rakhi's is a story of despair, but it ought to be a wake-up call to the leaders of her country. India's original people, the *adivasis*, have gained the least from seventy years of freedom. Their jungles have been denuded for timber. Their land has been stripped for minerals and their water polluted. No Indian child deserves the fate of Jeevan Munda, the *adivasi* boy who prepared to die because he could no longer go hungry. For a nation that aspires to be a world power, too many of its young are hungry, too many are forced to live in filth, and too many of them grow up, like Rakhi, as though they have nothing to lose.

That is why I think the stories of Anupam and Ankit, Varsha and Rakhi, Mani and Shaheen matter to the rest of us. From their generation could come an invention that changes the way we live, or a song that blows our minds, or a yearning, a hunger, to which we all have to pay attention.

Most of all, they reveal the fault lines in their own country. They will no doubt keep pushing India to be a more genuine democracy.

Narendra Modi, the current prime minister, knows he will have to address the needs of ordinary Indians—and fast. He has, after all, stoked their ambitions—perhaps more than any other Indian leader. The son of a tea seller, he has stood alongside the president of the United States of America, in a pin-striped suit with his name stitched in gold thread, hundreds of times. I am who I am. I wear me on my sleeve. I wear me up and down. The ultimate reinvention. Bold—no matter what you think of his taste in suits.

Because India is so big, its trajectory is going to inevitably bear on the rest of the world. Any global consensus to end hunger or reduce childhood deaths or ensure equal rights for men and women all of it depends in large part on India's progress.

Yes, of course, China's size and economic power make it an important country to study. But India's challenges are sui generis and instructive, precisely because India is so young and because India is a democracy. That is to say, where goes India's young, so go the rest of us.

The first challenge stems from the sheer size of its youth bulge. How does a country's economy create meaningful jobs for at least 10 million people coming of age every year, especially in the age of automation? The world economy is not creating nearly as many jobs as it needs. Can India put its ambitious, young people to work, or will Indians spread across the world to work in countries that are aging? The countries of Western Europe, with their rapidly aging populations, certainly don't seem ready to open their doors to migrants from India—or anywhere else.

Related, how does India fix its schools so that the millions of children streaming into its classrooms learn how to read and master basic arithmetic? This is an urgent challenge. No country has ever faced an education challenge at India's scale. But if something works in India, I bet it could work in other big, developing countries with large cohorts of first-generation learners. Education innovators in India are trying to crack that code, not least Rukmini Banerji's organization, Pratham. (Her group is also offering vocational programs to prepare young people for work opportunities that are available—as cooks, beauticians, plumbers, etc.)

Third, how can a country famous for exporting doctors and nurses around the world ensure that its young people grow up healthy? Groups like the Naandi Foundation are drilling down to better understand how to curb childhood hunger. Economists with the Abdul Jameel Latif Poverty Action Lab at the Massachusetts Institute of Technology have shown that small incentives—for instance, a bag of lentils—can nudge mothers to immunize their children. India has a rich tradition of harvesting scarce water; hopefully, the ingenuity of Indian engineers will yield new solutions so children no longer die for lack of clean drinking water.

Prime Minister Modi's ambitious target to develop solar and other renewable energy sources can go a long way in arresting the degradation of the environment. This raises the next challenge: how can India be a global leader in growing its economy without spewing as much carbon into the atmosphere as the rich world has during the last century.

These are global challenges, but India's scale and diversity make them all the more urgent.

Fifth, how India tackles the growing divide between rich and poor can hold lessons for the rest of us. Its experiment with the cash transfer program—putting money directly in the hands of the poor, following Brazil's lead—deserves to be carefully studied.

India's raucous free speech arguments mirror the arguments that many Western countries are having about how much political speech, even offensive speech, we can tolerate in a world of competing beliefs. India's intellectual legacy—perhaps its greatest soft power in the world—is the idea that free expression does not have to be squelched in order for so many different kinds of people to live peacefully in one republic. That also calls for a unique culture of tolerance, as the Nobel Laureate Kailash Satyarthi says. That would make for a truly strong and muscular India.

Speaking of strong, the seventh and last test is how India treats its women and girls. It can bear on everything else: childhood immunizations, the quality of its schools, how the government spends its money. Indian women's groups have pushed mightily to be treated equally under the law. Groups like Jagori have urged cities to be smarter about safety by repairing sidewalks and installing streetlights. The Indian innovation of another era—ensuring that women are elected to village councils— has led to measurable changes. One of the yields is that nearly all Indian girls are going to primary school. That is phenomenal. Varsha is one among many.

What I've tried to show you is the vast talent, grit, and determination of ordinary Indians. Some of you may think that I've emphasized the stories of the marginalized—a rebel, a housemaid, a murdered girl—too much. All I can tell you is that they are Indians too. Their stories are just as important.

They do not reflect all of India, you could say. And you would be right. No single story can reflect the story of a billion Indians—not even seven stories.

As I was researching this book, I got to know a remarkable woman named Rebecca, who was setting out to understand something about India at noonday.

I met Rebecca on a bright, cool morning in the winter of 2011 at an orphanage in a leafy suburb of Bangalore. She walked through a black iron gate and into a cheerful courtyard of zinnias and swings. She wore a black cotton tunic, jeans, and sturdy hiking boots. Her eyes were beaming. Rebecca, who was then thirty-four, was here to meet a little girl who had been abandoned, and who had spent the first two years of her life in this tidy little orphanage. Rebecca had just been cleared to adopt her.

Rebecca was born in India too—and also, once, abandoned. She was briefly taken care of at an orphanage in India too, and then carried by a flight attendant on a Pan American Airways flight all the way to the United States, where a mom, a dad, and two older brothers were waiting to take her into their arms.

When I met her, she was returning to India, for the first time, thirty-four years later.

She was so looking forward to becoming a mother. It was all she could think about for a long time. All the same, in becoming a mother to an Indian girl, she was also looking back to her past, trying to fathom that which was hardest of all to fathom: Why was she abandoned, and why was her daughter? Why did India give up on so many of its girls?

The old mysteries began to come up in new ways. Who bore me? Why did she give me up? Rebecca did not know anything about her own birth parents, nor those of her daughter. She harbored no resentment either, nor suspicion.

"I am just more curious about my history and about where I came from," she told me, in her typically sensible, unmawkish way. "It feels kind of like wanting to know the origins of the universe."

She set out to learn as much as she could about herself. She took cheek swabs and put herself in a genetic data bank, on the off chance that she could find some biological kin that way. She sought out others like her—men and women who had been adopted from India by families in the United States. For an art project, she invited adult Indian adoptees to record their own stories. By the time she turned forty, in the summer of 2015, she planned to take her daughter to India regularly, so they could both be in touch with the country that created them.

It was one big quest to give herself a story, to answer the great who-am-I question. The trip to India seemed to make it more urgent, because sooner or later, she knew, her little girl would also ask: What's *my* story, Mama, how did I get here?

The one thing that provided her some comfort—if it can be called that—was to discover the depth of how badly India sometimes treats its daughters. Over the years, Rebecca read how frequently female fetuses are aborted, and how girls are left quietly in the dead of night at railway stations and temple gates.

"It's not about me" is how she put it. "It's bigger than me. I don't take it personally. I know it can happen."

I had first made contact with Rebecca in 2010 on an email Listserv of parents of adoptive Indian children. I wanted to know what questions my girl might have one day and whether those questions would bring her any pain. I wanted to know—naïvely, you might think—how to help her. I came to really admire Rebecca's cheerful, practical, and deeply empathetic outlook.

This book is very much an effort to understand the India that gave our daughters to us. For my part, becoming a parent changed the direction of this book entirely. It made me want to see India through the eyes of its young. It made the fault lines clearer.

In that sense, it is a love letter to my own girl. As Sly Stone would say, "Thank You (Falettineme Be Mice Elf Agin)."

With all the swerves of history
I cannot imagine your future
Would wish to dream it, see you
In your teens, as I saw my son,
Your already philosophical air
Rubbing against the speed of the city.
I no longer guess a future.
And do not know how we end
Nor where.

Though I know a story about maps, for you.

—From Michael Ondaatje's "The Story"

*A young Indian boy looks upward in Mumbai as he waits to sell
statues of Bhimrao Ambedkar on Ambedkar's death anniversary,
December 6, 2013.*

ACKNOWLEDGMENTS

My deepest debt is to the many women and men, boys and girls who let me into their lives and barrage them with questions year after year. It cannot be easy to be at the receiving end of a journalist's excessive curiosity. I hope I have done justice to their stories. Any mistakes are mine alone.

A huge shout-out to Sarah Chalfant, my champion at the Wylie Agency. Not only did she believe in a half-baked book idea years ago, she repeatedly helped me sharpen it, nudged me gently when I needed it, and lit a fire under me exactly when it mattered. She has been the toughest, best backup that a writer could hope for. My thanks also to many others at the Wylie Agency who worked on my behalf over the years, including Celia Kokoris, Rebecca Nagel, Edward Orloff, and Nadia Wilson.

This book should have been finished long ago. I thank my editor, Jill Bialosky, for her patience and intellectual rigor. My thanks also to her assistants, Angie Shih and Maria Rogers, for tending to every detail; to Trent Duffy for careful copyedits; and to Edward Claris for his legal eye.

In Oakland, California, my writing *didi* Constance Hale took the garbled pages that I shared with her and helped me understand what I was trying to say and, at every iteration, say it better.

In Delhi, Mandakini Gahlot helped with reporting. In New York, Barbara Kean went through the manuscript with a fine-toothed comb, saving me from more errors than I care to remember.

Among my many colleagues and teachers over the years at *The New York Times*, thanks to Joe Lelyveld, Matt Purdy, Paul Fishleder, Ian Fisher, Susan Chira, Jill Abramson, Dean Baquet, Damon Darlin, Joe Kahn, Michael Slackman, Rick Gladstone, and Greg Winter, who kept urging me to have a "real" vacation, which did not involve working on this book. A special thanks to the amazing Nicole Bengiveno, for making me look presentable in the author photo.

In the Delhi bureau of the *Times*, my deepest thanks to Hari Kumar and P. J. Anthony, my gurus and most vital guides, from navigating the warrens of the Foreign Registration Office to climbing a glacier in the Himalayas.

A great tribe of journalists and writers across India schooled me and sustained me with laughter, cocktails, and kebabs. They include Lydia Polgreen, Candace Feit, Heather Timmons, Paul Beckett, Barkha Dutt, Randeep Ramesh, Rama Lakshmi, Suhasini Haidar, Emily Wax, Nilanjana Roy, Devangshu Datta, Mihir Sharma, Pankaj Pachauri, Pramila Phatarphekar, Subir Bhaumik, Monideepa Banerjie, Ruchir Joshi, Anurag Chaturvedi, Nandini Ramnath, Kavitha Kumar, Krishna Prasad, Yusuf Jameel, Muzamil Jaleel (including for one special hike), Mini Kapoor, Mala and Tejbir Singh, Sagarika Ghose, Bharat Desai, and Ajay Umat. My gratitude goes to Deepu Sebastian Edmond, Parvez, and Vijay Murthy for their help with reporting in Jharkhand. Thanks to Dayanita Singh for one exquisite summer in Saligao; Falguni Sarkar and Purba Chatterjee for offering their home in Kolkata; William and Anjali Bissell for dinners, walks, and eye-opening conversations; and Ashutosh Sharma and his crew at Sadhana Travels for ferrying me hither and yon at a moment's notice.

My life in Delhi would have been unmanageable without a team of capable, gracious staff, chiefly Pan Singh, Chunni Lal, and Kiran Sewa. Also, through their eyes I saw every day what high aspirations they had for their children and how much they wanted their lives to be different from their own.

For teaching me about Indian history and politics, thanks to Ramachandra Guha, Mahesh Rangarajan, Yogendra Yadav, Pratap Bhanu Mehta, Rajdeep Sardesai, and, specifically on Bihar politics, Shaibal Gupta. On matters economic, thanks to Kaushik Basu, Sonalde Desai, Rinku Murgai, Jishnu Das, Adarsh Kumar and Yamini Aiyar, Nandan Nilekani, and Abhijit Banerjee. The chapter on education would not have been written without guidance from Rukmini Bannerji and her colleagues at Pratham. To help me understand the Maoist conflict I am grateful to Rahul Pandita, Salman Ravi, Shubrangshu Choudhury, Gautam Navlakha, and Hasan Zulfiqar in the West Bengal police department. Julfikar Ali Manik, as courageous a journalist as he is generous, taught me everything about Bangladesh and agreed to a trip to Rangpur on a moment's notice.

Thanks to friends who read various versions of these pages over the years and improved them greatly: Adrienne Johnson, Andrew Hsiao, Paul Elie, Raka Ray, Suketu Mehta, Ramachandra Guha, Tripti Lahiri, Shelley Thakral, Brij Kothari, and Naresh Fernandes (also for saving me years ago with chocolate chip cookies and walks in the park). My confidante and guide in pretty much everything, the super-smart Meenakshi Ganguly, read umpteen versions of nearly every chapter. Samar Halarnkar and Priya Ramani offered valuable advice at every stage of this project. Tsan Abrahamson had a very good tip.

Without my girls in Delhi, neither my daughter nor I would have ever felt truly at home in Nizamuddin: Ambika Nair, Menaka Guruswamy, and Tripti Lahiri.

My relatives in Calcutta—namely, Gautam Sen, Kalpana Sen, and Mitali Sen—generously shared their knowledge and love. I am especially grateful to my aunt Kalpana, for letting me run off on a reporting trip and selflessly stepping in to take care of my daughter, at a time when she was mourning her own mother's death. In Delhi, my aunt Tapati Sen told me richly detailed stories of the Partition era.

My mother- and father-in-law, Hans and Marga van de Weerd, repeatedly volunteered to care for my daughter when I needed to work. Bernadette Joseph demanded that I finish the book and gave me her home for a long weekend writing retreat.

My parents, Sandip and Sipra Sengupta, made sure I am capable of making my own way in the world. Joe Wood reminded me that I belong in any world I choose. My sister, Sohini, and my cousin, Momita, are my anchors in times of joy and blinding grief. Their husbands, Chirag Menon and Gavin Hampson, keep spoiling me with love, music, and the best sirloin ever.

Finally, thanks to my husband, Hans van de Weerd, who asked no questions about how "the book" was going and let me descend into my writing cave nearly every weekend and every vacation, year after year. Our daughter tolerated my absences when she would much rather have played with me or danced to Lauryn Hill. As I was working through most of our most recent summer vacation together, she said (rightly with some exasperation), "C'mon, Mama. Just get done with it!" Thank you.

NOTES

INTRODUCTION: ASPIRATION, LIKE WATER

1. Some of the most intense effects of the emergency were felt by the poor in the slums of Delhi. It is best documented in Emma Tarlo, *Unsettling Memories: Narratives of the Emergency in Delhi* (Berkeley: University of California Press, 2003). The political backdrop to the emergency is chronicled in Bipan Chandra, *In the Name of Democracy: JP Movement and the Emergency* (New Delhi: Penguin India, 2003), while an extremely revealing insider's account of the Indira Gandhi administration can be found in *Indira Gandhi: The "Emergency" and Indian Democracy*, by her onetime adviser P. N. Dhar (New Delhi: Oxford University Press, 2000).

2. My father recalls that the Reserve Bank of India at the time restricted how much foreign currency one could take out of the country.

3. The phrase "city of dreadful night" is a coinage by Rudyard Kipling, who did not mean it as a compliment. I borrowed it in "A Walk in Calcutta," my essay about Calcutta for the travel section of *The New York Times*, May 3, 2009, available at www.nytimes.com/2009/05/03/travel/03calcutta.html.

4. Wendy Doniger, *Karma and Rebirth in Classical Indian Traditions* (Berkeley: University of California Press, 1980).

5. The latest world population projections by the United Nations, released in July 2015, predict that by 2022, India and China will have roughly 1.4 billion people each; after that India will grow faster, reaching 1.5 billion by 2030. The projections are available at http://esa.un.org/unpd/wpp/publications/files/key_findings_wpp_2015.pdf. David Bloom, a Harvard University demographer, has written most persuasively and expansively about this notion, positing what benefits India can reap because of its demography and also what the challenges are.

6. The growth rates in India's gross domestic product, or GDP, averaged between about 4 percent and nearly 10 percent between 1990 and 2014, as this chart shows: http://planningcommission.nic.in/data/datatable/0814/table_1.pdf. However, China and India were hardly comparable in economic terms. The per capita income of the average Indian, while growing steadily since 1991, was about $1570 in 2013, or less than one-fourth the per capita income of the Chinese, according to the World Bank (http://data.worldbank.org/country/india).

7. Elisabeth Bumiller and Somini Sengupta, "Bush and India Reach Pact That Allows Nuclear Sales," *The New York Times*, March 3, 2006, available at www .nytimes.com/2006/03/03/international/asia/03prexy.html.

8. Sheryl Gay Stolberg and Jim Yardley, "Countering China, Obama Backs India for U.N. Council," *The New York Times*, November 8, 2010, available at www .nytimes.com/2010/11/09/world/asia/09prexy.html?_r=0.

9. McKinsey Global Institute, the economics research arm of the consultancy firm, concluded, "Income levels will almost triple, and India will climb from its position as the twelfth-largest consumer market today to become the world's fifth-largest consumer market by 2025." This May 2007 report, "The 'Bird of Gold': The Rise of India's Consumer Market," is available at www.mckinsey .com/insights/asia-pacific/the_bird_of_gold.

10. The American urge to see India in its own image dates back to the early days of Indian independence. Daniel Patrick Moynihan, the U.S. ambassador to India between 1973 and 1975, describes it like this in his rich diplomatic memoir *A Dangerous Place*, written with Suzanne Weaver (New York: Little, Brown, 1978): "India was going to be like America, and America in turn was going to be like India," he wrote of the mood in the 1950s and early 1960s. "An innocent enough affair of the heart you might suppose. And yet its end brought great bitterness in India, and there was little for an ambassador to do in its aftermath but wait until the Indians were prepared to settle for a more traditional relationship of diplomacy rather than tutelage."

11. Salman Rushdie, *Midnight's Children* (London: Jonathan Cape, 1981). I have read it repeatedly and been enriched, moved, and entertained by it every time. My term "noonday's children" is a hat tip to him.

12. Nandan Nilekani, *Imagining India: Ideas for the New Century* (New Delhi: Penguin India, 2008).

13. United Nations figures available at https://data.un.org/Data.aspx?q=united+ states+of+america&d=WHO&f=MEASURE_CODE%3AWHS9_88%3B COUNTRY_ISO_CODE%3AUSA.

14. The World Bank defines abject poverty worldwide as $1.25 a day, adjusted for purchasing power parity. According to its latest data, from 2011, 23.6 percent of the population were in that category. Data available at http://povertydata .worldbank.org/poverty/country/IND.

15. Some sixty-five years after the partition of British India, Guneeta Singh Bhalla, a young Berkeley physicist and the granddaughter of a Partition survivor from India, initiated a remarkable oral history project to capture the stories of Partition survivors and preserve them online. Known as the 1947 Partition Archive, it describes itself as "a people-powered non-profit organization dedicated to documenting, preserving and sharing eye witness accounts from *all* ethnic, religious and economic communities affected by the Partition of British India in 1947." See my "Potent Memories from a Divided India," *The New*

York Times, August 13, 2013, available at www.nytimes.com/2013/08/14/arts/ potent-memories-from-a-divided-india.html?_r=0. The best nonfiction work that I have read on Partition and its aftermath is Urvashi Butalia's *The Other Side of Silence: Voices from the Partition of India* (Durham, N.C.: Duke University Press, 2000).

16. Granville Austin, *The Indian Constitution: Cornerstone of a Nation* (New Delhi: Oxford University Press, 1999), 33.

17. Sunil Khilnani's book *The Idea of India* (New York: Farrar, Straus and Giroux, 1998) is a groundbreaking work examining this singular trajectory.

18. Jean Drèze and Amartya Sen, *An Uncertain Glory: India and Its Contradictions* (London: Penguin, 2014), table A.5: Time Trends.

19. The World Bank: http://data.worldbank.org/indicator/SI.POV.2DAY; also see *Perspectives on Poverty in India: Stylized Facts from Survey Data* (Washington, D.C.: The World Bank, 2011).

20. Ramachandra Guha, *India After Gandhi: The History of the World's Largest Democracy* (New Delhi: Picador India, 2007).

"HI–FI": HOW TO OUTRUN FATE

1. John F. Richards, "The Opium Industry in British India," *The Indian Economic and Social History Review* 39 (2002): 149–80, available at http://ier.sagepub .com/content/39/2-3/149.extract. Arvind N. Das discusses peasant rebellions in twentieth-century Bihar in *Agrarian Movements in India* (London: Frank Cass, 1982). Prakash Kumar offers a fascinating history of indigo production in Bihar: "Facing Competition: The Story of Indigo Experiments in Colonial India, 1897 1920," PhD diss., Georgia Institute of Technology, 2004, available at https://smartech.gatech.edu/bitstream/handle/1853/7627/kumar_prakash_ 200412_phd.pdf.

2. V. S. Naipaul has written about Indian migration to Trinidad in *The Loss of El Dorado* (London: Andre Deutsch, 1969) and in a fictional account in *A House for Mr. Biswas* (London: Andre Deutsch, 1961). His first trip to India in the early 1960s yielded the travelogue *An Area of Darkness* (London: Andre Deutsch, 1964). More recently, Gaiutra Bahadur's *Coolie Woman: The Odyssey of Indenture* (Chicago: University of Chicago Press, 2014) explores the story of her great-grandmother's migration from Bihar to British Guiana.

3. Dalits were once referred to as untouchables, then by Mohandas K. Gandhi as *harijans* (literally, "the children of God"). The term "Dalit" signifies those who are suppressed, and it is how they refer to themselves. They are part of what the government calls its "Scheduled Castes," and eligible for affirmative action benefits, including set-asides in government universities and government jobs. Human Rights Watch documented violence against Dalits in a landmark

report entitled *Broken People: Caste Violence Against India's "Untouchables"* (New York: Human Rights Watch, 1999)—see especially chapter 4; the report is available at www.hrw.org/reports/1999/03/01/broken-people-0. In addition, South Asia Terrorism Portal keeps a chronology of massacres in central Bihar (1977–2001), available at www.satp.org/satporgtp/countries/india/terrorist outfits/massacres.htm.

4. Research in neighboring Pakistan by the World Bank economist Jishnu Das found that the children of women with just one year of formal schooling studied for at least an hour each day: Tahir Andrabi, Jishnu Das, and Asim Ijaz Khwaja, "What Did You Do All Day?: Maternal Education and Child Outcomes," *The Journal of Human Resources* 47 (Fall 2012): 873–912, available at www.hks.harvard.edu/fs/akhwaja/papers/WhatDidYouDoAllDay.pdf.

5. Jeffrey Witsoe, *Democracy Against Development: Lower-Caste Politics and Political Modernity in Postcolonial India* (Chicago: University of Chicago Press, 2013). William Dalrymple briefly describes the early days of Yadav's Bihar in *The Age of Kali: Indian Travels and Encounters* (London: HarperCollins, 1998). And Sankarshan Thakur wrote a political biography of Yadav in *The Making of Laloo Yadav: The Unmaking of Bihar* (New Delhi: HarperCollins India, 2000).

6. I quoted this social worker in "Push for Education Yields Little for India's Poor," *The New York Times*, January 17, 2008, available at www.nytimes.com/ 2008/01/17/world/asia/17india.html.

7. H. H. Risley, *The Tribes and Castes of Bengal: Ethnographic Glossary, Vol. 1* (Calcutta: Bengal Secretariat Press, 1891). A more contemporary encyclopedia of India's official Scheduled Castes can be found in K. S. Singh's *The Scheduled Castes* (New Delhi: Oxford University Press, 1999). The nineteenth-century treatise is by Jogendra Nath Bhattacharya: *Hindu Castes and Sects: An Exposition of the Origin of the Hindu Caste System and the Bearing of the Sects Towards Each Other and Towards Other Religious Systems* (Calcutta: Thacker, Spink, 1896). The British bureaucrat John C. Nesfield described the pecking order in *A Brief View of the Caste System of the North-western Provinces and Oudh* (Allahabad: North-Western Provinces and Oudh Government Press, 1885).

8. Karla Hoff and Priyanka Pandey, "Belief Systems and Durable Inequalities: An Experimental Investigation of Indian Caste," published online by the London School of Economics, available at http://sticerd.lse.ac.uk/dps/bpde2004/hoff.pdf.

9. Somini Sengupta, "A Vision of Stars Grounded in the Dust of Rural India," *The New York Times*, June 15, 2005, available at www.nytimes.com/2005/06/25/ world/asia/a-vision-of-stars-grounded-in-the-dust-of-rural-india.html.

10. The 2014 Annual Status of Education Report is available at http://img.aser centre.org/docs/Publications/ASER%20Reports/ASER%202014/national findings.pdf.

11. The University of Maryland and the National Council of Applied Economic Research carried out the Indian Human Development Survey in 2011–2012.

The dropout rates are used with permission from the lead author, Sonalde Desai, professor of sociology at the University of Maryland.

12. Karthik Muralidharan "Priorities for Primary Education Policy in India's Twelfth Five-Year Plan," April 4, 2013, available on the University of California–San Diego site, http://pdel.ucsd.edu/_files/paper_2013_karthik.pdf.

13. The World Bank calculated a weighted average of teacher absenteeism rates. The data is available at http://siteresources.worldbank.org/DEC/Resources/36660_Teacher_absence_in_India_EEA_9_15_04_-South_Asia_session_version.pdf.

14. J. P. Naik, *Policy and Performance in Indian Education (1947–74)*, published by the Azim Premji University, is available at http://182.18.153.100/sites/default/files/userfiles/files/Policy%20and%20performance%20in%20Indian%20Education%20-%20Naik.pdf.

15. A more recent examination of the Korean education system by the journalist Amanda Ripley describes it as a "hamster wheel," where kids study all the time, including in evenings, with tutors, where much of their real learning seems to take place. "In Korea, the hamster wheel created as many problems as it solved," Ripley writes in *The Smartest Kids in the World and How They Got That Way* (New York: Simon and Schuster, 2013). If nothing else, she concludes, it prepares them for the hamster wheel of the modern economy.

16. Provisional results of the 2011 Indian census are available at http://censusindia.gov.in/2011-prov-results/data_files/india/Final_PPT_2011_chapter6.pdf. Brij Kothari, a professor at the Indian Institute of Management in Ahmedabad, and his colleague Tathagata Bandyopadhyay tested 11,462 individuals in four Indian states on their basic ability to read a simple paragraph from a Class 2 text in their native language, Hindi, and found that the census estimates for those states had been overestimated by 16 percentage points.

17. Myron Weiner, *The Child and State in India: Child Labor and Education Policy in Comparative Perspective* (Princeton, N.J.: Princeton University Press, 1990), available at http://press.princeton.edu/titles/4838.html.

18. Numerous country-specific studies are cited at www.cgdev.org/files/2844_file_EDUCATON1.pdf; and at www.copenhagenconsensus.com/publication/post-2015-consensus-education assessment-psacharopoulos.

19. Author interviews with Karthik Muralidharan in 2013. A lecture he has posted online also offers some of his findings and can be viewed at www.fsmevents.com/younglives/session04/onDemand.html.

20. Diarrhea statistics are in a 2012 UNICEF report, "Pneumonia and Diarrhoea: Tackling the Deadliest Diseases for the World's Poorest Children," available at http://data.unicef.org/corecode/uploads/document6/uploaded_pdfs/corecode/Pneumonia_Diarrhoea_2012_35.pdf. Malnutrition rates worldwide are compared in the International Food Policy Research Institute's Global Hunger Index, which concluded in its 2014 report that India suffers from serious hunger,

at levels comparable to far poorer countries like Angola, Nepal, and Uganda; the report is available at www.ifpri.org/publication/2014-global-hunger-index-challenge-hidden-hunger. There is a world map available at http://public .tableau.com/profile/ifpri.td7290#!/vizhome/2014GHI/2014GHI. That conclusion was based on a survey carried out in 2013 and 2014 by the United Nations children's agency, which found that 30 percent of children under five were underweight. In an article entitled "Of Secrecy and Stunting," *The Economist* reported on it on July 5, 2015 (www.economist.com/news/ asia/21656709-government-withholds-report-nutrition-contains-valuable-lessons-secrecy-and). The Indian Ministry of Women and Child Development published a fact sheet on the 2013–2014 Rapid Survey on Children: www.wcd .nic.in/issnip/National_Fact%20sheet_RSOC%20_02-07-2015.pdf. This latest estimate on childhood malnutrition represents a significant decline from 2005–2006, when India's own National Family Health Survey concluded that 42.5 percent of children under five were underweight. (http://dhsprogram .com/pubs/pdf/frind3/00frontmatter00.pdf). The decline came amid a period of high economic growth and rising average household income, but there were huge disparities between poor northern states, like Bihar, and southern states, like Karnataka. India's ranking among nations improved, but it was nothing worth boasting of: among 128 countries on which data was available to IFPRI, India came in at 120.

GATES: KEEPING OUT THE LIVES OF OTHERS

1. Somini Sengupta, "Inside Gate, India's Good Life; Outside, the Servants' Slums," *The New York Times*, June 9, 2008, available at www.nytimes.com/ 2008/06/09/world/asia/09gated.html.
2. The arguments grew especially heated in 2013, when Jagdish Bhagwati, a Columbia University economics professor, issued a series of broadsides against Amartya Sen, a Harvard University economics professor. Both were celebrated economists, born and raised in India. Both favored economic liberalization. Bhagwati, in a book cowritten with Arvind Panagariya, argued that economic growth, market driven and encouraged by liberal state policies, would lift Indians out of poverty. Sen argued for more public funding for basic services, including health and education.
3. Across the developing world, the threshold for people living in extreme poverty is $1.25 a day, in terms of consumption, not income. By virtue of its population, India is home to the largest concentration of poor—about 33 percent of all the world's extremely poor people are Indians—according to the United Nations Millennium Development Goals report: www.un.org/millenniumgoals/2014 %20MDG%20report/MDG%202014%20English%20web.pdf. How India

compares with other countries is contained in a draft report by Pedro Olinto and Hiroki Uematsu of the World Bank's Poverty Reduction and Equity Department: "The State of the Poor: Where Are the Poor and Where Are the Poorest?" available at www.worldbank.org/content/dam/Worldbank/document/State_of_the_poor_paper_April17.pdf.

4. See the World Bank's table "Poverty Headcount Ratio at $2 a Day (PPP)," available at http://data.worldbank.org/indicator/SI.POV.2DAY/countries.

5. Gaurav Datt, Rinku Murgai, and Martin Ravallion, "India's (Uneven) Progress Against Poverty Since 1950" (mimeo, Department of Economics, Georgetown University, 2015). Cited with permission from Ravallion.

6. Between 2009 and 2011, the bottom 10 percent saw the greatest improvement in their living standards, at about 6 percent a year, according to an analysis by the World Bank, its chief economist, Kaushik Basu, said in an interview in 2015.

7. The World Bank measures inequality by the standard Gini coefficient. A chart that shows India's inequality measurement compared with the other nineteen largest economies in the world is available at http://forumblog.org/2014/02/emerging-world-worry-inequality/.

8. http://planningcommission.nic.in/reports/peoreport/peoevalu/peo_icds_v1.pdf.

9. The government reports a sharp decline in child labor, from over 12 million in 2001 to just under 4.5 million in 2011. The census data is available at http://labour.gov.in/upload/uploadfiles/files/Divisions/childlabour/Census-2001%262011.pdf. The International Labour Organisation cites older government data, available at www.ilo.org/legacy/english/regions/asro/newdelhi/ipec/responses/index.htm. UNICEF compares India's share of child workers with those in other countries in its State of the World's Children report, available at www.unicef.org/sowc2011/pdfs/SOWC-2011-Main-Report_EN_02092011.pdf.

10. The United Nations Office on Drugs and Crime's assessment report on India, "Current Status of Victim Service Providers and Criminal Justice Actors in India on Anti Human Trafficking," is available at www.unodc.org/documents/southasia/reports/Human_Trafficking-10-05-13.pdf.

11. In 2012, a year after Phoolo was taken, the Delhi newspapers were ablaze with news of another child abduction. A thirteen-year-old girl came forward to complain of an uncle who had sold her to an agent, who had in turn sold her to work for a couple, both doctors, in south Delhi. The girl told child welfare officials she was fed two chapatis a day and beaten when her work was not satisfactory. When her masters went on vacation, leaving her locked inside the apartment, she climbed out onto the balcony and screamed for help. She too was from an *adivasi* village in Jharkhand.

12. "*Mama*" literally signifies a maternal uncle, though in this case, it refers to someone feared, because they have a gun. "*Jungle ka-mama-log*" refers to uncles of the jungle. "*Bhai*" is the word for brother, and in this case "*bhai-log*" connotes men who are older and demand submission.

13. World Bank, "Poverty and Social Exclusion in India" (2011). Extracts from the study are available at http://siteresources.worldbank.org/EDUCATION/Resources/278200-1121703274255/1439264-1288632678541/7520452-12925329 51964/Session3_Das_Dec20.pdf.

14. "Government of India Rapid Survey on Children 2013–2014," available at www .wcd.nic.in/issnip/National_Fact%20sheet_RSOC%20_02-07-2015.pdf. That is significantly better than in 2005–2006, when the National Family Health Survey, on which a World Bank analysis relied, found that 55 percent of *adivasi* children were underweight, compared with about 43 percent among Indian children as a whole. An earlier analysis by the World Bank found sharp disparities among the well-being of Indian children as a whole and *adivasi* children. That analysis, cited previously, relied on data from the 2005–2006 National Family Health Survey.

15. The International Food Policy Research Institute compiles statistics by country for its Global Hunger Index; see www.ifpri.org/sites/default/files/publications/ghi14.pdf, table 2.1.

16. www.naandi.org/wp-content/uploads/2013/12/HUNGaMA-Survey-2011-The-Report.pdf.

17. Martin Ravallion, "A Comparative Perspective on Poverty Reduction in Brazil, China and India" (Washington, D.C.: The World Bank Development Research Group, 2009), available at http://elibrary.worldbank.org/doi/pdf/10.1596/1813-9450-5080.

18. Skeptics point out that even with the digital identification efforts that are designed to marginalize middlemen, India is unlikely to get rid of them entirely. Indeed, there have been reports of Indian citizens paying middlemen to procure digital identification.

19. Rukmini S., "Just 5 Percent of Marriages Are Inter-Caste: Survey," *The Hindu*, November 13, 2014, available at www.thehindu.com/data/just-5-per-cent-of-indian-marriages-are-intercaste/article6591502.ece. The article cited India Human Development Survey data, which had been collected by the University of Maryland and the National Council on Applied Economic Research.

20. Helene Cooper, *The House at Sugar Beach: In Search of a Lost African Childhood* (New York: Simon and Schuster, 2008).

21. Among industrialized countries, the United States ranks close to the bottom on public spending for family benefits. Things could have been different: in 1971, the U.S. Congress passed a bill that would have established a federally funded network of child-care centers. President Richard Nixon vetoed the legislation, suggesting that such a "radical" piece of legislation could diminish parental authority. His statement is available at www.presidency.ucsb.edu/ws/?pid=3251.

22. Gregory Clark, an economics professor at University of California–Davis, wrote

about the relationship between ancestry and economic mobility in "Your Ancestors, Your Fate," *The New York Times*, February 23, 2014, available at http://opinionator.blogs.nytimes.com/2014/02/21/your-fate-thank-your-ancestors/.

GUERRILLA: PAYING FOR BROKEN PROMISES

1. Many such killings are chronicled by the South Asia Terrorism Portal, which tracks insurgencies in India, including by the Maoists; see www.satp.org/satp orgtp/countries/india/maoist/timelines/2010/westbengal.html.
2. Ibid.
3. Jhumpa Lahiri paints a rich portrait of this generation in Calcutta in the novel *The Lowland* (New York: Alfred A. Knopf, 2013).
4. Human Rights Watch counted thirty-six schools in Jharkhand and sixteen schools in Bihar that Maoists attacked in 2009 alone; see www.hrw.org/en/node/86827.
5. Dilip D'Souza wrote about this doctor, Binayak Sen, in Chhatisgarh, in his book *The Curious Case of Binayak Sen* (New Delhi: HarperCollins India, 2012). Arun Ferreira wrote a memoir of his time in prison, on charges of being a Maoist, in *Colours of the Cage: A Prison Memoir* (New Delhi: Aleph Book Company, 2014).
6. Somini Sengupta, "In India Maoist Guerrillas Widen 'People's War,'" *The New York Times*, August 13, 2006, available at www.nytimes.com/2006/04/13/world/asia/13maoists.html.
7. Conversation with Monideepa Banerjie, the reporter who covered the Lalgarh insurgency for the television news station NDTV.

STRONGMAN: ASPIRATION GETS INTO POLITICS

1. Rashtriya Swayamsevak Sangh, or RSS, is literally translated as the National Volunteer Organization, a name that is more neutral than its mission. Established in 1925 by Keshav Baliram Hedgewar and driven by what its founders saw as a need to build a strong Hindu nation, it has chapters across the country. The FAQs on its website are instructive: see www.rss.org//Encyc/2012/10/23/Basic-FAQ-on-RSS.aspx. Books about the group include Walter K. Andersen and Shridhar D. Damle, *The Brotherhood in Saffron: The Rashtriya Swayamsevak Sangh and Hindu Revivalism* (Delhi: Vistaar Publications, 1987); and Christophe Jaffrelot, *The Hindu Nationalist Movement and Indian Politics* (London: C. Hurst & Co., 1996).
2. Only men are entitled to join the Sangh. There are women in the Hindu radical

movement, but they do not belong to the Sangh. There is a parallel organization to the RSS for Hindu women, which doesn't have the same political influence or name recognition as the RSS.

3. Ramachandra Guha, ed., *Makers of Modern India* (New Delhi: Penguin, 2010).

4. This amendment to the Constitution of India can be viewed at http://india code.nic.in/coiweb/amend/amend26.htm.

5. Agency for International Development case report, "India Drought 1972/1973," available at http://pdf.usaid.gov/pdf_docs/pnadq774.pdf.

6. Bipan Chandra, *In the Name of Democracy: JP Movement and the Emergency* (New Delhi: Penguin India, 2003), and Emma Tarlo, *Unsettling Memories: Narratives of India's Emergency* (Berkeley: University of California Press, 2003).

7. "Prime Minister Indira Gandhi Responds to Charges That Democracy in India Is Dead" *Saturday Review*, August 9, 1975, available at www.unz.org/Pub/SaturdayRev-1975aug09-00010?View=PDF.

8. A cable made available by Wikileaks describes the telephone call from the Indian foreign ministry to a political counselor at the U.S. embassy, informing the Americans of the expulsion of Lewis Simons of *The Washington Post*; see www.wikileaks.org/plusd/cables/1975NEWDE08681_b.html. Simons recalls his expulsion on July 1, 1975, in "Mrs. Gandhi Turns to Son in Crisis," an essay published in John Elliot, Bernard Imhasly, and Simon Denyer, eds., *Foreign Correspondent: Fifty Years of Reporting South Asia* (New Delhi: Viking, 2008), available at https://books.google.com/books?id=GlM7e_1dCjoC&pg=PA97&lpg=PA97&dq=lewis+simons+emergency+india+1975&source=bl&ots=aLjR bpBcOX&sig=KGM0n5w3GN0h9ir7DDGN50gxuu8&hl=en&sa=X&ei=QQl mVar2BcmYyASkjYOwCQ&ved=0CCEQ6AEwAQ#v=onepage&q=lewis%20 simons%20emergency%20india%201975&f=false.

9. Celia W. Dugger, "Religious Riots Loom over India's Politics," *The New York Times*, July 27, 2003, available at www.nytimes.com/2002/07/27/international/asia/27INDI.html.

10. Human Rights Watch, "India: A Decade on, Gujarat Justice Incomplete," February 24, 2012, available at www.hrw.org/news/2012/02/24/india-decade-gujarat-justice-incomplete.

11. Gardiner Harris and Hari Kumar, "Stiff Sentence for Former Gujarat Minister," *The New York Times*, September 1, 2012, available at http://india.blogs.nytimes.com/2012/08/31/stiff-sentence-for-former-gujarat-minister/.

12. The most senior among these Congress party leaders was Jagdish Tytler. In 2005, he resigned from his post as a cabinet minister in the Congress-led coalition government. See Hari Kumar, "Minister Quits over Riot Report," *The New York Times*, August 11, 2005.

13. Zahir Janmohamed wrote a revealing account, in the blog of *The New York Times*, of the evangelical Christians, Jewish leaders, human rights activists, and

Indian-American critics of Modi who teamed up to get the U.S. Congress to impose the visa ban: http://india.blogs.nytimes.com/2013/12/05/u-s-evangel icals-indian-expats-teamed-up-to-push-through-modi-visa-ban/.

14. Somini Sengupta, "Hindu Radical Is Re-elected in India," *The New York Times*, December 24, 2007, available at www.nytimes.com/2007/12/24/world/ asia/24india.html.

15. Somini Sengupta, "Shadows of Violence Cling to Indian Politician," *The New York Times*, April 28, 2009, available at www.nytimes.com/2009/04/29/world/ asia/29india.html.

16. In December 2012, writing in a newsmagazine called *Tehelka*, Shashi likened Modi's critics to the Turkish strongman Kemal Ataturk and the ouster of his heirs by politicians who flirted with political Islam, such as Reyep Tayyip Erdogan; see http://blog.tehelka.com/the-curious-case-of-indian-media-and-gujarat/ #sthash.0fb2UTzz.dpuf).

17. The political start-up, a company called Niti Central, was funded principally by a Mumbai technology magnate named Rajesh Jain.

18. See www.ipaidabribe.com/bribe-trends#gsc.tab=0.

19. Modi's session with Reuters was one of the most important political interviews of the 2014 campaign season: Ross Colvin and Satarupa Bhattacharjya, "Special Report: The Remaking of Narendra Modi," Reuters India, July 12, 2013, http://in.reuters.com/article/2013/07/12/india-modi-gujarat-bjp-idINDEE 96B00Y20130712.

20. Shashi's team had come up with the name of the website. It was based on the number of seats—272—that the BJP needed for an absolute majority in the lower chamber of parliament. Modi added to the name; he insisted that it should be called India272+, making it clear that a simple majority, which no party had achieved in twenty years, was not enough.

21. The digital strategy had some notable flops too. Once, a Modi supporter posted a fake endorsement by Julian Assange, which was roundly ridiculed. Another time, an automated tool, known as a bot, kept sending Twitter replies to anyone who posted anything mentioning Modi. It was a nuisance, even to his supporters.

22. IndiaSpend's analysis of voting data was summarized in an article available on its website. See Saumya Tewari, "Look Carefully Where India's Young Voters Are," May 27, 2014, available at www.indiaspend.com/cover-story/ look-carefully-where-indias-young-voters-are-76889.

23. http://twiplomacy.com/blog/twiplomacy-study-2014/.

24. www.prsindia.org/media/media-updates/profile-of-the-16th-lok-sabha-3276/.

25. Modi made a famous speech about the need to build toilets rather than temples in 2013; see www.ndtv.com/india-news/make-toilets-before-temples-narendra -modi-tells-students-in-delhi-536464. Economists and public health experts

have concluded that India's poor sanitation is to blame for childhood malnutrition and disease—see, for instance, www.thelancet.com/journals/langlo/article/PHS2214-109X%2814%2970307-9/fulltext.

26. Around the one-year anniversary of Modi's taking office, U.S. Ambassador to India Richard Verma said in a speech at the Center for Strategic and International Studies in Washington that the Indian government needed to do more to encourage foreign investment, including streamlining regulations. "This will take not just welcoming words" is how he put it, "but decisive actions." A link to his address is available at http://csis.org/event/recent-developments-us-india-relationship.

27. Gujarat schools went the furthest in pushing the Hindu right's agenda. They began using books by Dinanath Batra, whose crusade against the University of Chicago professor Wendy Doniger succeeded in getting every copy of Doniger's book on Hinduism voluntarily destroyed by her publisher, Penguin India. In Batra's books, children learned that ancient Indians had invented cars and that "Akhand Bharat" should be restored, which would mean expanding India's current borders to include Afghanistan, Pakistan, and Bangladesh. See www.outlookindia.com/article/ramayana-mahabharata-are-true-accounts-of-the-periodnot-myths/291363.

28. "Hindus to the Fore," *The Economist*, May 23, 2015, available at www.economist.com/news/special-report/21651334-religious-pluralism-looking-less-secure-hindus-fore. See also Gardiner Harris, " 'Reconversion' of Religious Minorities Roils India's Politics," *The New York Times*, December 23, 2004, available at www.nytimes.com/2014/12/24/world/asia/india-narendra-modi-hindu-conversions-missionaries.html?_r=0.

29. Amy Kazmin, "India's Raghuram Rajan Warns Against Intolerance," *Financial Times*, November 1, 2015, available at http://www.ft.com/intl/cms/s/0/86f8b6cc-807c-11e5-8095-ed1a37d1e096.html#axzz3rBqgkBsm.

30. www.niticentral.com/2015/05/25/narendra-modi-bats-rahul-dravid-style-in-test-match-with-t-20-expectations-314215.html.

FACEBOOK GIRLS: SPEAKING UP, TESTING DEMOCRACY'S CONSCIENCE

1. Suketu Mehta's magnificent book on his hometown, *Maximum City: Bombay Lost and Found* (New York: Alfred A. Knopf, 2004), contains a chapter about Thackeray and the political evolution of his Shiv Sena party. Among other things, Thackeray was responsible for rechristening the city with its Marathi name, Mumbai.

2. The 2012 figure was an estimate from Socialbakers, a social media analytics firm: www.socialbakers.com/facebook-statistics/india. Socialbakers has stopped making country-by-country estimates, and Facebook itself does not

release its own numbers. The following year, Jana, another social media analytics firm, estimated that Facebook users in India were just shy of the numbers in the United States and growing fast. That was reported by Quartz, a business news site: http://qz.com/150274/india-facebook/.

3. https://freedomhouse.org/sites/default/files/resources/FOTN%202014%20 Summary%20of%20Findings.pdf.

4. Americans especially will find some of these fundamental rights in the Constitution of India familiar. They are remarkably aspirational, considering how poor, fragile, and besieged the country was at its birth. The Constitution is posted at http://lawmin.nic.in/olwing/coi/coi-english/coi-indexenglish.htm.

5. Lawrence Liang, "Reasonable Restrictions and Unreasonable Speech," in *Sarai Reader 2004: Crisis/Media* (Delhi: The Sarai Programme, Center for the Study of Developing Societies, 2004), available at http://archive.sarai.net/ files/original/e8cc962416f0a1f2da6bc009347fa387.pdf.

6. I wrote about the film *Parzania*, which was screened elsewhere in India, in "Response to the Film 'Parzania' Raises the Question: Can Gujarat Confront Its Brutal Past?" *The New York Times*, February 21, 2007, available at www .nytimes.com/2007/02/21/arts/21iht-indfilm.html?_r=0. Nilanjana Roy, a writer and critic, compiled a list of significant banned books from independence to 2012 on her website: http://nilanjanaroy.com/2012/09/30/banned-books -week-banning-books-in-india/.

7. William F. Grimes, "Maqbool Fida Husain, India's Most Famous Painter, Dies at 95," *The New York Times*, June 10, 2011, available at www.nytimes.com/ 2011/06/10/arts/design/maqbool-fida-husain-indias-most-famous-painter -dies-at-95.html.

8. My colleagues at *The New York Times* have written extensively about China's efforts to tighten restrictions on Internet access in 2015, available at www .nytimes.com/2015/01/30/world/asia/china-clamps-down-still-harder-on -internet-access.html. They have also written about tools to evade censorship: http://sinosphere.blogs.nytimes.com/2015/03/30/q-and-a-adam-fisk-on -evading-internet-censorship-in-china/.

9. Data from comScore, a market research firm: www.comscore.com/Insights/ Press Releases/2013/8/comScore-Releases-the-2013-India-Digital-Future -in-Focus-Report.

10. A software tool made by a California-based firm called Blue Coat allowed Indian officials to either block certain websites or scour the web for content that the government considers to be illegal, according to a worldwide study carried out by the Citizen Lab, a human rights monitoring group based at the University of Toronto. Blue Coat's software is used by many repressive authoritarian states in the Middle East, including Saudi Arabia. See https://citizenlab .org/2013/01/planet-blue-coat-mapping-global-censorship-and-surveillance -tools/. In addition, the Bangalore-based Center for Internet and Society tal-

lied a total of two hundred separate surveillance tools in use in India, used by government agencies, Internet service providers, and telecommunications firms: http://cis-india.org/internet-governance/blog/surveillance-industry-india.pdf.

11. Between July and December 2014, the most recent statistics available before this book went to press, India sought information on 4684 users. By comparison U.S. authorities sought information on 20,986 users; Germany, 3883; France, 3752; and the United Kingdom, 2755. See www.google.com/transparency report/userdatarequests/countries/?t=table.

12. According to Facebook's government requests report for the most recent reporting period, India requested information on 7281 Facebook users or accounts. By comparison, the United States sought information on 21,731 users or accounts. The United Kingdom was third on the list, with information requested on 2890 users or accounts. Facebook posts the data at https://govt requests.facebook.com/.

13. The Center for Internet and Society at Stanford Law School posted the text of the legislation and a summary of court decisions affecting the legislation: http://cyberlaw.stanford.edu/page/wilmap-india.

14. Turkey came in a distant second: Facebook restricted access to 3624 pieces of content there. Third was Germany, which prohibits neo-Nazi content, with 60. See https://govtrequests.facebook.com/country/India/2014-H2/. Likewise, Twitter's report on government takedown requests is posted at https://trans parency.twitter.com/removal-requests/2014/jul–dec.

15. The judgment is available at http://supremecourtofindia.nic.in/FileServer/2015-03-24_1427183283.pdf.

16. In posting its new policies, Twitter maintained that its previous policies had been too narrow and limited the company's ability to act on "certain kinds of threatening behavior." See https://blog.twitter.com/2015/policy-and-product-updates-aimed-at-combating-abuse.

APOSTATES: WHEN THEY DARED TO LOVE

1. Delhi is poised to be home to 36 million by 2030, according to "World Urbanization Prospects," a study conducted by the United Nations Population Division. By the time of the study's release, in 2014, the majority of humanity was for the first time living in cities, rather than in the countryside. India, China, and Nigeria are expected to account for 37 percent of the projected growth of the urban population between 2015 and 2050, according to the same report. This raises enormous challenges for health, education, and infrastructure, but also potentially portends a change in social norms in many countries. Data

tables are available at www.un.org/en/development/desa/news/population/world-urbanization-prospects-2014.html.

2. Ankit is a common male name. This Ankit is no relation to the young man of the same name in a previous chapter.

3. The national news station NDTV was among the television outlets that aired such interviews; see www.ndtv.com/cities/delhis-triple-honour-killing-family-says-well-done-421643.

4. The India Human Development Survey found that only 25 percent of women surveyed in 2011–2012 said they had met their husbands before their wedding day. The principal author of the survey, Sonalde Desai, referred to the finding in a March 19, 2014, opinion piece in *The Hindu*, a daily national newspaper, available at www.thehindu.com/todays-paper/tp-opinion/declining-sex-ratios-seen-in-gender-scorecard/article5802855.ece. The survey also found that barely 5 percent of marriages were across caste lines. That finding was reported by Rukmini S. in a November 13, 2014, article in *The Hindu*, available at www.thehindu.com/data/article6591502.ece.

5. The same British-era law is part of the criminal code across most countries of the Commonwealth, with the exception of a few, like New Zealand, that have repealed it. In Malaysia, for instance, Section 377 of its Penal Code was used to prosecute an opposition politician, Anwar Ibrahim, in February 2015.

6. A Bangalore-based group of lawyers who support gay rights posted a transcript of the Supreme Court proceedings: http://orinam.net/377/wp-content/uploads/2013/12/SC_Transcripts_Hearings.pdf.

7. www.unaids.org/en/resources/infographics/20140108freeequal/.

8. The Iyers are a high-caste community from Kerala. *The Times of India* covered it as a news story: "Mother Seeks Groom for Son in First Gay Matrimonial Ad," May 21, 2015, available at http://timesofindia.indiatimes.com/city/mumbai/Mother-seeks-groom-for-son-in-first-gay-matrimonial-advertisement/articleshow/47363670.cms. Harish Iyer wrote his own version of what happened on the NDTV website; see www.ndtv.com/opinion/im-gay-this-is-what-it-took-to-place-matrimonial-ad-for-me-764603.

9. Somini Sengupta, "Innocence of Youth Is Victim of Congo War," *The New York Times*, June 23, 2003, available at http://www.nytimes.com/2003/06/23/world/innocence-of-youth-is-victim-of-congo-war.html.

CURSE: A FATHER'S FEARS, A DAUGHTER'S DREAMS

1. In 2004, for instance, right before I moved to India, Indian soldiers were accused of raping a woman named Thangjam Manorama in the northeastern

state of Manipur, which was racked by an insurgency and where security forces were by law immune from prosecution. That rape so incensed the women of Manipur they stood naked in front of the gates of a paramilitary base with a banner that screamed "INDIAN ARMY. RAPE US."

2. Jason Burke, "Delhi Rape: How India's Other Half Lives," *The Guardian*, September 10, 2013, available at www.theguardian.com/world/2013/sep/10/delhi-gang-rape-india-women.

3. Jagori, a feminist group in Delhi, has been conducting safety audits in Indian cities for years, asking women and girls what it would take for them to feel safer in public spaces. The December 2012 gang-rape has drawn new attention to its work. See www.unwomen.org/en/news/stories/2013/5/better-lighting-wider-pavements-steps-towards-preventing-sexual-violence-in-new-delhi.

4. Jagori, Safe Cities Free of Violence Against Women and Girls Initiative, "Report of the Baseline Survey Delhi 2010," available at www.jagori.org/wp-content/uploads/2011/03/Baseline-Survey_layout_for-Print_12_03_2011.pdf. The study was cited in www.unwomen.org/en/what-we-do/ending-violence-against-women/facts-and-figures#sthash.cSb5daoV.dpuf.

5. www.hindustantimes.com/newdelhi/78-delhi-women-sexually-harassed-in-2012-survey/article1-983731.aspx.

6. The World Health Organization report is available at http://apps.who.int/iris/bitstream/10665/85239/1/9789241564625_eng.pdf. In addition, a United Nations report found that 120 million girls under twenty—or one in ten—are subjected to sexual violence. How India ranks among nations worldwide can be found in a U.N. report on the status of women at http://apps.who.int/iris/bitstream/10665/85239/1/9789241564625_eng.pdf.

7. Kavita Krishnan, "Nirbhaya Film: Solidarity Is What We Want, Not a Civilising Mission," *Daily O*, March 3, 2015, available at www.dailyo.in/politics/kavita-krishnan-nirbhaya-december-16-indias-daughter-leslee-udwin-mukesh-singh-bbc/story/1/2347.html.

8. National crime records are quoted in this assessment by a committee appointed by the Planning Commission of India: http://planningcommission.nic.in/aboutus/committee/strgrp12/str_womagency_childrights.pdf.

9. Priya Ramani, "Sorry Boss, We Found Our Voice," *Mint*, November 21, 2013, available at www.livemint.com/Opinion/dtKZjcSz9I3iCZs6z748GJ/Sorry-boss-we-found-our-voice.html.

10. Raghbendra Chattopadhyay and Esther Duflo, "Women as Policy Makers: Evidence from a Randomized Policy Experiment in India," *Econometrics* 72, no. 5 (September 2004), available at http://economics.mit.edu/files/792.

11. The national census in 2011 found the mean age of marriage to be 21.2 for women; the data is available at www.censusindia.gov.in/vital_statistics/SRS_Report/9Chap%202%20-%202011.pdf. The smaller government survey, called the Rapid Survey of Children 2013–14, was carried out by the Ministry

of Women and Child Development among more than 100,000 households; it is available at www.wcd.nic.in/issnip/National_Fact%20sheet_RSOC%20_02-07-2015.pdf.

12. World Bank figures, country by country, are available at http://data.worldbank .org/indicator/SL.TLF.CACT.FE.ZS. A separate study, published in October 2014, found slightly higher rates; see Ruchika Chaudhury and Sher Varick, "Female Labour Force Participation in India and Beyond," available at www .ilo.org/wcmsp5/groups/public/---asia/---ro-bangkok/---sro-new_delhi/ documents/publication/wcms_324621.pdf. Most women are concentrated in low-wage work, particularly in the agricultural sector.

13. Prabhat Jha, Maya A. Kesler, Rajesh Kumar,Faujdar Ram, Usha Ram, Lukasz Aleksandrowicz, Diego G. Bassani, Shailaja Chandra, and Jayant K. Banthia, "Trends in Selective Abortions of Girls in India: Analysis of Nationally Representative Birth Histories from 1990 to 2005 and Census Data from 1991 to 2011," *The Lancet* 377, no. 9781 (June 4, 2011): 1921–28, available at www.the lancet.com/journals/lancet/article/PIIS0140-6736%2811%2960649-1/fulltext.

14. www.cia.gov/library/publications/the-world-factbook/fields/2018.html. India measures it slightly differently, enumerating the number of girls born per every 1000 boys. The 1941 census, carried out just before independence, found that for every 1000 boys under the age of six, there were 935 girls. By 2001, that had fallen to 933, and by 2011, the number improved slightly for the first time in decades, to 940 girls for every 1000 boys. The 2011 Indian census data on the sex ratio is summarized on the Census of India website: www.census2011.co.in/ sexratio.php. The 1941 Census figures are available at www.censusindia.gov.in/ Census_And_You/old_report/Census_1941_tebles.aspx.

15. These figures were obtained from the Indian Ministry of Child Development in response to a Right to Information request.

16. Seema Jayachandran and Rohini Pande, "The Youngest Are Hungriest," *The New York Times*, August 10, 2014, available at www.nytimes.com/2014/08/10/ opinion/sunday/the-youngest-are-hungriest.html.

17. Valerie M. Hudson and Andrea M. den Boer, *Bare Branches: The Security Implications of Asia's Surplus Male Population* (Cambridge, Mass.: MIT Press, 2004).

18. Lena Edlund, Hongbin Li, Junjian Yi, and Junsen Zhang, "Sex Ratios and Crime: Evidence from China's One-Child Policy" (Bonn: Institute for the Study of Labor, December 2007), available at http://ftp.iza.org/dp3214.pdf.

EPILOGUE

1. In certain sites in Calcutta, for instance, the presence of bacteria found in fecal matter is more than 100 times the recommended level, according to numbers from the Indian government figures that were analyzed by the news site India-

Spend. See www.indiaspend.com/cover-story/rs-986-cr-30-years-ganga-water-quality-plunges-67807.

2. The International Labour Organization estimates that four out of five workers in the countries across South Asia, the biggest being India, are in vulnerable jobs; see www.ilo.org/wcmsp5/groups/public/---dgreports/---dcomm/---publ/documents/publication/wcms_337069.pdf.